# Forecasting in Business and Economics

# Forecasting in Business and Economics

C. W. J. GRANGER

*University of California, San Diego*

ACADEMIC PRESS

*A Subsidiary of Harcourt Brace Jovanovich, Publishers*

New York   London   Toronto   Sydney   San Francisco

ACADEMIC PRESS, INC.
111 Fifth Avenue, New York, New York 10003

*United Kingdom Edition published by*
ACADEMIC PRESS, INC. (LONDON) LTD.
24/28 Oval Road, London NW1   7DX

ISBN 0-12-295180-8

LIBRARY OF CONGRESS CATALOG CARD NUMBER: 79-91742

PRINTED IN THE UNITED STATES OF AMERICA

80 81 82 83    9 8 7 6 5 4 3 2 1

# Contents

# Preface

This text arose from my being asked to give a course on economic and business forecasting to senior undergraduates in the Management Science sequence at the University of California, San Diego. My immediate reaction was to glance at the available texts, but, as so often seems to be the case, I found none that I viewed as acceptable. Some concentrated on just a single forecasting technique; others were just uncritical lists of alternative methods, some lacked depth or content, and some even were wrong. I have attempted to write a text that will provide a clear-cut strategy for tackling a forecasting problem. The importance of the selection of a relevant information set is emphasized together with the question of how to evaluate one's forecasts once they have been prepared. With this strategy in mind, a variety of forecasting techniques and problems, of increasing scope and complexity, are discussed.

I hope that the text will be suitable for senior undergraduates in economics, business, commerce, and management, and also for MBA and starting graduate students in these and other fields, such as operations research and production engineering. Some basic knowledge of statistics is assumed, and I have tried to treat the readers as being both intelligent and motivated. The layout of much of the first half of the book parallels, at a lower level, the recently published *Forecasting Economic Time Series* by Paul Newbold and myself, Academic Press, 1977. Because of the availability of this more advanced and rigorous book I do not attempt to prove every statement made in this text.

The students in my forecasting course have certainly helped in the evolution of the contents of the book, and I would like to thank those who made constructive comments. I would like to thank Liz Burford for her excellent typing, and I also would like to thank Dennis Kraft and Mark Watson for their careful reading through the page proofs. They must share in the blame for any minor errors that remain, any gross errors must be attributed to the author.

CHAPTER

# 1

# Basic Concepts of Forecasting

*Any astronomer can predict just where every star will be at half past eleven tonight;
he can make no such prediction about his daughter.*

James Truslow Adams

## 1.1 A SCENARIO

Consider this statement about a day in the future:

September 28, 1989, will be a Thursday. By 11 A.M. the sun will be
shining brightly on the Scripps Beach at La Jolla, a few miles north of
San Diego in California. The surf will consist of four-foot breakers
from the southwest at fourteen-second intervals.

It will be high tide, with a height of $+2.3$ feet. After a brief spell of
body surfing and enjoying the 20°C temperature, I shall put on my mask
and snorkel and start exploring the kelp beds just beyond the pier. I will
find a quarter lost by another diver many months ago and find that a
particularly attractive barnacle is attached to it. I use the quarter to buy
an *Evening Tribune* and get no change.

This little scenario or view about the future contains a number of predictions or forecasts.[1] These predictions are all time specific, in that a definite
time and date are specified, together with a particular location.

There is absolutely no possibility of the scenario being fully accurate
about what will occur. At this time one cannot forecast the future perfectly,

---

[1] The words *prediction* and *forecast* will be considered to be completely interchangeable in
what follows.

1

that is, without error. It does not require much imagination to realize how dull and mentally debilitating life would be if everything about the future were known with complete accuracy. Fortunately, such a possibility is by no means in sight.

Let us now examine some of the details of the scenario:

(i)   the date. September 28, 1989, merely specifies when the scenario is to occur.

(ii)   the day. That this date will be a Thursday is not a forecast but merely a designation of a name to a date according to a widely accepted method of designating such names, known as the Gregorian calendar. This calendar has given such names to all dates into the indefinite future. An assumption is being made that the same calendar will be in use in 1989.

(iii)   tide-height. The mechanism that causes tides is very well known and depends on the movement of the moon and various other members of the solar system. As these movements can be predicted with great accuracy, it is possible to calculate a tide height for virtually any beach in the world, although the calculation is not necessarily an easy one. Thus a forecast of tide height can be made, and one would expect very little error in the forecast, although previous wind conditions may affect the actual value somewhat. The only assumption required to make this forecast is that the tide-generating mechanism does not change in any significant fashion before 1989.

(iv)   sun shining, surf conditions, ocean temperature. These can all be considered to be forecasts made by observing what typically happens at Scripps Beach in La Jolla on September 28. For example, one might record sea temperature at 11 A.M. on all previous September 28s for which readings exist, average these values, and use this average to forecast what will occur at the same date in the future. It would clearly be wrong to average temperatures over all past days, as ocean temperature varies greatly from one part of the year to the next, a feature known as the seasonal variation. Clearly such forecasts could be very wrong, but it is difficult to see how they might be improved. Local weather effects in 1989 depend so greatly on the future movements of air masses and the mechanism that moves these masses through the atmosphere is so complicated that there is virtually no hope of making a really accurate forecast of what will occur several years hence. Unlike the astronomers and oceanographers, who have a very high quality model for the movement of planets and oceans, the meteorologist has only a very imperfect model for the atmosphere due to the extra order of complexity involved.

(v)   my personal behavior. Much of this is very doubtful, requiring not only that I be around in 1989 and sufficiently healthy to enjoy the ocean but also that I learn how to snorkel. Given that I am sufficiently healthy and wealthy, the prediction could be self-fulfilling, as I could ensure that I am in La Jolla and do body surf and so forth.

(vi)  finding a quarter with a barnacle. This is just pure fantasy. Such a thing could occur but is extremely unlikely. Any detail of this kind can be thought of as being merely the use of artistic license by the writer.

(vii)  spend a quarter to buy an *Evening Tribune*. The San Diego evening paper at this time is the *Evening Tribune* and currently costs 15 cents, having gone up from 10 cents fairly recently. By looking at the history of price increases in the economy at large, one might well forecast that what now costs 15 cents will be costing 25 cents by 1989. In fact, such a price is possibly optimistic. There has been a noticeable upward drift in prices, known as a trend, and, by simply assuming that this drift will continue, the price of the paper in 1989 may be estimated. The mechanism by which prices will change is by no means well understood, so the forecast is based on an extension, or extrapolation, of what has been observed in the past.

(viii)  use of centigrade. There is one possibly implied forecast in the scenario, that temperatures will be officially measured in degrees centigrade in California in 1989, rather than in degrees Fahrenheit as now. This is an example of a forecast about a change in the way society operates, albeit a very minor one. It is not based on any model of the society or on a great deal of past data but is just a suggestion about the consequences of discussions that are now occurring. In this case, it is not a particularly important forecast, since one can easily convert from centigrade to Fahrenheit without any error, $20°C$ being equal to $68°F$.

Even this simple scenario brings out a number of important points about forecasting. The most important of these is that things to be forecast vary greatly in their degree of predictability. One can have much greater confidence in the forecast for tide height than in that for ocean temperature, and even less confidence in the forecast of the price of an evening paper. Whereas some variables can be predicted with considerable accuracy, others are almost entirely unpredictable, as will be shown later. It should also be clear that the methods that can be used to forecast can vary greatly and will depend upon data availability, the quality of models available, and the kinds of assumptions made, amongst other things. This means that forecasting is generally not easy, which is one reason why the topic is so interesting.

## 1.2  SOME FORECASTING SITUATIONS

Many million dollars are spent annually on prediction in the United States alone, making forecasting big business. Who forecasts and why? The major consumers of specific forecasts are government officials and servants, federal, state, and local, together with management, particularly that part belonging to the higher echelons, in all types of business. Some typical forecast situations are the following:

(i)   A company has to forecast future sales of each of its products to ensure that its production and inventory are kept at economical levels while controlling the likelihood of being unable to meet orders.

(ii)   A firm is considering putting capital into a new investment. To decide whether the investment is a worthwhile one, it has to forecast the returns that will result in each of the next few years.

(iii)   A cigarette manufacturing company is considering introducing a new brand and has to predict the likely sales for this brand and also the effect of sales on its other brands.

(iv)   A government wants to forecast the values of some important economic variable, such as the unemployment rate, if it takes no action or if it alters one of its controls, such as the marginal tax rate. Such forecasts are necessary for policy decision.

(v)   A town council forecasts the demand for junior school places in some part of the town in order to decide whether or not an extra school is required, or if an existing school should be expanded.

Forecasting is by no means confined to business and government, as there are plenty of situations in which some kind of forecasting is needed in the lives of individuals. An example is deciding what career choice will give good total value in terms of job satisfaction and adequate monetary reward. One has to predict how well he will like a job, what kind of advancement possibilities exist, and whether the career is oversubscribed or not. Similarly, if one is making an investment such as buying a house, getting married, or having a further child, it is necessary to ask if the advantages will outweigh the disadvantages and to predict what these will be. These types of predictions are generally very difficult and liable to huge errors and are very rarely made in any formal or specific manner.

It is important to note one common feature of all these forecasting situations—that they lead to *decisions*. The government official, the manager, or the individual requires forecasts in order to decide what to do right now or how to plan for the near future. The forecaster is the producer of information and the decision maker is the consumer. It is clearly important for there to be no misunderstanding between the forecaster and the decision maker about what is being forecast, what information is being utilized, and what assumptions underlie the forecast.

There are, of course, some forecasts that have nothing to do with decisions, such as those that might be contained in an article entitled "Religion in Iceland in 50 Years Time" or "What Life Will Be Like in the Year 3078." Such offerings may be highly entertaining and are sometimes useful in helping forecasters free their minds from unnecessary restrictions, but they have to be classified with most science fiction as not serious forecasting. The majority of forecasting techniques described in later chapters will be aimed at being useful in decision making.

### Exercises

In order to get yourself in the mood for thinking about how the future can be investigated, consider each of the following personal questions and give forecasts:

(a)  What will you be doing next weekend?
(b)  How will you spend your next summer vacation?
(c)  When will you get married, and how many children will you have, if any?
(d)  If taking a forecasting course, what mark or grade will you receive in the course?

As a final example of a situation familiar to all students that requires a forecast, suppose you are taking a lecture course from a professor you have not had before. As his or her first introductory lecture drags on, one's mind naturally turns to the question of when the lecture will end. Suppose the time-table indicates that the lecture will start at 10 A.M. and finish by 11 A.M. So that students can get from one class to another, it is generally understood that teachers will finish by ten minutes to the hour. However, from experience you know that some professors so dislike teaching that they finish as early as they dare, while others are (expletive deleted) and so enjoy the sound of their own voice that they keep on going to within a minute or two of the hour, resulting in an unseemly rush to your next class. What forecast do you make about when the lecture will end? As you have very little information to go on, you will probably take a neutral course and guess at 10:50 A.M. but realize that the actual time of finishing will very likely lie in the period 10:40–10:59 A.M. After you have attended the course for a few weeks, you will have gathered some useful information in predicting the time the next lecture will finish. You may have observed, for example, that the lecture always ends between 10:46 and 10:52 A.M., with an average of 10:49 A.M. Thus, an appropriate forecast would be 10:49 A.M., and the expected interval within which the finish time will lie is now much smaller. Thus, the acquisition of relevant information can help greatly in improving the forecast. After a couple of more weeks observation, rather more subtle effects might be noticeable. You may notice, for instance, that the lecturer has the tendency to follow a longer than average lecture by one that is shorter than average, or you may find that the lectures are generally becoming longer as the sequence continues. Such patterns in the data can obviously be utilized in making improved forecasts. A great deal of attention will be paid in what follows to discussing what information should be gathered and how it should be used, particularly how patterns in the data sequence can be picked out and utilized to form better forecasts.


## 1.3   TYPES OF FORECASTS

It should already be clear that there are several types of forecasts that need to be made and that they each require different approaches.

The first classification depends on the length of time into the future one is looking. When making statements about the near future, the forecasts are called *short run*, when considering the very distant future, they are called *long run*, and the intermediate case involves *middle-run* forecasts. Such a statement having been made, it now has to be admitted that there is no precise definition of what constitutes short, middle, or long run, as this depends on the variable being forecast and the type of data available, amongst other things. In weather forecasting, the short run might be up to 24 hours ahead, and the long run 2 weeks or more, whereas if one is forecasting an economic variable such as unemployment, short run is up to 10–15 months and long run 4 years and more, although these are purely personal views.

It is generally true that the further ahead one forecasts the less well one does, in that larger errors are likely to occur. The reason for this is that usually the information available for making a forecast is more relevant in the short run than in longer runs.

In the extremely short run, forecasting is often trivial. For instance, if you ask yourself, "Where will I be in two seconds time?" the answer will have to be "Right here, or extremely nearby," as it is impossible to move very far in a couple of seconds. There is frequently a certain momentum in the course of events and this helps greatly in forecasting in the short run but is of very little relevance in the long run. It is also possible to make quite a reputation "predicting" things that have already occurred or have been planned but which are not yet publicly known. Again, such an approach does not help in the long run.

Three important types of forecasts may be called event outcome, event timing, and time series forecasts. These will now be considered in turn.

### 1.3.1   Event Outcome Forecasts

You know that an event will occur in the future with virtual certainty, but what will be the outcome of the event? For example, consider the following:

(i)   A baby is to be born. What sex will it be?

(ii)   An election is to occur. Who will win?

(iii)   A new brand of soap is to be introduced. Will it succeed? What will its sales be?

(iv)   A new premier is about to take over power in Moscow. How will this affect Russian foreign policy?

(v)   A new law is about to come into operation legalizing the use and sale of marijuana for adults. What will be the consequences?

The main problem with forecasting the outcome of a future event is that the event may be unique, so that really relevant information may be difficult or expensive to acquire. Take example (i), the sex of an unborn baby. It is very easy to note that in the United States in recent years 51.3% of all babies have been boys and, of course, 48.7% have been girls. Thus, one could make a forecast of the form "with probability 0.513 the baby will be a boy." By observing the proportions of boys and girls born in the families of the mother and father, one might want to alter this probability, since some families produce a predominance of girls, for instance. Much better information could be acquired by performing chemical tests on the mother-to-be and quite possibly a very definite prediction could be made with considerable confidence, particularly as the birth date draws near.

The main approach to event outcome forecasting is to seek or generate relevant data. For example, to predict the outcome of an election one conducts a poll of electors, and to forecast the success of the introduction of a new brand of soap the company will perform various market tests. These are examples of increasing one's information set; the usual limitations to doing this depend on the state of the relevant technology and the cost of gathering the information.

### 1.3.2   Event Timing Forecasts

This class of forecasts considers questions of the form, when, if ever, will an event occur. Examples are the following:

(i)   When will the next British election occur?

(ii)   When will the next turning point of the economy happen?

(iii)   When will our company's main competitor introduce a new brand?

(iv)   When will the company president retire?

  (v)   When will the bank change its interest rate?

  (vi)  When will your sister get married?

In some of these cases there exists a sequence of similar events in the past, such as the timing of British elections. By observing the pattern of the times between the events, it might be possible to forecast when the next event will occur. However, the usual procedure is to look for *leading indicators*, which are events that are likely to precede the one we are trying to forecast. For instance, the competitor company may book an exceptional amount of television advertising time or be observed doing market testing, or one's sister may announce her engagement. This approach is used intensively when considering turning points in the economy, as will be discussed in Chapter 7.

### 1.3.3   Time Series Forecasts

A time series is a sequence of values usually recorded at equidistant time intervals. Examples are

  (i)   hourly temperatures taken at the base of the Statue of Liberty,

  (ii)  daily closing prices of IBM shares,

  (iii) weekly automobile production by the Chevrolet division of General Motors,

  (iv) monthly unemployment rate or balance of payments deficit, and

  (v)  annual births in California.

As an example of the appearance of a time series, Fig. 1.1 shows the plot of quarterly U.S. Government surplus or deficit figures, using an annual rate, in billions of current dollars, for the period 1952–1974.

Suppose one observes such a time series, denoted by $x_t$ for the value at the time period $t$, over the period from $t = 0$ up to $t = n$, where $n \equiv$ now. In time series forecasting we are interested in making statements about what value the series will take at some future time period $n + h$, where $h =$ hence. Thus $h$ represents the number of time periods into the future the forecaster is looking. If $h = 1$, then one-step forecasts are being made. For example, if $x_t$

1952 53 54 55 56 57 58 59 60 61 62 63 64 65 66 67 68 69 70 71 72 73 1974

*Fig. 1.1*   Government surplus or deficit (quarterly).

represents the number of U.S. firms that go bankrupt in month $t$, this series might be observed over a 50 month period, $t = 1, \ldots, 50$, ending in August 197$x$, and one may want to forecast the values taken by this series for September 197$x$ ($h = 1$) and December of the same year ($h = 4$). As the reasons for any individual company going bankrupt are so complex, the series $x_t$ may be considered to be a sequence of random variables. In particular, when standing at time $n$ and contemplating the value that will occur at time $n + h$, one has very little reason to suppose it possible to forecast this value with perfect accuracy, except by incredible luck. Thus $x_{n+h}$ is a random variable, when viewed at time $n$, and so should be characterized in probability terms. In particular, one could talk about its distribution function or its probability density function, plus summary statistics such as mean and variance. As will be seen later, these distributions will be conditional ones, given the information available at time $n$ upon which a forecast is based.

Figure 1.2 shows the situation being considered. To fully characterize $x_{n+h}$, the value to occur at time $n + h$, one needs a complete probability density function, so that statements such as prob$(163 < x_{n+h} \leq 190) = 0.42$ can be made, for any interval. It will generally be quite impossible to completely determine the shape of the density function without making some very strong and highly unreal assumptions about the form of this function. A rather less ambitious procedure is to try to place confidence intervals about the forthcoming value $x_{n+h}$, so that a statement of the form

$$\text{prob}(B < x_{n+h} \leq A) = 0.95$$

can be made. The points A and B are shown in Fig. 1.2 and enable the forecaster to put limits on the value being forecast with a reasonably high degree of confidence of being correct. An example of such a forecast interval is to say, "I believe the price of potatoes in California will be in the range 6¢–8¢ per pound by the end of 197$x$, with probability 0.95." If your forecasting procedure were a good one and a whole sequence of such forecasts were made, you would expect that the true prices of potatoes or whatever would be outside the stated intervals only about 5% of the time. If you can go through

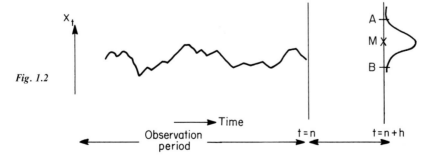

Fig. 1.2

life being wrong only 5% of the time, things should turn out very well for you. Such intervals are called *interval forecasts*. Confidence intervals are sometimes given in practice, although much less often than they should be, but forecasters are usually content with providing just a *point forecast*, that is, a single guess for $x_{n+h}$ that in some way well represents the whole distribution of possible values. An obvious candidate for such a value is an average, such as the mean shown in Fig. 1.2. Some examples of point forecasts are the following:

(i)   My wife will drink 17 cups of coffee next week.

(ii)   There will be 35 near misses by pairs of commercial airlines over the United States next year.

(iii)   We expect 142 minor accidents in our manufacturing plant over the next three months.

Most forecasts used in government and business are point forecasts. Chapters 3 and 4 will be particularly concerned with the formulation of such forecasts for a time series.

A whole sequence of point forecasts, for $h = 1, 2, 3, \ldots, H$, will be called a *trace forecast*, but the method of making such forecasts presents no new problem. As an example of the use of a trace forecast, consider the manager of a chocolate factory who has to buy cocoa on the international cocoa commodity market. Such markets are often very volatile, resulting in widely changing prices. If the manager has sufficient cocoa in his inventory to meet production needs in the near future, he, or she, may use a trace forecast to decide the best time to enter the cocoa market and purchase further stocks of the commodity, presumably trying to buy at the lowest available price.

## Exercises

1.   Make point forecasts and also 95% confidence interval forecasts, if possible, of each of the following variables:
   (a)   How many hours of television will you watch tomorrow? Next week?
   (b)   How many books will you read purely for enjoyment over the next three months?
   (c)   Over the next week, how many cans of beer (cups of tea, mugs of coffee, or whatever turns you on) will you drink?
   (d)   How many head-turning girls (boys, cars, horses, or whatever) will you see tomorrow?
2.   Classify the type of forecast involved in each of the following situations:
   (a)   A university announces it will admit a much larger proportion of

"minority students." How will this affect the average grades of future graduating classes?

(b) A company decides to lower the price of its product. How will sales be affected?

(c) A manager is planning a new factory to be started in 5 years time and is interested in the possibility of nuclear power eventually providing very cheap electricity. Should he plan on putting electric or gas heating in the factory?

(d) In order to decide whether or not a desalination plant to produce fresh water is required, a town council asks for a forecast of future water requirements for its area.

(e) The date of the day of reckoning is required by a company considering making a very long-term loan.

## 1.4 INFORMATION SETS AND COST FUNCTIONS

Before forming a forecast, it is necessary to assemble the set of information that is to be used to make the forecast. For example, if time series forecasting, the forecast might be formed from the observed past and present values of the series. In this case, the *information set* available at time $n$, denoted $I_n$, will consist of

$$I_n : x_{n-j}, \qquad j \geq 0,$$

which will be called the single series information set. Most of the forecasts considered in Chapters 2 and 3 will use only this set. However, on other occasions wider information sets may be utilized, consisting of the past and present of the series to be forecast, together with the past and present values of other series that might be thought relevant, which can be written formally

$$I_n : x_{n-j}, y_{n-j}, z_{n-j}, \text{etc.,} \qquad j \geq 0.$$

Thus, for example, suppose a forecast of next month's unemployment rate is required. A forecast might be made from just the previous values of this series by utilizing some observed pattern. This would be the single-series forecast. However, it might be thought that the past and present values of an index of production and also of government expenditure, in real terms, would contain relevant information which, if it could be properly used together with past unemployment figures, would provide a better forecast. This would be a forecast based on a multiseries information set. In general, you would expect to forecast better the wider the information set used, provided the relevant information in the set has been fully extracted. Certainly, as the contents of the information set is increased you would not expect to do any worse at forecasting. At some point, any further extension of the information set is likely to provide such insignificant improvements in the forecasts that the work involved in trying to use the extra information will not be worthwhile, unless a particularly relevant series has previously been omitted, of course.

An information set will be called *proper* if it contains the past and present terms of the series to be forecast. The use of improper information sets will usually lead to suboptimal forecasts, although this is not inevitably so.

In most circumstances, the information set will be assumed to contain just numerical data. However, on occasions information of a nonnumerical kind may become available that appears particularly significant, such as rumors that an important government official is resigning, that a President is secretly seriously ill, that two rival companies are considering merging, or that your main competitor is about to introduce a new brand formulation. This type of information, including opinions about some situation by experienced managers, salesmen, or economists, is often extremely important but is very difficult to handle within a purely statistical framework. Some possible ways of using nonnumerical information will be discussed in Section 8.3.

On some occasions a very poor forecast can result due to a poor choice of information set. For example, in the late 1950s, a commission was set up in Britain to consider the future demand for medical school places. They decided that very few, if any, new places were required to meet the future demand for doctors in England. In fact, the number of doctors available in England fell far short of demand in the next decade or so. The reason for the inaccurate forecast is that it was not realized that about one in four of the doctors would emigrate. This mistake was due to two factors which were badly estimated, the number of doctors who would go to the United States, which proved to be a major market, and—a serious underestimate—the number of doctors who were already emigrating in the 1950s. This underestimate occurred because official estimates of this figure only considered those who emigrate by *sea* and totally ignored the large percentage who went by air. If the information set had included figures for air emigration, the forecast would have been much improved and a superior policy decision reached, leading to new medical schools being instituted.

In the discussion so far, statements of the kind "one procedure will produce better forecasts than another" have been used without defining what is meant by "better" or having a specific criterion by which forecasting methods can be ordered. As there is a natural desire to use the best available methods of forecasting that are affordable, it is imperative to have a criterion so that forecast methods can be compared.

Assume that someone is going to base a decision on your forecast. It follows that when you make an error, there will be in consequence a cost to the decision maker because he did not make the optimum decision. Generally, the larger the magnitude of the error, the larger will be this generated cost. For example, suppose that you work for a cake maker who uses no preservatives and advertises that he sells no cakes not made within the previous 24 hours. The cakes are actually made during the night hours and sold from the maker's shops the following day. Any cakes that are not sold are thrown away and have no value. Your task is to forecast sales for tomorrow, and the number of cakes made is always put equal to your forecast. If your forecast is too high, then more cakes will be made than can be sold, so that wastage will occur. If your forecast is too low, insufficient cakes will be made and so the profits that could have been made on those extra cakes would be lost. As you see, the forecaster cannot win except by making perfect forecasts, and this is virtually impossible to achieve. Let us put some figures to these costs. Suppose that each cake costs exactly 70¢ to make and that the cakes sell for $1 each. If you forecast that ten more cakes will be sold than actually are, the cost is $10 \times 70¢ = \$7$, which is cost of the cakes that were made unnecessarily. If you underestimate the number of cakes that could have been sold, the cost is $10 \times 30¢ = \$3$, since 30¢ profit is made per cake. In this example, the cost function of making an error $e$, denoted by $C(e)$, is given by

$$C(e) = \begin{cases} 70e & \text{if } e > 0 \\ 30(-e) & \text{if } e < 0 \\ 0 & \text{if } e = 0, \end{cases}$$

costs being in cents. In this case, it is seen that the cost function, which is plotted in Fig. 1.3, is not symmetric, takes the value zero when no error is made, is never negative, and is increasing in size as the errors become larger in magnitude. In more realistic situations, the cost functions will be expected to have similar properties, although they could be symmetric about $e = 0$ and need not consist of straight lines.

In practice, it is unlikely that the decision maker can provide you with a

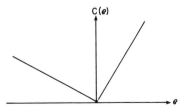

**Fig. 1.3**   Nonsymmetric cost function.

precise cost function partly because the company accountant may not be up to costing the effect of a single suboptimal decision amongst many and partly because the costs involved will occur in the future and so would have to be forecast. For this reason what is invariably done is that the forecaster assumes that a particular cost function, chosen for his own convenience, is a sufficiently good approximation to the decision maker's true cost function. The function usually chosen is

$$C(e) = Ae^2,$$

where $A$ is some positive constant. It will be seen later that the value of $A$ is quite irrelevant and so can be taken to be unity. Thus, the cost of an error is just the error squared. The obvious problem with this choice for $C(e)$ is that it is a symmetric function, whereas actual cost functions are often nonsymmetric. It is possible for the decision maker to take into account the fact that an incorrect cost function has been used, but to do this he has to have a good estimate of his true function, which is rarely the case in practice. Thus, the choice of an error-squared cost function is justifiable only on pragmatic grounds, but it is unclear how any additional costs that this may involve to the decision maker can be reduced.

With this preamble, it is now possible to give a criterion for choosing between forecasting methods, as follows:

**Criterion.** For a given cost function $C(e)$, the best of a set of alternative forecasting methods is that which results in the lowest expected (or average) cost.

Suppose $f(1)$, $f(2)$ are a pair of forecasting methods which when applied to a series of forecasting situations result in forecast errors $e_j(1)$, $e_j(2)$, $j = 1, \ldots, N$, respectively. Then using the squared-error criterion, $f(1)$ is the better method if

$$\frac{1}{N} \sum_{j=1}^{N} e_j^2(1) < \frac{1}{N} \sum_{j=1}^{N} e_j^2(2),$$

so that it produces the lower average squared error.[2] If both sides of this inequality were multiplied by the same positive constant, the inequality would not be altered, which is why the constant $A$ is of no consequence in the preceding formula. Even the $1/N$ term can be dropped. The advantage of the squared-error cost function is that it corresponds to a *least-squares*

---

[2] If a general cost function $C(e)$ were used, the criterion would read

$$\frac{1}{N} \sum_{j=1}^{N} C(e_j(1)) < \frac{1}{N} \sum_{j=1}^{N} C(e_j(2)).$$

*criterion* and so allows the use of much standard and well-understood statistical theory and practice relating to regression problems.

As an example of using this criterion, suppose you consider three alternative forecasting methods to predict daily cake sales and that the resulting errors over ten trading days are given in Table 1.1. The resulting average costs are shown in Table 1.2, using both the square error and the true cost function, as shown in Fig. 1.3.

Note that method (2) appears superior under both forms of the average least-cost criterion, whilst method (1) is consistently worst. The actual values in the cost table do not matter, as they are only used to find the method with the lowest figure in a column. To make a proper ranking of the methods, it is generally advisable to use more than ten error values if possible. One may also wish to apply a test of significance to the average cost values, but discussion of how this can be done is delayed until Chapter 8.

Suppose that the number $N$ of errors to be used in our least-squares criterion is very large and that a wide selection of possible forecasting methods are available. In fact, suppose that one can speak of all possible forecasting methods using a particular information set $I_n$. Then the method with the lowest average cost, that is, the smallest average squared error, may be called the *optimum forecast* based on $I_n$, although strictly it is the optimum least-

**TABLE 1.1**

*Forecast Errors from Three Forecasting Methods*

| Forecasting method | Day | | | | | | | | | |
|---|---|---|---|---|---|---|---|---|---|---|
| | 1 | 2 | 3 | 4 | 5 | 6 | 7 | 8 | 9 | 10 |
| (1) | −10 | 8 | 4 | 1 | 11 | −2 | 4 | 6 | −4 | 2 |
| (2) | 3 | −2 | 5 | −3 | 1 | 2 | −1 | 0 | −5 | −2 |
| (3) | 6 | 5 | −7 | 6 | −2 | 1 | −3 | −1 | 6 | 4 |

**TABLE 1.2**

*Average Costs of Three Forecasting Methods*

| Method | Cost function | |
|---|---|---|
| | Squared error | True |
| (1) | 37.8 | $3 |
| (2) | 8.2 | $1.16 |
| (3) | 18.3 | $2.35 |

squares forecast. Some theoretical properties of optimum forecasts are discussed in Section 4.5. It is generally too difficult to consider all possible forecasts based on $I_n$, even if this information set contains just numerical data. The form of a forecast usually considered is that which uses the data in $I_n$ in a linear fashion. Thus, for example, if a single-series information set is used, $I_n: x_{n-j}, j \geq 0$, then a forecast of $x_{n+h}$ will be considered of the form

$$f_{n,h} = \sum_{j=0}^{m} \gamma_j x_{n-j}$$

and will be called a *linear forecast*.

If some appropriate $m$ is chosen and the parameters $\gamma_j$ are then chosen so that the forecast is the best available according to our criterion, one has an optimal, linear, least-squares, single-series forecast.

### Exercises

1.  If you were asked to forecast how many students would graduate from a particular university, what information set would you ask for? What if you were asked to forecast the number of students entering the university in two years time?
2.  Two methods of forecasting the number of companies going bankrupt in California per month produce the following errors:

|          |     |     |     | Month |     |      |     |     |
| -------- | --- | --- | --- | ----- | --- | ---- | --- | --- |
| Method   | 1   | 2   | 3   | 4     | 5   | 6    | 7   | 8   |
| (1)      | 16  | 11  | -3  | -14   | 9   | -11  | 3   | -3  |
| (2)      | 12  | -1  | -8  | -2    | 3   | 8    | -6  | -9  |

On this evidence, which method appears superior, using
(a)  a squared-error cost function and
(b)  the cost function

$$C(e) = \begin{cases} e, & e \geq 0, \\ -e, & e \leq 0? \end{cases}$$

### 1.5  A NOTE ON NOTATION

The following notation will be used frequently throughout this text, but particularly in the early chapters, and so is worth memorizing:

$n$   now, the time period at which the forecast is made;

$h$   hence, the number of time periods ahead one is forecasting;

$x_t$   the basic time series under consideration;

$x_n$   the latest value available in this time series;

$I_n$   the information set upon which a forecast is based;

$A_n$   the set of assumptions made by the forecaster;

$x_{n+h}$   the value of the series to be forecast, the exact value of which is not known until time period $n + h$;

$f_{n,h}$   the forecast made at time $n$, looking ahead $h$ periods, and so is a forecast of $x_{n+h}$;

$e_{n,h}$   $x_{n+h} - f_{n,h}$, the resulting $h$-step forecast error, and not known until time $n + h$.

Strictly the forecast $f_{n,h}$ should be written $f_{n,h}(I_n, A_n)$, since it will depend on the information set used plus any assumptions made, but this extended notation is too uncomfortable for use. It is nevertheless worth noting whenever possible the form of $I_n$ and of $A_n$ being used. For example, $I_n$ may consist of the past and present of a couple of time series, plus a batch of rumors, and $A_n$ may contain assumptions that there will be no major breakdown in the running of society or in the physical laws operating in the universe, plus the belief that the economy can be well approximated by a linear model. These kinds of assumption are almost inevitably made, although they are dropped in Chapter 11.

## QUESTIONS

1. List the major factors that you think will determine U.S. beef production in the next 20 years.
2. Produce point and 95% confidence interval forecasts of
    (a) how many films you will watch (other than on television) in the next year, and
    (b) how many cups of coffee you will drink in the next week.
3. Two methods of forecasting the number of companies going bankrupt in California per month produce the following errors:

|  | Month | | | | | | | |
| --- | --- | --- | --- | --- | --- | --- | --- | --- |
| Method | 1 | 2 | 3 | 4 | 5 | 6 | 7 | 8 |
| (1) | 6 | 11 | −13 | −14 | 19 | −10 | 23 | −31 |
| (2) | 12 | −10 | −28 | −21 | 13 | 18 | −16 | −9 |

On this evidence, which method appears superior, using
(a)   a squared error cost function and
(b)   the cost function

$$C(e) = \begin{cases} e^2, & e \geq 0 \\ -4e, & e < 0? \end{cases}$$

CHAPTER

# 2

# Trend-Line Fitting
# and Forecasting

The best qualification of a prophet is to have a good memory.

Marquis of Halifax

## 2.1  INTRODUCING TRENDS

Many aspects of society, and particularly the economy, when put into numerical form seem to have been steadily increasing throughout this century; population, prices, and number of crimes committed are three of the most widely discussed. A time series that appears to contain a smoothly increasing (or decreasing) component is said to contain a trend term. Some examples from the United States are shown in Table 2.1, in which figures for just a few selected years are given. There is no difficulty in finding many other examples from virtually any country in the world. Some of the trends are due to increases in population, others to improvements in technology and increases in wealth. When these two effects are multiplied together, very dramatic trends can occur, as seen for total horsepower in the table. Although most trends are upward, this is not necessarily so, as seen in the figures for child deaths per 1000 births shown in the table. Average hours worked per week in developed economies provides another example.

Although many important series appear to be trending from visual inspection of their plot against time, it is not at all easy to define trend. As an example of this difficulty, suppose that temperatures are recorded outside Nassau Hall at Princeton University on a spring day each five minutes from 5 A.M. until 3 P.M., giving a series of 120 values. Almost certainly the temperatures will have been steadily increasing over this period and so the data

19

**TABLE 2.1**[a]

| Year | Population (million) | Total horsepower (1000s) | No. of vehicles (1000s) | Autos per capita | Telephones per capita | Death rate per 1000[b] |
|------|------|------|------|------|------|------|
| 1890 | 63 | NA[c] | NA[c] | — | 3.6 | — |
| 1900 | 76 | 100 | 8 | 0.0001 | 17.6 | 162.4 |
| 1910 | 92 | 7714 | 312 | 0.005 | 82 | 131.8 |
| 1920 | 106 | 280,000 | 9237 | 0.076 | 123 | 92.3 |
| 1930 | 123 | 1,420,000 | 26,749 | 0.187 | 163 | 69.0 |
| 1940 | 132 | 2,511,000 | 32,453 | 0.208 | 165 | 54.9 |
| 1950 | 151 | 4,403,000 | 49,161 | 0.267 | 281 | 33.0 |
| 1960 | 179 | 10,367,000 | 73,826 | 0.342 | 408 | 27.0 |
| 1970 | 203 | 19,325,000 | 108,375 | 0.435 | 584 | 21.4 |
| 1973 | 211 | 23,029,000 | 125,157 | 0.464 | 655 | 18.0 |

[a] Source: Statistical Abstract of the United States, 1977, U.S. Dept. of Commerce, U.S. Govt. Printing Office, Washington, D.C.

[b] Age under 1 year.

[c] NA: not available.

will appear to contain a trend. If this trend line is extended out beyond 3 P.M., very unfortunate temperatures will be reached by about midnight, but, of course, this does not happen. The apparent "trend" we saw in the data was just the upward swing of a daily cycle in temperature level. There is also an annual cycle in temperature in Princeton which could be misleading if a very long series of hourly reading were used, over the months of February to June, say. For the moment, these examples will be used just to point out difficulties in interpreting an apparent trend. Some further implications will be considered later.

Table 2.2 shows total U.S. personal consumption data for the period 1947–1975. These data are used throughout this chapter to provide examples of the forecasting techniques being considered. The "smoothed" series is explained later in this section. The data up to 1964 are to be used to fit broad curves, and after 1964 to evaluate forecasts made using these curves.

Figure 2.1 shows these data plotted. Incidentally, it is always good practice to plot a time series before starting to analyze it so that any very special features can be noted, such as extraordinary values due to a strike or a particularly severe winter, say. That the series contains a trend appears clear, but there are also fluctuations about the smooth trend line. For a long time, the basic approach to time series analysis was to assume that the series are made up of three identifiable components, a very smooth trend curve, a set of long swings, undulations, or cycles, plus a rather unimportant residual or "hash" consisting mainly of short fluctuations. As will be clear

**TABLE 2.2**[a]

| Year | Total U.S. personal consumption (billions of 1958 dollars) | Smoothed data |
|---|---|---|
| 1947 | 206.3 | 206.3 |
| 1948 | 210.8 | 209.45 |
| 1949 | 216.5 | 214.39 |
| 1950 | 230.5 | 225.67 |
| 1951 | 232.8 | 230.66 |
| 1952 | 239.4 | 236.78 |
| 1953 | 250.8 | 246.59 |
| 1954 | 255.7 | 252.97 |
| 1955 | 274.2 | 267.83 |
| 1956 | 281.4 | 277.33 |
| 1957 | 288.2 | 284.94 |
| 1958 | 290.1 | 288.55 |
| 1959 | 307.3 | 301.68 |
| 1960 | 316.1 | 311.77 |
| 1961 | 322.5 | 319.28 |
| 1962 | 338.4 | 332.66 |
| 1963 | 353.3 | 347.11 |
| 1964 | 373.7 | 365.72 |
| 1965 | 397.7 | |
| 1966 | 418.1 | |
| 1967 | 430.1 | |
| 1968 | 452.7 | |
| 1969 | 469.1 | |
| 1970 | 477.5 | |
| 1971 | 496.3 | |
| 1972 | 526.8 | |
| 1973 | 552.1 | |
| 1974 | 539.5 | |
| 1975 | | |

[a] Source: Survey of Current Business, U.S. Dept. of Commerce, U.S. Govt. Printing Office, Washington, D.C., various issues.

later, this particular decomposition is no longer universally accepted. Figure 2.2 shows a constructed series made up of the three components. If a series is so composed, the relative importance of the three components depends largely on how far ahead one is forecasting. In the very short run, the trend and cycle components may have changed very little, so forecasts of the third component are the most important. However, when long-run forecasting, the trend term is usually dominant and the other two components are of relatively minor importance. In the middle run all three components could be important.

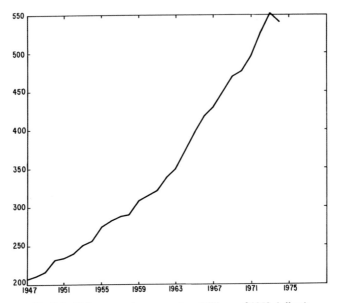

***Fig. 2.1***   U.S. personal consumption (billions of 1958 dollars).

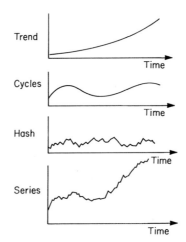

***Fig. 2.2***   Constructed series.

This chapter is concerned with methods of estimating the trend and then forecasting over the long run. The other two components are thus of lesser interest and it is usually worthwhile removing or at least reducing their importance before analyzing the trend. This is done by *smoothing* the series and this is best achieved by use of a *filter*, which is a linear transformation of the original series. A possible smoothing filter is to form a series $y_t$ from the given series $x_t$ by

$$y_t = \frac{1}{2m + 1} \sum_{j=-m}^{m} x_{t-j},$$

and this is called a (two-sided) moving average. However, as "future" $x$'s are used to form $y_t$, in practice one loses data at each end of the series by use of such a filter. A better filter generates $y_t$ from $x_t$ by the interactive formula

$$y_1 = x_1, \qquad y_t = ky_{t-1} + (1 - k)x_t, \qquad t = 2, \dots, n.$$

The larger the value of $k$, the greater the smoothing achieved. Typical appropriate values for $k$ would be 0.7 for monthly data, 0.5 for quarterly data, and 0.3 for a series recorded annually. The smoothed personal consumption series, with $k = 0.3$, has been shown in Table 2.2.

It is important to note that if the series is smoothed, and then a forecast made of $Y_{n+h}$ when at time $n$, $f_{n,h}^y$, then the corresponding forecast of $X_{n+h}$ is given by

$$f_{n,h}^x = \frac{f_{n,h}^y - kf_{n,h-1}^y}{1 - k}.$$

*It should be emphasized* that the methods discussed in the next two sections do not necessarily provide good forecasts relative to methods discussed in later chapters. These trend-curve methods are occasionally useful and allow discussion of a number of important points about forecasting strategy and provide examples of some of the ideas introduced in Chapter 1.

## 2.2   CHOOSING AND ESTIMATING A CURVE

Suppose that a sales manager of some manufacturing company looks at the chart of sales over the last few years and sees a smooth curve of one of the shapes shown in Fig. 2.3. There are innumerable curves that might fit some of these shapes, but if one is interested in just simple curves involving only a few parameters, the following are good candidates:

(1)   the straight line $C(t) = a + bt$;
(2)   the exponential curve $C(t) = \exp(a + bt)$, so that $\log C(t) = a + bt$;
(3)   the parabolic curve $C(t) = a + bt + ct^2$;
(4)   the modified exponential curve $C(t) = a + br^t$;
(5)   the Gompertz curve given by
$\log C(t) = a + br^t$, with $0 < r < 1$;
(6)   the logistic curve $C(t) = 1/(a + br^t)$, with $0 < r < 1$, so that $1/C(t) = a + br^t$.

**Fig. 2.3**

Looking at the different sales curves, appropriate curves might be

  (i)  Things going great
      exponential curve, with $b$ positive,
      modified exponential, $r > 1, b > 0$,
      parabolic curve, $b$ and $c$ positive;
  (ii)  things going well
      where the only curve appropriate is the straight line with $b > 0$;
  (iii)  Sales easing off
      modified exponential, $r < 1, b > 0$,
      parabolic curve, $c$ negative, $b$ positive,
      Gompertz curve, $b > 0$,
      logistic curve, $b > 0$;
  (iv)  Nothing happening
      straight line $C(t) = a$, so $b = 0$;
  (v)  Situation steadying
      modified exponential, $b$ negative,
      parabolic curve, $b$ negative, $c$ positive,
      Gompertz curve, $b$ negative,
      logistic curve, $b$ negative;

(vi) Steadily worse
    straight line, with $b < 0$; and
(vii) Awful
    exponential curve, with $b$ negative,
    modified exponential, with $b$ negative,
    parabolic curve, with both $b$ and $c$ negative.

It is seen that in several cases a unique curve is not a possibility. When this occurs all the possible curves should be fitted and then a criterion applied to see which fits best, as will be illustrated. Two of the set of six curves introduced above may be unfamiliar to many readers, the Gompertz and logistic curves. Their use is a rather specialized one, as they tend to a limit, or asymptote, as $t$ becomes large, this limit taking the value $e^a$ for the Gompertz and $1/a$ for the logistic. They are thus only appropriate for variables for which there is a clear upper limit which will virtually be reached not too distant in the future, such as the percent of homes in the U.S. that have electrification. However, for many series, it is not clear if there is an upper limit. Consider the total number of automobiles per 1000 population in some developed country, for instance. If one has a clear-cut idea of what the upper limit will be, this should be used for $e^a$ or $a^{-1}$ rather than an estimate of these quantities. If the variable is not near any limit and the limit is estimated from the available data, some very strange forecasts of the eventual limit values can result.

Having chosen one or a few curves to fit to the data, the next stage is to estimate its parameters from the data. The curves used need not be one of those mentioned above if one has a preference for some other curve, but it should be remembered that the more complicated the curve, involving more parameters, the more difficult will be the estimation stage.

Because of the least-squares criterion suggested in Chapter 1 for choosing between forecasting methods, the obvious way to estimate the parameters in some curve $T(t)$ is to choose values for these parameters that minimizes

$$I = \sum_{t=1}^{n} (x_t - C(t))^2,$$

where $x_t$ is the given or smoothed series, whichever is being used. If $C(t) = a + bt$, then some simple calculus and algebra gives as estimates

$$\hat{b} = \frac{\sum_{t=1}^{n} tx_t - \frac{1}{2}(n + 1) \sum_{t=1}^{n} x_t}{\frac{1}{12}n(n^2 - 1)}$$

and

$$\hat{a} = \frac{1}{n} \sum_{t=1}^{n} x_t - \frac{1}{2}(n + 1)\hat{b}.$$

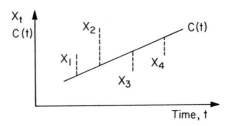

**Fig. 2.4**   Least-squares fit.

These estimates ensure that the sum of squares of the distance between the line and the data points, as shown in Fig. 2.4, is made as small as possible.

For some of the curves, it is very difficult to find parameter estimates in this way, so when possible a transformed least-squares estimate is obtained instead. For example, the parameters of the exponential trend can be fitted by taking logarithms of both the data and trend curve, so that

$$\log C(t) = a + bt$$

is fitted to $\log x_t$, provided all data values are positive. Most computer centers will have least-squares curve fitting programs in their statistics package so the tedious task of actually doing the calculations oneself can be avoided.

However, even these days there are occasions when access to a computer is not possible, or is too costly, so an alternative, much simpler but sub-optimum method of estimation will be described, known as the three-point method. As all of the curves considered above involve no more than three parameters, three points on the curves will determine exactly all other points. For the two-parameter curves, the straight line and the exponential, two points are enough to completely determine the parameters and thus all other points. One could start by just choosing two or three actual data points and then making the curves go through these, but even after smoothing there can be values that lie off the trend curve, and if these were used in the three-point method very poor estimates could result. To reduce this problem, averages of adjacent points might be used. However, the most important points are clearly the very last few, as they probably contain the most information about the future, so it is suggested that later points be given greater weight than earlier ones, so that weighted averages are used. The actual formulas are as follows:

Suppose the available data are $x_t$, $t = 1, \ldots, n$, and that $n$ is an odd integer. (If $n$ is even, it is simplest to merely drop the earliest piece of data.) Denote by $R$, the weighted average of the first five terms, i.e.,

$$R = \tfrac{1}{15}(x_1 + 2x_2 + 3x_3 + 4x_4 + 5x_5);$$

denote by $S$ the weighted average of the middle five terms, i.e.,

$$S = \tfrac{1}{15}(x_{d-2} + 2x_{d-1} + 3x_d + 4x_{d+1} + 5x_{d+2})$$

where $d = (n + 1)/2$ and as $n$ is odd, $d$ will be an integer; and further denote by $T$ the weighted average of the last five terms, i.e.,

$$T = \tfrac{1}{15}(x_{n-4} + 2x_{n-3} + 3x_{n-2} + 4x_{n-1} + 5x_n).$$

The weighted sums are divided by 15 because this is the sum of the weights used.

To understand the method, consider the fitting of the straight line

$$C(t) = a + bt.$$

If the observed series lay exactly on this line, we would have

$$R = \tfrac{1}{15}[(a + b) + 2(a + 2b) + 3(a + 3b) + 4(a + 4b) + 5(a + 5b)],$$

so

$$R = a + \tfrac{11}{3}b$$

and

$$T = \tfrac{1}{15}([a + (n - 4)b] + 2[a + (n - 3)b] + 3[a + (n - 2)b]$$
$$+ 4[a + (n - 1)b] + 5[a + nb])$$
$$= a + (n - \tfrac{4}{3})b.$$

Solving for $a$ and $b$, one has

$$b = \frac{T - R}{n - 5}, \qquad a = R - \frac{11}{3}b.$$

In practice, of course, the data will not exactly lie on the line but will vary about it, so the estimates of a and b are taken as

$$\hat{b} = \frac{T - R}{n - 5} \quad \text{and} \quad \hat{a} = R - \frac{11}{3}\hat{b}.$$

Suppose a straight line is fitted to the smoothed personal consumption data of Table 2.2 for the period 1948–1964, then $n = 17$, and

$$R = \tfrac{1}{15}(209.45 + 2 \times 214.39 + 3 \times 225.67 + 4 \times 230.66 + 5 \times 236.78)$$
$$= 228.12$$

and

$$T = \tfrac{1}{15}(311.77 + 2 \times 319.28 \times 332.66 + 4 \times 347.11 + 5 \times 365.72)$$
$$= 344.36,$$

so

$$\hat{b} = (344.36 - 228.12)/12 = 9.687$$

and

$$\hat{a} = 228.12 - \tfrac{11}{3}(9.697) = 192.6.$$

Thus, the fitted straight line trend is

$$C(t) = 192.6 + 9.687t,$$

with $t = 1$ in 1948.

In Table 2.3 all the fitted terms are shown and can be compared to the original data. The same method can be used for fitting the exponential curve, but using the logarithms of the data, the values of which are also shown in Table 2.3. Using the log data, one gets

$$R = 5.4291, \qquad T = 5.8403,$$

**TABLE 2.3**

| Year | Data | $t$ | Weights | Fitted straight line | Log (base $e$) Data | Weights | Fitted exponential curve |
|---|---|---|---|---|---|---|---|
| 1948 | 209.45 | 1 | 1 | 202.28 | 5.3444 | 1 | 208.01 |
| 1949 | 214.39 | 2 | 2 $R$ | 211.98 | 5.3677 | 2 $R$ | 215.27 |
| 1950 | 225.67 | 3 | 3 = 228.12 | 221.67 | 5.419 | 3 = 5.4291 | 222.78 |
| 1951 | 230.66 | 4 | 4 | 231.35 | 5.4409 | 4 | 230.56 |
| 1952 | 236.78 | 5 | 5 | 241.04 | 5.4571 | 5 | 238.60 |
| 1953 | 246.59 | 6 | | 250.72 | 5.5077 | | 246.93 |
| 1954 | 252.97 | 7 | 1 | 260.41 | 5.5332 | | 255.55 |
| 1955 | 267.83 | 8 | 2 $S$ | 270.10 | 5.5903 | | 264.46 |
| 1956 | 277.33 | 9 | 3 = 280.21 | 279.78 | 5.6252 | | 273.69 |
| 1957 | 284.94 | 10 | 4 | 289.47 | 5.6522 | | 283.24 |
| 1958 | 288.55 | 11 | 5 | 299.16 | 5.6648 | | 293.13 |
| 1959 | 301.68 | 12 | | 308.85 | 5.7094 | | 303.35 |
| 1960 | 311.77 | 13 | 1 | 318.93 | 5.7424 | 1 | 313.94 |
| 1961 | 319.28 | 14 | 2 $T$ | 328.22 | 5.7662 | 2 $T$ | 324.89 |
| 1962 | 332.66 | 15 | 3 = 344.36 | 337.91 | 5.8072 | 3 = 5.9403 | 336.23 |
| 1963 | 347.11 | 16 | 4 | 347.59 | 5.8497 | 4 | 347.96 |
| 1964 | 365.72 | 17 | 5 | 357.28 | 5.9019 | 5 | 360.11 |

giving

$$\hat{a} = 5.3033, \qquad \hat{b} = 0.0343,$$

so that the trend curve is given by

$$\log C(t) = 5.3033 + 0.0343t.$$

The method of fitting the other curves is very similar, it being merely a matter of forming $R$, $S$, and $T$ and then applying the formulas given in Table 2.4. However, if only a short series is available, say $n < 10$ if fitting a two-parameter, or $n < 15$ if fitting a three-parameter curve, slightly different definitions of $R$, $S$, and $T$ are used, that is, weighted averages over just three terms:

$$R = \tfrac{1}{6}(x_1 + 2x_2 + 3x_3),$$
$$S = \tfrac{1}{6}(x_{d-1} + 2x_d + 3x_{d+1}),$$

and

$$T = \tfrac{1}{6}(x_{n-2} + 2x_{n-1} + 3x_n)$$

where $d = (n + 1)/2$ as before.

The list of formulas to apply to fit the curves is given in Table 2.4.

Four different possible trend curves were fitted to the consumer expenditure data, the linear, exponential, parabolic, and modified exponential curves. The estimated parameters were found to be

   (i)   linear[1]: $\hat{a} = 192.6$, $\hat{b} = 9.687$;
  (ii)   exponential: $\hat{a} = 5.3033$, $\hat{b} = 0.0343$;
 (iii)   parabolic: $\hat{a} = 201.96$, $\hat{b} = 6.449$, $\hat{c} = 0.1675$;
 (iv)   modified exponential: $\hat{a} = 3.131$, $\hat{b} = 197.790$, $\hat{r} = 1.0355$.

Table 2.5 shows the original data, plus the fitted values of these four curves. The question remains, which curve fits best? Our criterion states that we should look at the average squared error, but this will not quite give a fair comparison since a curve involving three parameters has an advantage over one with just two, even if neither is the correct curve. The criterion used is designed to at least partly remove this possible bias:

$$\bar{S} = [\text{sum of squared errors (i.e., difference between data and curve)}]/(n - m),$$

where $m$ is the number of parameters involved in the curve, so that $m = 2$ for the linear and exponential curves and $m = 3$ for the others.

---

[1] If the linear function had been fitted by least squares, the coefficients would have been $\hat{a} = 191$, $\hat{b} = 9.69$, which are very similar to the two-point estimates.

**TABLE 2.4**

*Formulas for Estimating Parameters Using the Three-Point Method*

| Ordinary series | Short series |
| --- | --- |
| (R, S, T weighted average of 5 terms) | (R, S, T weighted average of 3 terms) |

(1)   Straight line, $C(t) = a + bt$

$$\hat{b} = \frac{T - R}{n - 5}$$

$$\hat{b} = \frac{T - R}{n - 3}$$

$$\hat{a} = R - \tfrac{11}{3}\hat{b}$$

$$\hat{a} = R - \tfrac{7}{3}\hat{b}$$

(2)   Exponential curve, $C(t) = \exp(a + bt)$

As for straight line, but using logarithms of data when forming $R$, $S$, and $T$.

(3)   Parabolic curve, $C(t) = a + bt + ct^2$

$$\hat{c} = \frac{2(R + T - 2S)}{(n - 5)^2}$$

$$\hat{c} = \frac{2(R + T - 2S)}{(n - 3)^2}$$

$$\hat{b} = \frac{T - R}{n - 5} - \frac{(3n + 7)}{3}\hat{c}$$

$$\hat{b} = \frac{T - R}{n - 3} - \frac{(3n + 5)}{3}\hat{c}$$

$$\hat{a} = R - \tfrac{11}{3}\hat{b} - 15\hat{c}$$

$$\hat{a} = R - \tfrac{7}{3}\hat{b} - 6\hat{c}$$

(4)   Modified Exponential curve, $C(t) = a + br^t$

$$\log \hat{r} = \frac{2}{n - 5} \log \frac{T - S}{S - R}$$

$$\log \hat{r} = \frac{2}{n - 3} \log \frac{T - S}{S - R}$$

$$\hat{a} = \frac{TR - S^2}{R + T - 2S}$$

$$\hat{a} = \frac{TR - S^2}{R + T - 2S}$$

$$\hat{b} = \frac{k(S - R)^2}{R + T - 2S}$$

$$\hat{b} = \frac{k(S - R)^2}{R + T - 2S}$$

where $k = 15/(\hat{r} + 2\hat{r}^2 + 3\hat{r}^3 + 4\hat{r}^4 + 5\hat{r}^5)$     where $k = 6/(\hat{r} + 2\hat{r}^2 + 3\hat{r}^3)$

(5)   Gompertz curve, $\log C(t) = a + br^t$

Same as for modified exponential curve, but using logarithms of data when forming $R$, $S$, and $T$.

(6)   Logistic curve, $1/C(t) = a + br^t$

Same as for modified exponential curve, but using the reciprocals of the data when forming $R$, $S$, and $T$.

**TABLE 2.5**

| $t$ | Data | Straight line | Exponential | Modified exponential | Parabolic |
|---|---|---|---|---|---|
| 1 | 209.45 | 202.23 | 208.01 | 207.94 | 208.58 |
| 2 | 214.39 | 211.98 | 215.27 | 215.21 | 215.53 |
| 3 | 225.67 | 221.67 | 222.78 | 222.74 | 222.81 |
| 4 | 230.66 | 231.35 | 230.56 | 230.54 | 230.44 |
| 5 | 236.78 | 241.04 | 238.60 | 238.61 | 238.39 |
| 6 | 246.59 | 250.72 | 246.93 | 246.97 | 246.68 |
| 7 | 252.97 | 260.41 | 255.55 | 255.63 | 255.31 |
| 8 | 267.83 | 270.10 | 264.46 | 264.59 | 264.27 |
| 9 | 277.33 | 279.78 | 273.69 | 273.87 | 273.57 |
| 10 | 284.94 | 289.47 | 283.24 | 283.48 | 283.20 |
| 11 | 288.55 | 299.16 | 293.13 | 293.44 | 293.17 |
| 12 | 301.68 | 308.85 | 303.35 | 303.74 | 303.47 |
| 13 | 311.77 | 318.53 | 313.94 | 314.41 | 314.10 |
| 14 | 319.28 | 328.22 | 324.89 | 325.46 | 325.08 |
| 15 | 332.66 | 337.91 | 336.28 | 336.91 | 336.38 |
| 16 | 347.11 | 347.59 | 347.96 | 348.76 | 348.02 |
| 17 | 365.72 | 357.28 | 360.11 | 361.03 | 360.00 |

The results for the four fitted curves of our example are given in the accompanying tabulation.

| | $m$ | $\bar{S}$ |
|---|---|---|
| linear | 2 | 39.0 |
| exponential | 2 | 10.3 |
| parabolic | 3 | 11.4 |
| modified exponential | 3 | 11.8 |

From the $\bar{S}$ value over the fitting period, it is clear that the straight line is the poorest approximation to the data but that there is virtually no reason to choose amongst the other three curves. In the circumstances, it is probably best to retain all three curves, make forecasts from them and average these values to get the eventual forecast. Within a few years, evidence will have accumulated on the relative abilities of the curves to actually forecast. The best curve can then be picked and its parameters reestimated and then used to forecast further ahead. The next section discusses how the forecasts are made and how well our curves actually did forecast.

## 2.3   FORECASTING USING TREND CURVES

To forecast for a particular year corresponding to $t = t_0$, using the curve $C(t)$, one simply calculates $C(t_0)$ and then corrects for the smoothing filter, if used, by applying the formula at the end of Section 2.1. Thus, for example, if the parabolic curve is being used,

$$C(t) = 201.96 + 6.449t + 0.167t^2.$$

Then to forecast for 1974, which corresponds to $t = 27$ as $1947 = 1$, one forms

$$C(27) = 201.96 + 6.449 \times 27 + 0.1675 \times (27)^2$$

$$= 498.19.$$

Similarly, the forecast for 1973 is

$$C(26) = 482.86.$$

Thus, the forecast for the original, unsmoothed series for 1974 is

$$f_{17, 10} = \frac{498.19 - 0.3 \times 482.86}{1 - 0.3} = 504.76.$$

The whole set of forecasts for the original, unsmoothed series for the years 1965–1977 is shown in Table 2.6, together with the actual values where available. Are the forecasts good or bad? This question is virtually impos-

**TABLE 2.6**

| Year | $t$ | Actual values | Linear | Exponential | Modified exponential | Parabolic |
|------|-----|---------------|--------|-------------|----------------------|-----------|
| 1965 | 18 | 397.7 | 371.12 | 378.20 | 379.18 | 377.59 |
| 1966 | 19 | 418.1 | 380.80 | 391.48 | 392.53 | 390.38 |
| 1967 | 20 | 430.1 | 390.49 | 405.22 | 406.35 | 403.50 |
| 1968 | 21 | 452.7 | 400.18 | 419.44 | 420.66 | 416.97 |
| 1969 | 22 | 469.1 | 409.87 | 434.16 | 435.48 | 430.75 |
| 1970 | 23 | 477.5 | 419.56 | 449.40 | 450.83 | 444.89 |
| 1971 | 24 | 496.3 | 429.24 | 465.18 | 466.72 | 459.36 |
| 1972 | 25 | 526.8 | 438.93 | 481.50 | 483.18 | 474.15 |
| 1973 | 26 | 552.1 | 448.62 | 498.40 | 500.23 | 489.28 |
| 1974 | 27 | 539.5 | 458.30 | 515.90 | 517.87 | 504.76 |
| 1975 | 28 |       | 467.99 | 534.01 | 536.15 | 520.56 |
| 1976 | 29 |       | 477.68 | 552.75 | 555.07 | 536.70 |
| 1977 | 30 |       | 487.36 | 572.15 | 574.65 | 553.18 |

sible to answer. All one *can* say is whether one technique appears superior to another, and at this point there is no other technique available for comparison. It is certainly to be expected that the forecasts will be made with error. In 1964 it would have been virtually impossible to forecast the occurrence of a strong depression in 1974–1975, for example. The exponential curves forecast U.S. consumer expenditure (in 1958 dollars) within 2% in 1975, the most recent available figure at the time of writing, which for many purposes would be considered a rather acceptable level of error for a forecast looking 11 years into the future. However, the forecasts for earlier years were less impressive, although errors were generally less than 5%. The occurrence of the inflation-induced depression of 1974–1975 has made the forecasts for 1975 more respectable. Without this dip in growth, the forecasts would have continued too low. This downward bias would have been quickly noticed within a few years of our base year of 1964. Presumably, exponential curves fitted in 1968, say, would have performed rather better in later years but may have been too high in 1975. Overall, the example does suggest that trend curves do produce forecasts of some value for several years into the future, perhaps surprisingly so, given the basic lack of sophistication in model selection that is used.

The obvious problem with trend-curve fitting is the lack of any real theory underlying the forecasts, and this is true whatever method is used to estimate the parameters of curves. The set of curves considered is necessarily arbitrary, even if a wider set is used than those discussed in the previous section. The curve fitting process appears to be just "number crunching," and the method of forecasting consists of the blind hope that whatever mechanism generated the trend in the past will continue to work in the future. It is the main weakness of this approach that absolutely no attempt is made to understand this underlying mechanism.

The hope that things will continue in the future as they have in the past is clearly wrong on occasions. An example is provided by pollution levels in air and water in recent years. After years of increasing pollution in some locations, not only has the situation stabilized but the direction of trend has actually reversed. Air pollution levels in Pittsburgh and London are cases in point, as is the pollution content of some rivers such as the Thames in London, where some species of fish have recently been observed that have been hitherto absent throughout the twentieth century. There is a river in the eastern part of the United States that was so polluted that the oil and junk floating on its surface made it into an official fire hazard for a period, but it is now much improved. A second possible example of a change in trend appeared in a news item whilst this section was being prepared. By 1975, there were approximately a quarter of a million swimming pools in California, with sales of new pools running at about 12,000 a year. As virtually no existing pools were being removed, the total number was obviously trending upward. However, worries of a natural gas shortage led the state senate to pass a new law forbidding any new pool to be heated by gas, which is virtually the only practical way of doing it at this time. One would certainly expect the slope of the trend of total pools to be changed, at the very least. Whether this is a temporary change in the trend or a permanent one depends on the development of new technology to provide heat for pools not using natural gas. The question of whether the timing of such technological developments can be forecast will be discussed in Chapter 10.

A rather different example of the problems encountered when venturing outside one's normal range of experience comes from the situation faced by the sailors when they first left the Mediterranean Sea. For the first time they encountered substantial tides and initially had considerable difficulty in coping with this phenomenon. Any forecaster who extrapolates to an economy or society outside of previous experience has to be ready for similar difficulties.

It should be emphasized again that trend-curve forecasting cannot be recommended with complete confidence but can be a useful member of a parcel of alternative methods and does sometimes produce really worthwhile predictions.

The more important lessons of this chapter so far are derived from the approach taken to fitting and evaluating a technique. The basic steps in this approach are

   (i)   the choice of a set of possible curves or models (the identification stage),
   (ii)   the estimate of the parameters of the model (the estimation stage), and
   (iii)   the use of a criterion to evaluate the relative goodness of fit of the models (the diagnostic checking stage).

A different example of the use of these stages will be provided by the techniques described in the next chapter.

## 2.4   TREND REMOVED BY DIFFERENCING

The fitting of trend curves is not the only method available for treating series apparently containing a trend. In the first section of this chapter a simple filter was introduced that removed the unsmooth components of a series leaving only the smooth or trend part. It is also possible to find filters that remove a trend, so that the remaining, relatively unsmooth parts can be forecast using methods to be outlined in the next two chapters and the original series then forecast by unraveling the filter. A simple example of how this is done comes from considering the effect of differencing a series. If the original series is $x_t$, the differenced series is

$$y_t = x_t - x_{t-1},$$

so that $y_t$ is just the change in $x_t$. Suppose that $x_t$ is just the straight line

$$x_t = a + bt.$$

Then

$$y_t = (a + bt) - (a + b(t - 1)) = b,$$

so although $x_t$ contains a trend, $y_t$ does not. More generally, suppose that $x_t$ consists of a linear trend plus some other, nontrending component $x'_t$ having zero mean, so that

$$x_t = a + bt + x'_t.$$

Then

$$y_t = b + (x'_t - x'_{t-1}).$$

If some method of forecasting the $y_t$ is devised, producing forecasts $f_{n,h}^{(y)}$ in the notation of Chapter 1, then noting that

$$x_{n+h} = y_{n+h} + x_{n+h-1},$$

one obtains forecasts of $x_{n+h}$ by

$$f_{n,1}^{(x)} = f_{n,1}^{(y)} + x_n,$$
$$f_{n,h}^{(x)} = f_{n,h}^{(y)} + f_{n,h-1}^{(x)}.$$

Provided that the mean of $y_t$, which is an estimate of $b$, is nonzero, the sequence of forecasts $f_{n,h}^{(x)}$ for $h = 1, 2, \ldots$ will contain a linear trend.

If the true trend curve is not linear, differencing the series once will not do a complete job of trend removal. There are various ways around this problem. Some trends are "locally linear," that is, can be well approximated over sections by straight lines, in which case differencing will remove most of the trend, but forecasting what remains may be complicated. If the trend is exponential, then by using the logarithm of the data the trend may be made linear and the differencing procedure applied. Finally, if the trend is parabolic in nature, it can be removed by differencing twice. This is seen by taking

$$x_t = a + bt + ct^2.$$

Then

$$y_t = x_t - x_{t-1}$$
$$= a + bt + ct^2 - (a + b(t-1) + c(t-1)^2)$$
$$= b + c(t^2 - (t^2 - 2t + 1))$$
$$= b + c + 2tc,$$

so that $y_t$ now contains a linear trend which can be removed by differencing $y_t$.

The use of differencing series to remove trends has become popular again in recent years, after a couple of decades of neglect, and has been found to be effective for most economic data. This point is discussed further in Section 3.7.

## 2.5   IRREGULARLY RECORDED DATA

Virtually all of the data considered in this book are assumed to be recorded at virtually constant intervals of time, such as each day, week, month, or quarter. However, occasionally the only data available, or the most appropriate, are recorded at irregular intervals. One of the advantages of using least-square regression methods is that they can be used with this type of data, particularly with the simple curves. Consider, for example, the data given in Figure 2.5, which show those years from 1864 to 1975 when the men's mile run was finished in record time together with the world records.

***Fig. 2.5***   World record times for the mile run.

The times have reduced from the 4 minutes and 56 seconds by Charles Lawes in 1804 through to the 3:59.4 by Roger Bannister in 1954, and on to the 3:49.4 by John Walker in 1975. The names of the other temporary record holders can be found in the standard reference books. The plot of the data, shown in Fig. 2.5, suggests that a straight line would be an appropriate curve to fit. If the record years are denoted by $x_j$ and the corresponding records by $y_j$, then the data consist of the pairs $(x_j, y_j)$, $j = 1, \ldots, n$. In this case, if the $x$ are recorded as the deviation in years from 1895 and the $y$'s in minutes, then the relationship takes the form

$$y = a + bx + \text{error.}$$

Standard least-squares regression theory finds that $a$ and $b$ are obtained as the solutions to the following equations:

$$\sum_j y_j = na + b \sum_j x_j,$$

$$\sum_j x_j y_j = a \sum_j x_j + b \sum_j x_j^2.$$

In this case, Oakley and Baker (1977) estimated the straight line relationship to be

$$y = 4.33907564 - 0.00644959x.$$

The number of figures shown is far more than usually recorded; a more usual form might be

$$y = 4.339 - 0.0064x.$$

If the world record for the one-mile run continues to evolve at the same rate, then the record will be at almost exactly 3 minutes and 40 seconds by the year 2000, according to either of these equations.

## QUESTIONS

Data definitions and sources (Table 2.7):

    A   U.S. infant mortality rate (deaths in first year) per 1000 live births.

    B   U. S. per capita consumption of fishery products, pounds of edible meat.

    C   U.S. net production of electrical energy, in billions of kilowatt-hours.

    D   Price of silver, cents per fine ounce, New York.

## TABLE 2.7

*Sample Data*

| Year | A | B | C | D |
|------|------|------|------|-----|
| | | Series | | |
| 1930 | 64.6 | 10.2 | 114 | 38 |
| 1931 | 61.6 | 8.8 | 109 | 28 |
| 1932 | 57.6 | 8.4 | 99 | 27 |
| 1933 | 58.1 | 8.7 | 102 | 34 |
| 1934 | 60.1 | 9.2 | 110 | 47 |
| 1935 | 55.7 | 10.5 | 118 | 64 |
| 1936 | 57.1 | 11.7 | 136 | 45 |
| 1937 | 54.4 | 11.8 | 146 | 44 |
| 1938 | 51.0 | 10.8 | 141 | 43 |
| 1939 | 48.0 | 10.7 | 161 | 39 |
| 1940 | 47.0 | 11.0 | 179 | 34 |
| 1941 | 45.3 | 11.2 | 208 | 34 |
| 1942 | 40.4 | 8.7 | 233 | 38 |
| 1943 | 40.3 | 7.9 | 267 | 44 |
| 1944 | 39.4 | 8.7 | 279 | 44 |
| 1945 | 38.3 | 9.9 | 271 | 51 |
| 1946 | 33.8 | 10.8 | 269 | 80 |
| 1947 | 32.2 | 10.3 | 307 | 71 |
| 1948 | 32.0 | 11.1 | 336 | 74 |
| 1949 | 31.3 | 10.9 | 345 | 71 |
| 1950 | 29.2 | 11.8 | 388 | 74 |
| 1951 | 28.4 | 11.2 | 433 | 89 |
| 1952 | 28.4 | 11.2 | 463 | 84 |
| 1953 | 27.8 | 11.4 | 514 | 85 |
| 1954 | 26.6 | 11.2 | 544 | 85 |
| 1955 | 26.4 | 10.5 | 629 | 89 |
| 1956 | 26.0 | 10.4 | 684 | 90 |
| 1957 | 26.3 | 10.2 | 716 | 90 |
| 1958 | 27.1 | 10.6 | 724 | 89 |
| 1959 | 26.4 | 10.9 | 797 | 91 |
| 1960 | 26.0 | 10.3 | 844 | 91 |
| 1961 | 25.3 | 10.7 | 881 | 92 |
| 1962 | 25.3 | 10.6 | 946 | 108 |
| 1963 | 25.2 | 10.7 | 1011 | 127 |
| 1964 | 24.8 | 10.5 | 1083 | 129 |
| 1965 | 24.7 | 10.9 | 1157 | 129 |

*Postsample Data*

| Year | A | B | C | D |
|------|---------------|------|------|-----|
| 1966 | 23.7 | 10.9 | 1249 | 129 |
| 1967 | 22.4 | 10.6 | 1317 | 154 |
| 1968 | 21.8 | 11.0 | 1436 | 214 |
| 1969 | 20.9 | 11.2 | 1552 | 179 |
| 1970 | 20.0 | 11.8 | 1639 | 177 |
| 1971 | 19.1 | 11.5 | 1718 | 154 |
| 1972 | 18.5 | 12.4 | 1853 | 169 |
| 1973 | 17.7 | 12.9 | 1959 | 256 |
| 1974 | 16.7 | 12.2 | 1968 | 471 |
| 1975 | 16.1 | 12.2 | 2003 | 442 |
| 1976 | not available | 12.9 | 2123 | 437 |

For the period 1930–1970, the data are taken from *Historical Statistics of the United States, Colonial Times to 1970*.[2] The more recent data are taken from the *Statistical Abstract of the United States, 1977*. The table numbers in these publications are tabulated below.

| Series | 1930–1970 | 1971 on |
|--------|-----------|---------|
| A | B 139 | 102 |
| B | L 294 | 1250 |
| C | S 32 | 992 |
| D | M 270 | 1186 |

1. Using just the data from the sample period 1930–1965 (Table 2.7) identify and fit trend lines to each of the four series. Do not look at the postsample data when picking trend curves.

   Compare your forecasts for the period 1966–1975 with the actual postsample values. Do you consider the forecasts to have been successful? If no, suggest reasons.

   If instead of using annual data, you had used data for just the odd years (1931, 1933, etc.), would your curves have forecast 1973 significantly worse?

2. Consider the time series

| $t$ | 1 | 2 | 3 | 4 | 5 | 6 | 7 | 8 | 9 | 10 | 11 | 12 |
|-----|---|---|---|---|---|---|---|---|---|----|----|----|
| $x_t$ | −3 | 1 | 0 | −1 | 3 | 5 | 6 | 8 | 5 | 11 | 8 | 12 |

   Smooth, using the filter $y_t = 0.5y_{t-1} + 0.5x_t$, fit a straight line by the two-point method, and forecast a value of $x_t$ for $t = 20$.

3. Suppose that you are given a puppy of a rare breed and with a rather unusual shape—low, thin, and long. By observing the puppy's growth during the first few weeks of your ownership, discuss how you would attempt to predict its eventual weight, height, and length.

4. The following table shows the men's world record pole vaults since 1957, when metal poles were introduced. Fit a trend curve to these figures. (Only the records standing at the end of record-breaking years are shown.)

---

[2] Published by the U. S. Department of Commerce, Bureau of the Census, U.S. Govt. Printing Office, Washington, D.C., 1975.

| Year | Record feet | Record inches | Year | Record feet | Record inches |
|------|------|--------|------|------|--------|
| 1957 | 15 | $8\frac{1}{4}$ | 1967 | 17 | $7\frac{3}{4}$ |
| 1960 | 15 | $9\frac{1}{4}$ | 1968 | 17 | 9 |
| 1961 | 15 | $10\frac{1}{4}$ | 1969 | 17 | $10\frac{1}{4}$ |
| 1962 | 16 | 2 | 1970 | 18 | $\frac{1}{4}$ |
| 1963 | 17 | $\frac{3}{4}$ | 1972 | 18 | $5\frac{3}{4}$ |
| 1964 | 17 | 4 | 1975 | 18 | $6\frac{1}{4}$ |
| 1966 | 17 | $6\frac{1}{4}$ | 1976 | 18 | $8\frac{1}{4}$ |

## FURTHER READINGS

Armstrong, J. Scott (1978). *Long-Range Forecasting, from Crystal Ball to Computer*, New York: Wiley.
   Wide-ranging discussion, with good, detailed examples.
Martino, J. P. (1972). *Technological Forecasting for Decision Making*, New York: Amer. Elsevier.
   Many excellent examples of trend curve fitting.
Oakley, C. O., and J. C. Baker (1977). "Least Squares and the 3.40 Minute Mile," *Mathematics Teacher* **70** (4), 322–324.

CHAPTER

# 3

# Forecasting from Time Series Models

*Some things are so unexpected that no one is prepared for them.*
Leo Rosten in "Rome Wasn't Burned in a Day"

## 3.1 WHITE NOISE

Before consideration of how a time series is analyzed and forecast, it is necessary to be introduced to a few simple but important models, that is methods by which a series can be generated. The simplest possible model gives a *purely random series*, otherwise known as *white noise*. This second name comes from engineering and cannot properly be explained without entering the murky environment of a method of analysis known as spectral analysis, so no explanation will be attempted. A series is white noise if it has virtually no discernable structure or pattern to it. If such a series is denoted by $\varepsilon_t$, for all values of $t$, the formal definition is that this series is white noise if correlation$(\varepsilon_t, \varepsilon_s) = 0$, all $t \neq s$, and if also the mean, or expected value, of $\varepsilon_t$ is a constant for all $t$. It is usual to take this constant to be zero, giving zero-mean white noise.

To appreciate this definition, it is perhaps best to consider some examples of purely random series.

   (i)   Suppose you stand on the street corner and record the numbers on the license plates of passing cars. There is very little reason to suppose that there is any relationship between one number observed and the next.

   (ii)   A teacher asks everyone in his class to write down an integer from 0 to 9 inclusive. If the first twenty students, going across the first row, then the second row, and so forth, read out their numbers, will this help the teacher predict the number that would be read out next? Again, there is likely to be no pattern to the numbers. If the teacher thinks that each integer is equally likely to occur, then all he can predict is that there is a probability of 0.1 that the next number will be a 0, a 1, a 2, etc. The numbers read out by the first few students may suggest to the teacher that certain integers are more likely to occur than others, so he may change his prediction to a statement such as "there is a probability of 0.05 that the next number will be 0, of 0.07 that it will be 1, of 0.11 of it being 2, etc." In this case, the earlier data may be helpful in making his prediction statement, but it is important to note that he will be indifferent between any possible *order* in which these earlier numbers are given to him. A time-series has a *structure*, strictly a temporal structure, if the order of the data not only matters but is of paramount importance. Examples will be given later.

(iii)   The winning numbers on a state lottery ticket or the British premium bonds, if recorded monthly, make up a white noise series. Having the sequence of past winning numbers will in no way help you predict the next winning number.

(iv)   A further example of a white noise series is the winning numbers in the numbers game. This game is, or was, played heavily in the lower income areas of the large eastern U.S. cities. You hand a slip of paper to a bookie with three integers on it, such as 275, plus your bet. If your number comes up, the organizers pay $600 for every $1 bet. The potential profit margin is huge, at about $400 for every $1,000 bet, which probably explains why the game is illegal and is said to be run by major criminal organizations whose names remind one of the Mediterranean. The rules of the game are simple, but how is the winning number to be chosen so that it cannot be "fixed?" The method used is to take the final three digits of the total amount of money bet at some specific horserace track that day, either in New York or Florida. This completely explains why this otherwise entirely useless statistic was historically printed by some New York newspapers.

Table 3.2 (Section 3.8) shows an example of a constructed white noise series. The main properties of these series are that

(i)   there is no correlation between terms, and
(ii)   previous values do not help forecast future values.

This second statement needs amending if the white noise has nonzero mean of unknown size, as then the sample mean of the observed values can be used to predict this population mean. Note that the order in which the numbers are observed is of no consequence when forming the sample mean.

If a least-squares criterion is used, it can be shown that the best forecast of all future values of a white noise series is just equal to the series mean.

From a forecasting point of view, a white noise series is rather uninteresting, but it will later be shown to be a particularly important model when evaluating forecasts.

### Exercises

1. Suggest two further examples of white noise series other than those mentioned in the text.

2. Do you think that any of the following provide examples of white noise series?
   (a) The number of companies going bankrupt in a month.
   (b) The daily changes in stock market prices.
   (c) The number of runs scored by a baseball team in a sequence of consecutive games (goals scored by a soccer team, points scored by a basketball team, or whatever).
   (d) The number of letters in succeeding words in a novel.
   (e) The number of letters in the names of succeeding months (January = 7, February = 7, March = 5, etc.).
   (f) The total number of telephone calls made in a day in some developed country.

## 3.2 MOVING AVERAGES

Most series observed in reality, particularly in economics, are much smoother than the white noise shown in Table 3.2. One method of forming smoother series is to use a moving average. If $\varepsilon_t$ is a white noise series, a simple moving average is the series $x_t$ generated by

$$x_t = \varepsilon_t + \beta\varepsilon_{t-1}, \tag{1}$$

although a better name would be weighted moving sum. If $\varepsilon_t$ has mean zero, then so will $x_t$. A numerical example of $x_t$ generated in this fashion, with $\beta = \frac{1}{2}$, is shown in Table 3.1A. A larger sample of this series is shown in Table 3.2. Although this particular moving average series could hardly be described as smooth, it is nevertheless smoother than the white noise series. It becomes somewhat smoother yet if $\beta$ is near unity, but a negative value of $\beta$ produces a series that is even less smooth than white noise, as a numerical example would show.

To examine the theoretical properties of this moving average series, values for the correlation between $x_t$ and $x_{t-j}$ are required, the so-called

TABLE 3.1A

| $t$ | $\varepsilon_t$ | $\frac{1}{2}\varepsilon_{t-1}$ | $x_t$ | $t$ | $\varepsilon_t$ | $\frac{1}{2}\varepsilon_{t-1}$ | $x_t$ |
|---|---|---|---|---|---|---|---|
| 0 | 0.02 | — | — | 5 | −0.04 | −0.09 | −0.13 |
| 1 | −0.12 | 0.01 | −0.11 | 6 | 0.00 | −0.02 | −0.02 |
| 2 | 0.20 | −0.06 | 0.14 | 7 | 0.16 | 0.00 | 0.16 |
| 3 | 0.06 | 0.10 | 0.16 | 8 | 0.06 | 0.08 | 0.14 |
| 4 | −0.18 | 0.03 | −0.15 | | | | |

*autocorrelations* of the series, because the series $x_t$ is checked to see if it is correlated with its own past. If two random variables $X$ and $Y$ are correlated, the formula used is

$$\text{corr}(X,\ Y) = \frac{\text{covariance}(X,\ Y)}{\sqrt{\text{variance}(X)\text{variance}(Y)}},$$

where, if $X$ and $Y$ both have zero mean, the terms used in the ratio are defined, using the expectation notation, by

$$\text{covariance}(X,\ Y) = E[XY]$$

and

$$\text{variance}(X) = E[X^2],$$

so

$$\text{variance}(Y) = E[Y^2].$$

However, it can be shown that for a moving average series variance$(x_{t-j})$ = variance$(x_t)$, so the autocorrelation formula becomes

$$\text{corr}(x_t,\ x_{t-j}) = \frac{E[x_t x_{t-j}]}{\text{var}(x_t)}.$$

Note that if $x_t$ is white noise, then all of these autocorrelations are zero, provided $j \neq 0$. By substituting for $x_t$, $x_{t-1}$ from the generating formula (1), it is seen that

$$E[x_t x_{t-1}] = E[(\varepsilon_t + \beta\varepsilon_{t-1})(\varepsilon_{t-1} + \beta\varepsilon_{t-2})]$$
$$= E[\varepsilon_t\varepsilon_{t-1}] + \beta E[\varepsilon_{t-1}^2] + \beta^2 E[\varepsilon_{t-1}\varepsilon_{t-2}] + \beta E[\varepsilon_t\varepsilon_{t-2}].$$

However, any term such as $E[\varepsilon_t\varepsilon_s]$, $t \neq s$, will be proportional to corr$(\varepsilon_t,\ \varepsilon_s)$, which is zero, so this formula simplifies to

$$E[x_t x_{t-1}] = \beta\ \text{var}(\varepsilon_t).$$

It follows that if $\beta$ is positive, then adjacent terms of $x_t$ will be positively correlated, so that an above average, i.e., positive, $x_t$ will be inclined to be followed by a further above average value, and similarly, a below average term is likely to be followed by a below average value. For a white noise series, $\beta = 0$, an above average value is equally likely to be followed by an above average or a below average value, because of the zero correlation between adjacent terms in the series. If $\beta$ is negative, then adjacent terms are negatively correlated, so an above average term is likely to be followed by a below average term, and so forth. It should thus be clear why the value of $\beta$ determines the relative smoothness of the moving average series. These ideas are illustrated in Figure 3.1.

Now consider correlations between nonadjacent terms. To do this, one has to look at

$$E[x_t x_{t-j}] = E[(\varepsilon_t + \beta\varepsilon_{t-1})(\varepsilon_{t-j} + \beta\varepsilon_{t-j-1})],$$

but if the right-hand side is expanded, all the terms are of the form $E[\varepsilon_t \varepsilon_s]$, $t \neq s$, provided $j > 1$, and so

$$E[x_t x_{t-j}] = 0, \qquad j > 1,$$

i.e.,

$$\text{corr}(x_t, x_{t-j}) = 0, \qquad \text{all } j > 11$$

Thus, for the model (1), there is no correlation between the present value of $x_t$ and all previous values apart from the most recent.

Suppose that you are told that a given series has been generated by model (1) and that also you are provided with the value of $\beta$, how would this information be used to forecast future values of the series? Further, suppose that the information set available to you is $I_n$: $x_{n-j}$, that is, just the past and present of the series to be forecast and consider the one-step forecast. At time $n$, you know from (1) that the next value of the $x_t$ series will be generated by

$$x_{n+1} = \varepsilon_{n+1} + \beta\varepsilon_n.$$

*Fig. 3.1* MA(1) scatter plots. (a) $\beta > 0$, (b) $\beta = 0$ (white noise), and (c) $\beta < 0$.

Of these two terms, the first is not forecastable, with the information being used, as it is the next term of a white noise series, but the second term is known at time $n$. It should be clear that the optimum forecast of $x_{n+1}$ is

$$f_{n,1} = \beta\varepsilon_n, \tag{2}$$

and this can be proved more formally. The one-step forecast error is

$$\begin{aligned} e_{n,1} &= x_{n+1} - f_{n,1} \\ &= (\varepsilon_{n+1} + \beta\varepsilon_n) - \beta\varepsilon_n \\ &= \varepsilon_{n+1}. \end{aligned} \tag{3}$$

Thus, it is convenient to write

$$\varepsilon_n = x_n - f_{n-1,1},$$

and so (2) becomes

$$f_{n,1} = \beta(x_n - f_{n-1,1}). \tag{4}$$

By using this formula, the whole sequence of one-step forecasts for different values of $n$ can be generated, although there is a starting-up problem. If it is known that the mean of the series to be forecast is zero, it is usual to start up the sequence of forecasts by putting $f_{0,1} = 0$. To see how this works in practice, we look again at the figures in Table 3.1A, for which $\beta = \frac{1}{2}$. The column $x_t - f_{t-1,1}$ in Table 3.1B gives estimates of $\varepsilon_t$, the true values of which are shown in the preceding column. It is seen that in this instance the two columns quickly becomes virtually identical. The number of figures after the decimal point carried in this table is much greater than can normally be justified but is necessary here to show the speed of convergence of the

TABLE 3.1B

| $t$ | $x_t$ | $\varepsilon_t$ | $x_t - f_{t-1,1}$ (with $f_{0,1} = 0$) | $f_{t,1} = \frac{1}{2}(x_t - f_{t-1,1})$ | $x_{t+1}$ |
|---|---|---|---|---|---|
| 0 | — | 0.02 | — | 0 | — |
| 1 | −0.11 | −0.12 | −0.11 | −0.055 | 0.14 |
| 2 | 0.14 | 0.20 | 0.195 | 0.0975 | 0.16 |
| 3 | 0.16 | 0.06 | 0.0625 | 0.03125 | −0.15 |
| 4 | −0.15 | −0.18 | −0.18125 | −0.0906 | −0.13 |
| 5 | −0.13 | −0.04 | −0.0394 | −0.0197 | −0.02 |
| 6 | −0.02 | 0.00 | −0.0003 | −0.00015 | 0.16 |
| 7 | 0.16 | 0.16 | 0.15985 | 0.0799 | 0.14 |
| 8 | 0.14 | 0.06 | 0.0601 | 0.03005 | |

estimated $\varepsilon_t$ terms to the actual values. It should also be noted that the optimum one-step forecast series $f_{t,1}$ does not closely match the terms being forecast, shown in the final column. This is because the error term, which is the unforecastable component of the value being forecast, is relatively important in this case. It is easily seen that

$$\text{var}(x_t) = E(x_t^2) = E[(\varepsilon_t + \beta \varepsilon_{t-1})^2]$$
$$= \text{var}(\varepsilon_t) + \beta^2 \text{var}(\varepsilon_{t-1}) + 2\beta E[\varepsilon_t \varepsilon_{t-1}]$$
$$= (1 + \beta^2) \text{var}(\varepsilon_t).$$

A frequently used measure of the forecastability of a series is $R^2$, defined by

$$R^2 = 1 - \frac{\text{variance forecast error}}{\text{variance series being forecast}},$$

which in this case becomes

$$R^2 = 1 - \frac{\text{var}(\varepsilon_t)}{(1 + \beta^2) \text{var}(\varepsilon_t)} = \frac{\beta^2}{1 + \beta^2},$$

so, if $\beta = \frac{1}{2}$, $R^2 = 0.2$, which might be considered low. Some problems with the interpretation of $R^2$ will be discussed in Chapter 5.

Forecasting more than one step ahead proves to be particularly easy for series generated by model (1). At time $n$ you know that $x_{n+2}$, for instance, will be generated by

$$x_{n+2} = \varepsilon_{n+2} + \beta \varepsilon_{n+1},$$

but both $\varepsilon_{n+2}$ and $\varepsilon_{n+1}$ are future terms in a white noise series and so are unforecastable. It follows that $x_{n+2}$ is not forecastable, and the optimum forecast is just

$$f_{n,2} = 0,$$

and similarly,

$$f_{n,h} = 0, \qquad h > 1,$$

and $R^2 = 0$ in all these cases. These results should be expected from the observation that $\rho_h = \text{corr}(x_t, x_{t-h}) = 0$ for $h \geq 2$.

A series generated by (1) is called a moving average of order 1, denoted by MA(1), because a single lag term appears on the right-hand side. The obvious generalization is a series generated by

$$x_t = \varepsilon_t + \beta_1 \varepsilon_{t-1} + \beta_2 \varepsilon_{t-2} + \cdots + \beta_q \varepsilon_{t-q}, \tag{5}$$

where $\varepsilon_t$ is again a zero-mean white noise series. This is called a moving average of order $q$ and denoted MA($q$). Using the same approach as with the simple MA(1) model, it is easy to show that

$$\text{corr}(x_t, x_{t-j}) = 0, \qquad j > q,$$

and consequently that the optimum $h$-step forecast is

$$f_{n,h} = 0 \qquad \text{for} \quad h > q.$$

To consider the one-step forecast made at time $n$, put $t = n + 1$ in (5) to get

$$x_{n+1} = \varepsilon_{n+1} + \left[\beta_1\varepsilon_n + \beta_2\varepsilon_{n-1} + \cdots + \beta_q\varepsilon_{n-q+1}\right].$$

All the terms within the square brackets are known at time $n$ and so these constitute the optimum one-step forecast,

$$f_{n,1} = \beta_1\varepsilon_n + \beta_2\varepsilon_{n-1} + \cdots + \beta_q\varepsilon_{n-q+1}, \qquad (6)$$

and the one-step forecast error will again be

$$e_{n,1} = x_{n+1} - f_{n,1} = \varepsilon_{n+1}. \qquad (7)$$

To actually form the optimum forecast, the values of past and present $\varepsilon_t$ are required. These are not directly observed but can be estimated by using (7), so that

$$\hat{\varepsilon}_t = x_t - f_{t-1,1}. \qquad (8)$$

After a starting up problem with the early terms these estimated values will usually closely approximate the true $\varepsilon_t$ values.

A similar procedure is used to form $f_{n,j}$ for $j \leq q$: One writes down the expression for $x_{n+j}$ and replaces every unknowable, future value of $\varepsilon_t$ by zero and all the knowable values by the estimates from (8).

There are a number of ways that a moving average model might arise in the real world. Consider a small commodity market, say the Prickly Pear Commodity Exchange of Uganda, if such a thing existed. A commodity market is a place where buyers and sellers of a metal or an agricultural crop meet and trade. The current selling price might be thought to arise from the classical supply and demand arguments, but in practice there is great uncertainty about future supply by the miners or farmers, and so the users of the market have to maintain inventories of the good. The presence of uncertainty leads to the presence of speculators on the market, which sometimes complicates matters. However, the Uganda Prickly Pear market will probably not have attracted the attention of speculators and suppose that it is currently in equilibrium, so that everyone involved agrees on what should be the correct price at this time. If now some extra, unexpected piece of information reaches the market, for example, that a sudden tropical storm has wiped out half of the entire crop of prickly pears in Cuba or that a research doctor in Baltimore has found that rats regularly washed in prickly pear juice developed skin cancer, then this news item will very likely induce a change in price. If $P_t$ is the price series, the next price might be determined by

$$P_{t+1} = P_t + \varepsilon_{t+1},$$

where $\varepsilon_{t+1}$ is the effect on price of the unexpected news item. This may be written

$$y_{t+1} = \varepsilon_{t+1},$$

where $y_t$ is the price change series. However, if the full impact of the news item is not immediately absorbed by the market, the price change on the next day might be formed by

$$y_{t+1} = \varepsilon_{t+2} + b\varepsilon_{t+1},$$

where $\varepsilon_{t+2}$ is the effect of yet a further news item and $b\varepsilon_{t+1}$ reflects the reassessment of the earlier piece of news. If a sequence of unexpected news items keep affecting the price on the market and their complete impact takes several days to work out, the price change series will be well represented by a moving average model.

For a further example, consider a maternity hospital. Let $\varepsilon_t$ be the number of new patients that arrive on day $t$ and suppose that this is a white noise series, so that the number arriving one day is unrelated to the number coming the next day. Suppose that typically 10% stay just one day, 50% two days, 30% three days, and 10% four days. The number of patients leaving the hospital on day $t$, $x_t$, will then be given by

$$x_t = 0.1\varepsilon_{t-1} + 0.5\varepsilon_{t-2} + 0.3\varepsilon_{t-3} + 0.1\varepsilon_{t-4} + \eta_t,$$

where $\eta_t$ is a white noise error term, because of random variations about the typical situation, so that $x_t \sim \text{MA}(4)$. Thus, one could predict how many patients will be leaving in one, two, three, or four days time but not in seven days time.

### Exercises

1.  $-0.50 \quad 0.40 \quad -0.81 \quad 0.00 \quad -0.24 \quad -0.36 \quad -0.39 \quad 0.79 \quad 0.98 \quad -0.17$
    $\quad 0.72 \quad -0.45 \quad 0.52 \quad -0.76 \quad -0.18 \quad -0.83 \quad 0.57 \quad -0.86 \quad 0.71 \quad -0.72$

are the first twenty terms of a white noise series $\varepsilon_t$, $t = 1, \ldots, 20$. Using these values, generate the MA(2) series $x_t$ given by

$$x_t = \tfrac{1}{3}(\varepsilon_t + \varepsilon_{t-1} + \varepsilon_{t-2})$$

for $t = 3, \ldots, 20$. From the plots of $\varepsilon_t$ and $x_t$ against time, which do you consider to be the smoother in appearance?

2.  You are told that the monthly change in sales of paperback books in a certain store obeys an MA(2) model of the form

$$x_t = \varepsilon_t + 0.6\varepsilon_{t-1} + 0.3\varepsilon_{t-2}$$

and are given the following recent values for $x_t$: $x_{20} = 180$, $x_{21} = -120$, $x_{22} = 90$, $x_{23} = 10$.

(a)  What forecast would you have made for $x_{20}$ and $x_{21}$ at time $t = 19$ if you had assumed $\varepsilon_{17} = -10$, $\varepsilon_{18} = 30$, $\varepsilon_{19} = 70$?

(b)  Using these same values for $\varepsilon_{17}$, $\varepsilon_{18}$, and $\varepsilon_{19}$, what do you forecast for $x_{24}$, $x_{25}$, $x_{26}$, and $x_{27}$ at time $t = 23$?

3.  Suppose that you are unsure whether a certain series has been generated by an MA(1) or an MA(2) model. How would the value of the second autocorrelation coefficient $\rho_2$ help you choose between these alternative models?

4.  Prove that the two series $x_t$ and $y_t$, generated by

$$x_t = \varepsilon_t + 0.8\varepsilon_{t-1}$$

and

$$y_t = \eta_t + 1.25\eta_{t-1},$$

where $\varepsilon_t$, $\eta_t$ are each zero-mean white noise series and $\mathrm{var}(\varepsilon_t) = 1$, $\mathrm{var}(\eta_t) = 0.64$, have identical autocorrelation sequences $\rho_k$, $k = 0, 1, 2, \ldots$. Prove that if $z_t$ is generated by

$$z_t = \theta_t + a\theta_{t-1} + b\theta_{t-2},$$

where $\theta_t$ is white noise, and if $b \neq 0$, the $z_t$ cannot have the same autocorrelation sequence as $x_t$ and $y_t$.

## 3.3   AUTOREGRESSIVE MODELS

An alternative way of producing a series with more structure than white noise is from an iterative generating equation of the form

$$x_t = \alpha x_{t-1} + \varepsilon_t \qquad\qquad (9)$$

where $\varepsilon_t$ is zero-mean white noise. Given the sequence $\varepsilon_t$, $t = 1, 2, \ldots, n$ and a starting value $x_0$, the series $x_t$ is formed by repeated application of (9).

For example, with $\alpha = 0.5$, $x_0 = 0.16$, we have the values shown in Table 3.1C.

**TABLE 3.1C**

| $t$ | $\varepsilon_t$ | $0.5x_{t-1}$ | $x_t$ | $t$ | $\varepsilon_t$ | $0.5x_{t-1}$ | $x_t$ |
|---|---|---|---|---|---|---|---|
| 0 | — | — | 0.16 | 4 | $-0.18$ | 0.075 | $-0.105$ |
| 1 | $-0.12$ | 0.08 | $-0.04$ | 5 | $-0.04$ | $-0.05$ | $-0.09$ |
| 2 | 0.20 | $-0.02$ | 0.18 | 6 | 0.00 | $-0.045$ | $-0.045$ |
| 3 | 0.06 | 0.09 | 0.15 | | | | |

A relationship such as (9) is known as a difference equation and has a solution of the form

$$x_t = x_0\alpha^t + (\varepsilon_t + \alpha\varepsilon_{t-1} + \alpha^2\varepsilon_{t-2} + \cdots + \alpha^{t-1}\varepsilon_1). \qquad (10)$$

That this is a solution to (9) can be seen by writing (10) as

$$x_t = \alpha[x_0\alpha^{t-1} + (\varepsilon_{t-1} + \alpha\varepsilon_{t-2} + \alpha^2\varepsilon_{t-3} + \cdots + \alpha^{t-2}\varepsilon_1)] + \varepsilon_t$$

and then noting that the expression in the square brackets is the same as (10) but with $t$ replaced by $t - 1$. It can be proved that this is a complete solution to the difference equation.

The series $\varepsilon_t$ is interpreted as a sequence of innovations or shocks to the system in the same way that news items affected the commodity market discussed at the end of the previous section. Without these shocks, $x_t$ would equal just the first term in (10), which is a very smooth curve.

Suppose now that the generating mechanism for $x_t$ did not start at time $t = 0$ but at $t = -N$. Then (10) becomes

$$x_t = x_{-N}\alpha^{t+N} + (\varepsilon_t + \alpha\varepsilon_{t-1} + \alpha^2\varepsilon_{t-2} + \cdots + \alpha^{t+N-1}\varepsilon_{-N+1}), \qquad (11)$$

where $x_{-N}$ is the starting value. This equation has two quite distinct interpretations depending on whether $\alpha$ lies inside the region from $-1$ to 1 or outside this region. If $N$ is large and $-1 < \alpha < 1$, then the first term in (11) will be negligible and the weight given to a shock that occurred a long time ago, $\varepsilon_{-N+1}$, will also be extremely small. However, suppose $\alpha > 1$; then the first term in (11) will be large in magnitude and the weights given to distant shocks will be much greater than those given to more recent ones. This second situation is said to correspond to an *explosive model*, since the mean of the series, which is the first term in (11), explodes dramatically as $t$ increases. This is also the case for the variance of $x_t$. These properties, together with the fact that innovations of the distant past are more important than recent ones, suggest that the model is of little use to approximate economic data and most other series met in practice. When $-1 < \alpha < 1$, the model produces a non-explosive, or *stationary* series. A more rigorous definition of stationarity will be discussed in Section 3.5. The marginal case when $\alpha = 1$ gives a series that is not explosive but is not really stationary. The series produced by taking $\alpha = 1$ are called random walks and belong to a class that is particularly important in practice and will be dealt with in Section 3.7. For the rest of this section it will be assumed that $-1 < \alpha < 1$ and that $N$ is very large, so that the solution to (9) is effectively

$$x_t = \sum_{j=0}^{\infty} \alpha^j \varepsilon_{t-j}. \tag{12}$$

For later use, it should be noted that

$$E[x_t \varepsilon_{t+1}] = 0, \tag{13}$$

as all terms resulting from substituting for $x_t$ from (12) are of the form $E[\varepsilon_s \varepsilon_{t+1}]$, $s < t+1$, and are all zero as $\varepsilon_t$ is white noise.

Squaring both sides of (12) and taking expectations gives

$$\text{var}(x_t) = E[x_t^2] = (1 + \alpha^2 + \alpha^4 + \alpha^6 + \cdots)\,\text{var}(\varepsilon_t) = \frac{\text{var}(\varepsilon_t)}{1 - \alpha^2} \tag{14}$$

using a well-known summation formula.[1]

The covariance between $x_t$ and $x_{t-1}$, since this series has zero mean, is

$$\begin{aligned}
\text{cov}(x_t, x_{t-1}) &= E[x_t x_{t-1}] \\
&= E[(\alpha x_{t-1} + \varepsilon_t)(x_{t-1})] \qquad \text{[from (9)]} \\
&= \alpha E[x_{t-1}^2] + E[\varepsilon_t x_{t-1}] \\
&= \alpha\,\text{var}(x_t),
\end{aligned}$$

the second term vanishing because of (13). It thus follows that

$$\text{corr}(x_t, x_{t-1}) = \frac{\text{cov}(x_t, x_{t-1})}{\text{var}(x_t)} = \alpha. \tag{15}$$

To achieve this result, the equality of $\text{var}(x_t)$ and $\text{var}(x_{t-1})$ has to be used, which can be proved to be true if $-1 < \alpha < 1$ and the series started up a long time ago.

From (15) it is seen that

$$\begin{aligned}
\text{corr}(x_t, x_{t-1}) &> 0 \qquad \text{if} \quad \alpha > 0, \\
&< 0 \qquad \text{if} \quad \alpha < 0,
\end{aligned}$$

[1] If $|x| < 1$, then $\sum_{j=0}^{\infty} x^j = 1/(1-x)$.

so the degree of smoothness of the series is determined by the size of $\alpha$, that is, most smooth for $\alpha$ near $+1$, very unsmooth for $\alpha$ near $-1$.

It is also easy to show that

$$\text{corr}(x_t, x_{t-k}) = \alpha^k \qquad \text{for all } k,$$

but the proof will be omitted. As there is always some correlation between a value of the series and all future values, it should be expected that something can be forecast for all future time periods.

Forecasting from model (9) is easily achieved. First consider how the next value will be generated when at time $n$,

$$x_{n+1} = \alpha x_n + \varepsilon_{n+1}.$$

The first term is known, provided we are given a value for $\alpha$, but the second term is not knowable from the information set $I_n: x_{n-j}, j \geq 0$. Thus the optimum forecast of $x_{n+1}$ is clearly

$$f_{n,1} = \alpha x_n.$$

Now consider the value to occur at time $n + 2$, which will be formed by

$$x_{n+2} = \alpha x_{n+1} + \varepsilon_{n+2}.$$

The second term is not knowable and so should be replaced by its optimum forecast made at time $n$, which is just zero. The first term is not known, but it can be forecast when at time $n$, giving the two-step forecast

$$f_{n,2} = \alpha^2 x_n.$$

Similarly,

$$x_{n+3} = \alpha x_{n+2} + \varepsilon_{n+2}$$

and replacing $x_{n+2}$ by its forecast $f_{n,2}$ one gets

$$f_{n,3} = \alpha^3 x_n,$$

and so forth, giving in general

$$f_{n,h} = \alpha^h x_n.$$

As $\alpha$ lies between $-1$ and $+1$, this will be very small for $h$ large, suggesting that the series is always somewhat forecastable but that the effect of the present on the distant future is negligible in extent.

It is worth noting that the one-step forecast error is

$$e_{n,1} = x_{n+1} - f_{n,1} = x_{n+1} - \alpha x_n = \varepsilon_{n+1},$$

so that the sequence of one-step errors is a white noise.

Autoregressive models can arise in various ways. For example, let $x_t$ equal this month's number of employed in a city. Suppose that typically the proportion of last month's unemployed that get jobs within the month is $1 - \alpha$, but that a further number $\varepsilon_t$ enter the unemployed and that $\varepsilon_t$ is a white noise. It follows that $x_t$ will be given by Eq. (9). This is not necessarily a realistic model for unemployment.

As a second example, consider a tank that contains $M$ units of a mixture of two liquid chemicals, A and B. Let $Z_t$ be the concentration level of A at start of week $t$, so that

$$Z_t = \frac{\text{total amount of A in tank, week } t}{\text{total amount of chemicals in tank } (= M)}.$$

During each week one unit of the mixture is removed from the tank for use and at the end of each week the tank is topped up from a set of one-unit barrels. Let the concentration level of A in the barrel used in week $t$ be $\varepsilon_t$, a white noise series. Note that $\varepsilon_t \geq 0$, so it is not a zero-mean white noise. The amount of A in the tank at the beginning of week $t$ is $MZ_t$ and so at the end of the week the amount of A in the tank is $(M - 1)Z_t$. To refill, an amount $\varepsilon_{t+1}$ of A is added to the tank, so that the amount of A at the start of week $t + 1$ will be

$$(M - 1)Z_t + \varepsilon_{t+1}$$

and the concentration level is now

$$Z_{t+1} = \frac{M - 1}{M} Z_t + \frac{\varepsilon_{t+1}}{M}.$$

These two examples both lead to models similar to (9), which generate series called *autoregressive of order 1*, as just $x_t$ with a single lag occurs on the right-hand side. This is denoted $x_t \sim \text{AR}(1)$. An obvious generalization is a series generated by

$$x_t = \alpha_1 x_{t-1} + \alpha_2 x_{t-2} + \alpha_3 x_{t-3} + \cdots + \alpha_p x_{t-p} + \varepsilon_t$$

and called an autoregressive series of order $p$, denoted $\text{AR}(p)$. In this case, $p$ starting values are required, $x_{-j}, j = 0, 1, \ldots, p$, and then together with the white noise series $\varepsilon_t$ the values of $x_t$ are calculated iteratively.

If this model arises and its coefficients are known, it is again easy to use to form forecasts. $x_{n+1}$ will be generated by

$$x_{n+1} = (\alpha_1 x_n + \cdots + \alpha_p x_{n-p+1}) + \varepsilon_{n+1},$$

the last term of which is not knowable at time $n$, so the optimum forecast is

$$f_{n,1} = \alpha_1 x_n + \cdots + \alpha_p x_{n-p+1}.$$

Similarly, $x_{n+2}$ will be generated by

$$x_{n+2} = \alpha_1 x_{n+1} + (\alpha_2 x_n + \cdots + \alpha_p x_{n-p+2}) + \varepsilon_{n+2}.$$

The last term is not knowable, the term in parentheses is entirely known at time $n$, and the first term is forecasted by $\alpha_1 f_{n,1}$, so that

$$f_{n,2} = \alpha_1 f_{n,1} + (\alpha_2 x_n + \cdots + \alpha_p x_{n-p+2}).$$

It is obvious how further forecasts are formed: One simply writes down the generating mechanism for the value to be forecast, with everything that is known part of the forecast and everything that is not known replaced by *its* optimum forecast.

As an example, suppose $x_t$ is generated by

$$x_t = 0.5x_{t-1} + 0.2x_{t-2} + \varepsilon_t$$

and that

$$x_n = 50, \qquad x_{n-1} = 40;$$

then

$$f_{n,1} = 0.5 \times 50 + 0.2 \times 40 = 33,$$

$$f_{n,2} = 0.5 \times 33 + 0.2 \times 50 = 26.5,$$

$$f_{n,3} = 0.5 \times 26.5 + 0.2 \times 33 = 19.85,$$

$$f_{n,4} = 0.5 \times 19.85 + 0.2 \times 26.5 = 15.225,$$

$$f_{n,5} = 0.5 \times 15.225 + 0.2 \times 19.85 = 11.58,$$

$$\vdots$$

The time series properties of the AR($p$) process are quite difficult to determine, but it can be shown that they greatly depend on the largest root of the equation

$$Z^p = \alpha_1 Z^{p-1} + \alpha_2 Z^{p-2} + \cdots + \alpha_{p-1} Z + \alpha_p.$$

Let $\theta$ be this largest root and denote by $|\theta|$ the absolute size of this root, so that a positive value is taken if $\theta$ is negative and the modulus if $\theta$ is a complex root. Theory states that if $|\theta| < 1$, then $x_t$ will not be an explosive series, but if $|\theta| > 1$, it will be explosive. Further, corr$(x_t, x_{t-k})$ is well approximated for $k$ not small by $A\theta^k$ if $\theta$ real and positive or will approximately lie in the region $\pm A|\theta|^k$ otherwise, where $A$ is some constant. This helps determine the shape of the plot of this correlation against $k$, which is a particularly useful diagram and will be discussed in Section 3.6.

## Exercises

1.  If you are told that the number of accidents in a factory in month $t$ obeys an AR(1) model of the form

$$x_t = 10 + 0.7x_{t-1} + \varepsilon_t,$$

where $\varepsilon_t$ is zero-mean white noise, and that $x_{19} = 20$, $x_{20} = 24$, $x_{21} = 16$, what forecasts would you make

(a)   for $x_{22}$, $x_{23}$, and $x_{24}$ at time $t = 21$?
(b)   for $x_{23}$ and $x_{24}$ at time $t = 20$?

2.  A company economist believes that a rival firm's quarterly advertising expenditures obey the AR(3) model

$$x_t = 0.2x_{t-1} + 0.6x_{t-2} - 0.3x_{t-3} + \varepsilon_t.$$

If the values for the last three quarters are $x_{10} = 180$, $x_{11} = 140$, and $x_{12} = 200$, forecast expenditures for the next three quarters, $t = 13$, 14, and 15.

3.  A time series is constructed on a computer by an AR(1) model. You are told that the series has zero mean, that the second autocorrelation is $\rho_2 = 0.64$, and that $x_{50} = 10$. Forecast $x_{51}$ and $x_{52}$. Why would knowing the value of $\rho_3$ help forecast $x_{51}$ but not $x_{52}$?

4.  If a series $x_t$ is generated by

$$x_t = 0.8x_{t-1} + \varepsilon_t,$$

where $\varepsilon_t$ is zero-mean white noise with variance 25, find the variances of the one-, two-, and three-stop forecast errors, i.e., $\mathrm{var}(e_{n,h})$, $h = 1$, 2, and 3.

## 3.4   MIXED AUTOREGRESSIVE–MOVING AVERAGE MODELS

A much wider class of models can be produced by mixing an autoregressive and a moving average, so that $x_t$ is generated by

$$x_t = \alpha_1 x_{t-1} + \alpha_2 x_{t-2} + \cdots + \alpha_p x_{t-p} + y_t, \tag{16}$$

where $y_t$ is a moving average of order $q$,

$$y_t = \varepsilon_t + b_1 \varepsilon_{t-1} + b_2 \varepsilon_{t-2} + \cdots + b_q \varepsilon_{t-q}.$$

This is a mixed autoregressive-moving average model of order $p$, $q$, denoted

ARMA($p$, $q$). A specific example is the ARMA(1, 1) generating process

$$x_t = 0.5x_{t-1} + \varepsilon_t + 0.3\varepsilon_{t-1},$$

so that given a starting value for $x_0$ and the white noise sequence $\varepsilon_t$, $x_t$ is formed iteratively.

Forecasting is straightforward by just using the rules given in the previous two sections, so that in the ARMA(1, 1) example, $x_{n+1}$ is formed by

$$x_{n+1} = 0.5x_n + \varepsilon_{n+1} + 0.3\varepsilon_n.$$

Then

$$f_{n,1} = 0.5x_n + 0.3\varepsilon_n = 0.5x_n + 0.3(x_n - f_{n-1,1})$$

by noting that the one-step forecast error is

$$e_{n,1} = \varepsilon_{n+1},$$

so

$$\varepsilon_n = e_{n-1,1} = x_n - f_{n-1,1}.$$

Further, $x_{n+2}$ is given by

$$x_{n+2} = 0.5x_{n+1} + \varepsilon_{n+2} + 0.3\varepsilon_n.$$

Both of the last two terms are best forecast by their mean values, which are taken as zero, so

$$f_{n,2} = 0.5f_{n,1},$$

and so forth.

The condition that the process generated by (16) be nonexplosive is exactly the same as that for the general autoregressive process, as discussed in the previous section.

Although these mixed models appear complicated and their statistical properties are difficult to derive, they are of real importance in practice. One reason for this is that there are good theoretical reasons for believing that mixed models are the most likely to be found in the real world, particularly in economics and business. This statement follows from the following theorem, which is stated without proof. If

$$x_t \sim \text{ARMA}(p_1, q_1), \qquad y_t \sim \text{ARMA}(p_2, q_2),$$

$x_t$, $y_t$ are independent series, and

$$z_t = x_t + y_t,$$

then typically

$$z_t \sim \text{ARMA}(P, Q),$$

where

$$P = p_1 + p_2,$$

$$Q = p_1 + q_2 \quad \text{or} \quad p_2 + q_1, \quad \text{whichever is larger.}$$

It is possible to invent situations where $P$ and $Q$ are less than the values shown here, but these situations are unlikely to occur in practice. To show the relevance of this theorem, suppose that a company makes two products sold to quite independent markets and that the two sales value per month series are $x_t$ and $y_t$. The total value of sales for the company is then

$$z_t = x_t + y_t.$$

If $x_t$ and $y_t$ are both AR(1) series, but with different parameters, then $z_t$ will be ARMA(2, 1). The condition of independence between $x_t$ and $y_t$ can be relaxed in realistic ways and the general form of the model still hold. As many series in economics and business are *aggregates*, the theorem implies that if each component obeys a simple AR model, then the sum of these components will be ARMA. Equally, if some components are AR and others MA, again their sum is a mixed process. The only case where an ARMA model does not arise is when all the components are moving averages.

Suppose now that some "true" economic series obeys an AR($p$) model but that this series can only be observed with a measure error, which might be assumed to be white noise (MA(0)) series. Then the observed series will be ARMA($p$, $p$) according to the above theorem. As virtually all economic and business series contain observation errors, the observed series is seen likely to be ARMA.

As many series are aggregates of components measured with error, the practical importance of ARMA models should be clear.

## 3.5[2]  STATIONARITY AND INVERTIBILITY

It has been shown in the last few sections that if a time series model is given, it is easily used to form forecasts. However, in practice a model is not given and one just starts with a set of data from which a model has to be derived. The first question to ask is, which model to choose to fit to the data. Should it be a moving average, an autoregressive, a mixed model, or something else? To assist with this decision a number of statistical tools can prove useful, but before these can be introduced and their interpretation discussed, a number of fundamental ideas need to be considered.

---

[2] This section is rather technical. A complete understanding of its contents is not necessary for what follows.

Suppose that $x_t$ is a time series with zero mean, so that $E[x_t] = 0$, for all $t$. Define $\mu_{t,k}$ by

$$\mu_{t,k} = \text{cov}(x_t, x_{t-k}) \equiv E[x_t x_{t-k}].$$

In general, this autocovariance will depend both on the time of observation $t$ and also on $k$, the distance in time between the two variables being considered, $x_t$ and $x_{t-k}$. However, a particularly useful class of time series models, known as *stationary* models, arise from assuming that $\mu_{t,k}$ does not depend on $t$, so that

$$\text{cov}(x_t, x_{t-k}) = \mu_k.$$

This means that the extent to which two terms in the time series are related depends only on the time interval between them and not on time itself. Essentially, this means that the generating function for the series does not itself change through time. Thus, for example, if $x_t$ were generated by the equation

$$x_t = \varepsilon_t + b(t)\varepsilon_{t-1}$$

and the parameter $b(t)$ alters with time, then the series would not be stationary. It should be noted that one implication of the definition of stationarity is that the variance of the series, which is $\mu_0$, also is time invariant. The definition of stationarity just given assumes that the series has zero mean, but this assumption can be replaced with no difficulty by one that takes the mean to be a constant for all time.

There are many ways in which a series encountered in the real world can be nonstationary, but the most important is that where the mean or level of the series is not a constant. This situation, known as *trend in mean*, was considered in Chapter 2. If a suitable trend curve can be found or if trend in mean can be effectively removed by differencing the series, then this particular form of nonstationarity can be removed. It is also quite common to meet series whose variability is changing through time, called a *trend in variance*. Such series can often be made stationary, or more nearly so, by considering the logarithms of the series values, which usually transfer the trend in variance to one in mean. More complicated types of nonstationarity can also occur but require techniques of such complexity and sophistication to handle them that they are not considered here.

Most series met in economics and business are probably nonstationary but can be made sufficiently near to stationarity for purposes of forecasting by removal of trend in mean by curve fitting or differencing, possible after taking logarithms, as discussed in Chapter 2. Why is the assumption of stationarity, or of achieved stationarity, such an important one? The main reason is the existence of a remarkable theorem.

**Wold's Theorem.**   Any stationary series can be considered to be the sum of two parts, a self-deterministic component and a moving average of possibly infinite order.

It will be recalled that a self-deterministic series is one that can be forecast perfectly, that is, without error, from its own past. It is now widely accepted that virtually all series arising in business and economics do not contain a self-deterministic component, except possibly a seasonal part, which is discussed later in Section 4.1. If this is so, then a nonseasonal series can always be represented by a MA($\infty$) model. In practice, this does not get us very far, except for the strong belief that all actual MA($\infty$) models that arise in practice can be very well approximated by either a MA($q$), AR($p$), or ARMA ($p'$, $q'$) models with at least one of these models having a modest number of parameters, so that one of $q$, $p$, or $p' + q'$ will not be large. If this is accepted, it now means that, given stationarity, the models considered above are sufficient to represent any series and so no further models need to be considered.[3]

It was shown in Section 3.3 that an AR(1) model could always be "solved" to provide an equivalent MA($\infty$) model and any AR($p$) can be similarly represented. A condition was also given to ensure that the moving average form was nonexplosive, the stationarity condition. If the AR($p$) model obeys this condition, then it will generate a stationary series. Precisely the same condition applied to the autoregressive part of an ARMA($p$, $q$) model will also ensure both stationarity and the correspondance of this mixed model to a nonexplosive MA($\infty$) model.

It can easily be shown that all moving average models of finite order are stationary. However, there is an alternative condition that has to apply to a moving average model to make it useful for forecasting purposes, known as *invertibility*. Consider the MA(1) model

$$x_t = \varepsilon_t + b\varepsilon_{t-1}, \tag{17}$$

which can be considered as a difference equation for the $\varepsilon_t$ series and has solution

$$\varepsilon_t = x_t - bx_{t-1} + b^2x_{t-2} - b^3x_{t-3} + \cdots + (-b)^kx_{t-k} + \cdots, \tag{18}$$

as can be checked by substituting this expression and the corresponding one for $\varepsilon_{t-1}$ into (17). It should be noted that in practice we only directly observe the $x_t$ series and the $\varepsilon_t$'s can only be estimated by an equation such as (18). Clearly, if $b$ is larger than, or equal to, unity in magnitude, the weights given to more and more distant $x_t$ values will increase in size, and again an explosive

---

[3] This is not strictly true. What is really being said is that no other *linear* models need be considered. Discussion of nonlinear models takes us into too deep water for a text of this level.

solution results, meaning that current $\varepsilon_t$ cannot be estimated from past $x_t$. If a nonexplosive solution such as (18) is found, the moving average is said to be invertible. For the MA(1) model, the condition for invertibility is just that $b$ is less than unity in magnitude, i.e., $b < 1$, ignoring the sign of $b$. For the MA($q$) model,

$$x_t = \varepsilon_t + b_1\varepsilon_{t-1} + \cdots + b_q\varepsilon_{t-q},$$

where the invertibility condition is that the root with the largest magnitude of the equation

$$Z^q + b_1 Z^{q-1} + \cdots + b_q = 0$$

should have magnitude less than 1. A theorem concerning invertibility is mentioned in Section 3.7.

## 3.6 THE CORRELOGRAM AND PARTIAL CORRELOGRAM

Suppose that you are considering fitting either an AR(1) or a MA(1) model to some data. In practice, of course, it would be rare to consider only these two models, as other alternatives would also need to be considered, but to provide an example this pair will do. Which model should be chosen? A diagram that may well prove helpful in making this choice is the plot of the autocorrelations

$$\rho_k = \text{corr}(x_t, x_{t-k})$$

or their estimates

$$r_k = \sum_{t=k+1}^{n} (x_t - \bar{x})(x_{t-k} - \bar{x}) \Big/ \sum_{t=1}^{n} (x_t - \bar{x})^2, \qquad \text{where} \quad \bar{x} = \frac{1}{n}\sum_{t=1}^{n} x_t,$$

against $k$. The first of these plots is known as the *theoretical correlogram* and the second is the *estimated correlogram*.

It was shown in Sections 3.2 and 3.3 that the AR(1) model

$$x_t = ax_{t-1} + \varepsilon_t$$

has

$$\rho_k = a^k, \qquad k = 0, 1, 2, \ldots,$$

and the MA(1) model

$$x_t = \varepsilon_t + b\varepsilon_{t-1}$$

has

$$\rho_1 = \frac{b}{1 + b^2}, \qquad \rho_k = 0, \quad k = 2, 3, \ldots .$$

Figures 3.5 and 3.6 (Section 3.8) show the theoretical and estimated correlograms for the AR(1) model with $a = 0.5$ and for the MA(1) model with $b = 0.5$, with the estimated curves based on a generated series of length $n = 200$. The plots are seen to be quite different in shape, although the difference is naturally rather less clear cut for the estimated correlogram. Returning now to the problem of choosing between an AR(1) or an MA(1) model, if the data are used to form a correlogram and if the resulting diagram is similar in shape to one of these in Figure 3.5 or 3.6, the appropriate model can be selected and fitted. This process of selecting what seems to be an appropriate model has been called the *identification* stage in model building.

The estimated correlogram is an important tool in identification, because the theoretical correlogram takes distinctive shapes for AR($p$) and MA($q$) models. The AR($p$) model has autocorrelations $\rho_k$ which, for large enough $k$, are approximated by

$$\rho_k = A\lambda^k,$$

where $\lambda$ is some constant less than 1 in magnitude, although it can be negative, and $A$ is a positive constant also less than 1. This means that for large enough $k$, particularly $k \geq p$, the correlogram will either decline steadily or will be bounded by a pair of declining curves, as shown in Fig. 3.2. For the MA($q$) model, the theoretical correlogram has a particularly distinctive shape, being zero for all $k > q$ but having no clear shape for $k \leq q$. An example is shown in Fig. 3.3.

It is clear that, in theory at least, the correlogram should enable one to both identify between an AR($p$) and an MA($q$) model, and an expert will be able to make a good guess at $p$ or $q$. In practice, the decisions are not always so easily made, so a second diagram should also be considered, known as the *partial correlogram*.

To appreciate this second curve, consideration has to be given to the

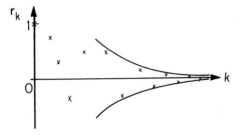

**Fig. 3.2**  Correlogram for AR($p$).

**Fig. 3.3**   Correlogram for MA($q$).

estimation of the parameters of an autoregressive model. First note that for the AR(1) model

$$x_t = a_{11}x_{t-1} + \varepsilon_t$$

we have

$$\rho_1 = a_{11},$$

and so an estimate of $a_{11}$ is just $r_1$, the estimate of $\rho_1$. For the AR(2) model

$$x_t = a_{21}x_{t-1} + a_{22}x_{t-2} + \varepsilon_t$$

it can be shown (by multiplying through by $x_{t-1}$, $x_{t-2}$ and taking expectations) that the following two equations hold:

$$\rho_1 = a_{21} + a_{22}\rho_1$$

and

$$\rho_2 = a_{21}\rho_1 + a_{22}.$$

By replacing $\rho_1$ and $\rho_2$ by their estimates, $r_1$ and $r_2$, these equations can be solved to give estimates for $a_{21}$ and $a_{22}$. Similarly, for the AR(3) model

$$x_t = a_{31}x_{t-1} + a_{32}x_{t-2} + a_{33}x_{t-3} + \varepsilon_t$$

the following three equations hold:

$$\rho_1 = a_{31} + a_{32}\rho_1 + a_{33}\rho_2,$$
$$\rho_2 = a_{31}\rho_1 + a_{32} + a_{33}\rho_1,$$
$$\rho_3 = a_{31} + \rho_2 + a_{32}\rho_1 + a_{33}.$$

Once more, replacing the $\rho$'s by their estimates, the equations can be solved to give estimates of the $a_{3j}$'s, $j = 1, 2, 3$. In general, the AR($p$) model

$$x_t = a_{p1}x_{t-1} + a_{p2}x_{t-2} + \cdots + a_{pj}x_{t-j} + \cdots + a_{pp}x_{t-p}$$

gives rise to equations

$$\rho_s = a_{p1}\rho_{s-1} + a_{p2}\rho_{s-2} + \cdots + a_{pj}\rho_{s-j} + \cdots + a_{pp}\rho_{s-p},$$

noting that $\rho_{-m} = \rho_m$ by definition. These equations are called the *Walker–Yule equations* and are used to provide estimates for the $a_{pj}$'s by replacing $\rho$'s by $r$'s and solving. Suppose we want to fit an autoregressive model, but are not sure of what order to use; then we could first fit a first-order model, then a second-order one, then a third-order, and so forth. Denote by $\hat{a}_{kk}$ the estimate of the coefficient of $x_{t-k}$ when a $k$th-order autoregressive is fitted; then the plot of $\hat{a}_{kk}$ against $k$ is called the *partial correlogram*. The name derives from the interpretation that $\hat{a}_{kk}$ is the estimated correlation between $x_t$ and $x_{t-k}$, after the effects of all intermediate $x$'s on this correlation are taken out. If the true model is AR($p$), then it is clear that the true value of $a_{kk}$ is zero for $k > p$. For example, if $p = 2$, then fitting a third-order model should give a zero coefficient to $x_{t-3}$ as this term does not enter into the model. Thus, the theoretical shape of the partial correlogram for an AR($p$) model is distinctive, being exactly the same as that for the correlogram (not partial) for an MA($p$) model. Interestingly enough, the theoretical shape of the partial correlogram for an MA($q$) model is exactly the same as the correlogram for an AR($q$) model.

To summarize the rules for identification:

(i)    If the correlogram "cuts off" after some point, say $k = q$, then the appropriate model is MA($q$).

(ii)    If the partial correlogram "cuts off" after some point, say $k = p$, then the appropriate model is AR($p$).

(iii)    If neither diagram cuts off at some point, but does decline towards zero in some steady fashion, the appropriate model is ARMA($p'$, $q'$) for some $p'$, $q'$.

There is thus seen to be a chance of identifying the appropriate model and even of providing an initial guess at the orders of the models in some cases. The rules are illustrated in simplified form in Fig. 3.2–3.4.

To become an expert in these rules and a few others to be discussed below requires a great deal of experience in data analysis. They outline a process that can only be acquired by considering many examples and learning from one's mistakes. It has been said to be so difficult that it should never be tried for the first time. This is perhaps a little too pessimistic and it is hoped that this section will at least give a feel for the kind of evidence that expert model builders use when deciding on a model.

## 3.7   THE BOX–JENKINS APPROACH TO MODEL BUILDING

A specific approach to model building has been proposed by Box and Jenkins (1970) and has proved to be very useful. To ease discussion, it will initially be assumed that the series considered has no seasonal component. This assumption is eased in Section 4.1. There are three stages to be used in model building:

(i)   *identification*, which is the choice of one or of just a few models that seem appropriate for further consideration,

(ii)   *estimation*, in which the parameters of the models are estimated from the data, and

(iii)   *diagnostic checking*, which involves applying various tests to see if the model(s) selected and estimated do really fit the data adequately, or if further models should be considered.

Let us consider these three stages in turn.

### 3.7.1   Identification

If the series being considered is stationary, one tries to use the correlogram and the partial correlogram to choose an appropriate model, as discussed in the previous section. With some practice, it is not too difficult to convince oneself that at most a couple of models are likely. If a single model cannot be selected at this point, then all of the alternative models should be retained. It is common for anyone considering identification for the first time to choose too high orders for his models, so that either $p$, $q$, or $p' + q'$ are about 5 or more rather than 1, 2, or 3. It is generally thought to be good policy to at least start with simple, low-order models and then move to higher-order ones only if the diagnostic stage suggests that this is necessary. This preference for simple models over more complicated ones, called *parsimonious parametrization* by Box and Jenkins, is based not on a belief that the world is necessarily simple but on the more pragmatic reason that a model with few parameters will be more satisfactorily estimated than one having many parameters. In what follows, if two models appear to fit the data equally well, the one with the fewest parameters will always be preferred. A specific example of the use of the identification procedure is given in the following section.

In practice, few series met with in business or economics appear to be stationary, but rather most contain either trends or long swings. This is particularly true when the series is a *level*, such as price, unemployment, or production, rather than a *rate* of change or return. To make such series amenable to the use of our identification procedure, Box and Jenkins strongly advocate differencing the data. To check whether or not differencing is required, the correlogram of the raw data is calculated and plotted. If this plot declines rather slowly, then differencing is indicated. In theory, a series that needs to be differenced to produce a stationary series has autocorrelations near unity for all lags, but in practice, as estimated autocorrelations are

**Fig. 3.4** Correlogram that requires differencing.

used based on a finite sample, the correlogram might look like Fig. 3.4. If, after differencing, the correlogram *still* has this shape, the series should be differenced once more, although it is rather rare for economic series to need to be differenced more than once. It is also rare for levels to require differencing less than once. Suppose that the series is differenced $d$ times before an interpretable correlogram of the kind discussed in the previous section is achieved and that the resulting series is identified to be ARMA($p'$, $q'$). The original series is then said to be an integrated mixed autoregressive-moving average series, denoted ARIMA($p'$, $d$, $q'$).

### 3.7.2   Estimation

In the sections above dealing with the moving average and autoregressive models, expressions were derived for autocorrelations given the coefficients of the models. For example, the first autocorrelation $\rho_1$ is given by

$$\rho_1 = a \tag{19}$$

for the AR(1) model

$$x_t = ax_{t-1} + \varepsilon_t \tag{20}$$

and by

$$\rho_1 = \frac{b}{1 + b^2} \tag{21}$$

for the MA(1) model

$$x_t = \varepsilon_t + b\varepsilon_{t-1}, \tag{22}$$

where $\varepsilon_t$ is white noise in each case. The estimation of parameters is achieved by reversing this process—given the autocorrelations, equations are obtained that can be solved for the parameters. Of course, in practice the actual autocorrelations for the models are not known but can be estimated from the available data, $\rho_k$ being estimated by

$$r_k = \frac{\sum_{t=1}^{n-k} (x_t - \bar{x})(x_{t+k} - \bar{x})}{\sum_{t=1}^{n} (x_t - \bar{x})^2}.$$

If $n$ is reasonably large, greater than 30 say, quite acceptable estimates are achieved for $k$ not too big. Thus, for example, from (19) the estimate of $a$ is

$$\hat{a} = r_1$$

and from (21) estimates of $b$ are

$$\hat{b} = \frac{-1 \pm \sqrt{1 - 4r_1^2}}{2r_1}. \tag{23}$$

It is interesting to note that for a MA(1) model $\rho_1 \leq \frac{1}{2}$, so, in theory at least, $\hat{b}$ should be real. It is also clear from (23) that two alternative estimates of $\hat{b}$ occur, but it can be shown that only *one* of these corresponds to an invertible moving average model, as discussed in Section 3.6. As for forecasting purposes, it is essential to have an invertible moving average, and so the value of $b$ that gives an invertible model is always strongly preferred. A more general theorem is available when estimating the coefficients of an MA($q$) model. Using the equations for $\rho_1, \rho_2, \ldots, \rho_q$ and replacing these quantities by their estimates $r_1, r_2, \ldots, r_q$ one gets $q$ nonlinear equations for the coefficients $b_1, b_2, \ldots, b_q$ of the MA($q$) model. There are many possible solutions for these parameters but *only one* solution set gives an invertible model. The computer programs available for solving the equations will always provide this invertible form. For low-order models, it is not too difficult to obtain estimates of parameters, but as orders increase the process soon becomes too complicated for analytical solutions and a computer program becomes necessary.

Once a model has been estimated, it can be taken to be a true model and forecasts formed in the manner discussed in earlier sections of this chapter. However, before using these forecasts, it is important to check that the model achieved is a satisfactory one. This is done by use of diagnostic checks.

### 3.7.3   Diagnostic Checking

The best way to investigate if a model is fitting the data satisfactorily is to see how well it performs outside of the sample period. That is, one set of data is used to identify and estimate a model and a later set is used to check how good the model is. However, frequently the amount of data available is insufficient for this approach to be used, so that models are identified, estimated, and diagnostically checked over the same data set. The usual test is to fit a model, estimate the residuals from it, form the correlogram of these residuals, and then see if this correlogram suggests that the residuals are a white noise as they should be. If the residuals had been formed from post-sample data, this would be a useful test, but when the sample is used for all purposes this test is rather weak and lacking in power. The best available approach seems to be to fit a slightly higher-order model and then to see if the extra parameters are significantly different from zero. For instance, if the model fitted is ARMA(1, 1), then the test involves fitting ARMA(2, 1) and ARMA(1, 2) models and then looking carefully at the coefficients of the extra terms. Details of how this should be done can be found in more specialized texts, such as those by Box and Jenkins (1970), Nelson (1973), and Granger and Newbold (1977).

Some numerical examples of the techniques discussed in Sections 3.6 and 3.7 are presented in the following section.

## 3.8  NUMERICAL EXAMPLES

In this section the correlograms and partial correlograms for six series are discussed. Five of these series were generated on a computer by the models discussed earlier in this chapter and the sixth series consists of real economic data. The six series are

E.  white noise, with zero mean and a variance of 1;

F.  MA(1) $x_t = \varepsilon_t + b\varepsilon_{t-1}$, with $b = 0.5$, $\varepsilon_t$ white noise;

G.  AR(1), $x_t = ax_{t-1} + \varepsilon_t$, with $a = 0.5$;

H.  AR(2), $x_t = 0.7x_{t-1} + 0.2x_{t-2} + \varepsilon_t$;

J.  ARIMA(0, 1, 1), $x_t - x_{t-1} = \varepsilon_t + 0.6\varepsilon_{t-1}$, so that differenced $x_t$ is MA(1);

K.  U.S. Index of Industrial Production, monthly data from January 1948 to October 1974, so that there are $n = 322$ terms.

The generated series were constructed for $t = 1$–200 for $E$–$G$ and for $t = 1$–300 for series $H$ and $J$, and the last 50 terms are shown in Table 3.2, together with the last 50 terms of series $K$.

As we look at the data listings in Table 3.2 some of the series are seen to be smooth, varying little from one term to the next, particularly series $H$–$K$, whereas others vary greatly, including frequent changes in sign, particularly series $E$, with series $F$ and $G$ being intermediate.

Table 3.3 shows the estimated correlograms and partial correlograms derived from the full series. The theoretical values for the correlations of

TABLE 3.2 *Fifty Terms of Sample Series*[a]

| k | E | F | G | H | J | K |
|---|---|---|---|---|---|---|
| 0 | 0.50 | — | — | — | — | — |
| 1 | −0.41 | −0.16 | 2.29 | −3.79 | 26.15 | 106.3 |
| 2 | 1.46 | 1.26 | 0.32 | −4.47 | 26.37 | 103.7 |
| 3 | 1.91 | 2.64 | −1.53 | −4.94 | 25.00 | 102.8 |
| 4 | 0.88 | 1.84 | −0.59 | −4.56 | 24.78 | 104.9 |
| 5 | −0.54 | −0.10 | 0.91 | −2.16 | 24.71 | 105.5 |
| 6 | −0.44 | −0.71 | −0.06 | −3.49 | 25.16 | 106.0 |
| 7 | 0.47 | 0.25 | −1.97 | −3.27 | 24.17 | 106.0 |
| 8 | 0.22 | 0.45 | 0.14 | −2.63 | 22.37 | 106.5 |
| 9 | 0.68 | 0.78 | −0.44 | −1.47 | 21.09 | 107.4 |
| 10 | 0.27 | 0.61 | 0.19 | −1.56 | 19.69 | 107.4 |
| 11 | 1.07 | 1.21 | 0.60 | −0.85 | 16.99 | 106.7 |
| 12 | −1.08 | −0.55 | 0.18 | −1.82 | 14.93 | 105.6 |
| 13 | 0.42 | −0.12 | 1.29 | −0.37 | 13.26 | 107.1 |
| 14 | 1.39 | 1.60 | 0.25 | −0.37 | 11.56 | 106.8 |
| 15 | 0.54 | 1.23 | −1.48 | −0.71 | 11.11 | 107.4 |
| 16 | −2.66 | −2.39 | −1.11 | −0.11 | 10.72 | 108.1 |
| 17 | 0.65 | −0.68 | −1.90 | 1.05 | 9.66 | 108.7 |
| 18 | −3.34 | −3.02 | −0.57 | −2.52 | 9.85 | 110.0 |
| 19 | −1.55 | −3.22 | −2.05 | −2.40 | 10.97 | 111.6 |
| 20 | −0.90 | −1.68 | −2.56 | −0.39 | 8.39 | 132.2 |
| 21 | 1.57 | 1.12 | −0.89 | −0.58 | 6.58 | 113.8 |
| 22 | −0.07 | 0.72 | 0.38 | 0.92 | 5.30 | 114.4 |
| 23 | 0.13 | 0.10 | 0.22 | 0.49 | 5.33 | 115.1 |
| 24 | 1.90 | 2.00 | 0.41 | 1.32 | 5.87 | 116.3 |
| 25 | −1.05 | −0.10 | 1.66 | 0.89 | 6.08 | 117.6 |
| 26 | −1.98 | −2.50 | −0.02 | 1.90 | 6.43 | 119.2 |
| 27 | −0.05 | −1.04 | 0.64 | 1.40 | 7.89 | 120.2 |
| 28 | −2.04 | −2.07 | 1.01 | 1.01 | 8.59 | 121.1 |
| 29 | −0.52 | −1.54 | −0.33 | 1.62 | 7.82 | 122.2 |
| 30 | 0.95 | 0.69 | 0.26 | 1.41 | 7.14 | 123.4 |
| 31 | −0.40 | 0.08 | 3.61 | −1.05 | 7.35 | 123.7 |
| 32 | 1.04 | 0.84 | 2.58 | −1.15 | 6.74 | 124.1 |
| 33 | −0.32 | 0.21 | 0.32 | −0.65 | 7.57 | 124.9 |
| 34 | 0.16 | 0.00 | 0.27 | −1.34 | 7.61 | 125.6 |
| 35 | −0.01 | 0.07 | 2.29 | −0.86 | 6.56 | 126.7 |
| 36 | −1.58 | −1.58 | 1.11 | 0.50 | 8.03 | 126.5 |
| 37 | −0.44 | −1.23 | 0.39 | −1.10 | 10.24 | 126.8 |
| 38 | 1.46 | 1.24 | −1.12 | −1.05 | 10.91 | 127.6 |
| 39 | −0.03 | 0.70 | −0.44 | −1.28 | 10.21 | 127.5 |
| 40 | −0.35 | −0.36 | 0.60 | −1.94 | 9.35 | 126.5 |
| 41 | 1.17 | 1.00 | 0.14 | −2.30 | 8.07 | 125.4 |
| 42 | −1.86 | −1.27 | −0.36 | −3.51 | 6.86 | 124.6 |
| 43 | 0.50 | −0.43 | 0.79 | −1.49 | 6.41 | 124.7 |
| 44 | −0.58 | −0.33 | 1.72 | −2.22 | 7.40 | 124.9 |
| 45 | 0.78 | 0.49 | 1.93 | −2.43 | 8.71 | 125.7 |
| 46 | 0.71 | 1.10 | 0.29 | −2.23 | 8.86 | 125.8 |
| 47 | −0.50 | −0.15 | −0.95 | −0.82 | 9.05 | 125.5 |
| 48 | 0.57 | 0.32 | −0.73 | −0.24 | 7.76 | 125.2 |
| 49 | −0.46 | −0.17 | −0.64 | 0.08 | 7.36 | 125.6 |
| 50 | 0.47 | 0.24 | 1.19 | 0.68 | 7.77 | 124.9 |

[a] *Note:* As the numbers shown are the last 50 terms, they are at times $n - 50 + k$, where $n$ is the sample size and $k$ is shown in the first column.

**TABLE 3.3**

*Estimated Correlograms and Partial Correlograms[a]*

| | Lag | | | | | | | | | | | | Standard error |
| --- | --- | --- | --- | --- | --- | --- | --- | --- | --- | --- | --- | --- | --- |
| | 1 | 2 | 3 | 4 | 5 | 6 | 7 | 8 | 9 | 10 | 11 | 12 | |
| *Series E* | | | | | | | | | | | | | |
| Correlation | 0.13 | -0.05 | 0.00 | -0.01 | 0.08 | 0.04 | -0.02 | 0.01 | -0.05 | -0.08 | -0.02 | 0.06 | 0.07 |
| Partial Corr. | 0.13 | -0.08 | 0.02 | -0.02 | 0.09 | 0.01 | -0.01 | 0.02 | -0.05 | -0.07 | -0.01 | 0.07 | 0.07 |
| *Series F* | | | | | | | | | | | | | |
| Correlation | 0.42 | 0.03 | -0.03 | -0.12 | -0.15 | -0.11 | -0.06 | 0.02 | 0.05 | 0.07 | 0.02 | -0.10 | 0.07 |
| Partial Corr. | 0.42 | -0.18 | 0.04 | -0.14 | -0.05 | -0.05 | -0.01 | 0.04 | -0.00 | 0.04 | -0.06 | -0.09 | 0.07 |
| *Series G* | | | | | | | | | | | | | |
| Correlation | 0.58 | 0.35 | 0.21 | 0.13 | 0.02 | -0.03 | 0.05 | 0.04 | 0.08 | 0.05 | -0.08 | -0.06 | 0.07 |
| Partial Corr. | 0.58 | 0.03 | -0.01 | 0.01 | -0.09 | -0.03 | -0.03 | 0.08 | 0.04 | 0.01 | -0.12 | 0.01 | 0.07 |
| *Series H* | | | | | | | | | | | | | |
| Correlation Levels | 0.90 | 0.84 | 0.78 | 0.71 | 0.66 | 0.61 | 0.57 | 0.53 | 0.49 | 0.45 | 0.42 | 0.37 | 0.06 |
| Differences | -0.23 | 0.03 | -0.01 | -0.01 | -0.08 | 0.03 | -0.04 | -0.01 | 0.03 | -0.06 | 0.08 | -0.03 | 0.06 |
| Partial Corr. Levels | 0.90 | 0.19 | -0.01 | -0.03 | -0.02 | 0.06 | -0.02 | 0.01 | -0.00 | -0.04 | 0.03 | -0.09 | 0.06 |
| Differences | -0.23 | -0.02 | -0.00 | -0.02 | -0.10 | -0.01 | -0.04 | -0.03 | 0.02 | -0.06 | 0.06 | -0.01 | 0.06 |
| *Series J* | | | | | | | | | | | | | |
| Correlation Levels | 0.98 | 0.95 | 0.92 | 0.89 | 0.86 | 0.84 | 0.81 | 0.78 | 0.75 | 0.72 | 0.69 | 0.66 | 0.06 |
| Differences | 0.42 | -0.01 | 0.04 | 0.07 | 0.02 | -0.08 | -0.08 | 0.05 | 0.13 | 0.02 | -0.06 | 0.03 | 0.06 |
| Partial Corr. Levels | 0.98 | -0.21 | 0.07 | 0.01 | -0.05 | -0.03 | 0.03 | 0.01 | -0.10 | -0.06 | -0.01 | 0.01 | 0.06 |
| Differences | 0.42 | -0.06 | -0.04 | -0.10 | 0.01 | -0.03 | 0.05 | 0.03 | 0.02 | -0.08 | -0.03 | -0.07 | 0.06 |
| *Series K* | | | | | | | | | | | | | |
| Correlation Levels | 0.99 | 0.98 | 0.97 | 0.96 | 0.95 | 0.94 | 0.93 | 0.92 | 0.91 | 0.90 | 0.89 | 0.88 | 0.06 |
| Differences | 0.40 | 0.21 | 0.15 | 0.11 | 0.03 | 0.06 | 0.07 | 0.04 | 0.07 | 0.05 | -0.03 | -0.19 | 0.06 |
| Partial Corr. Levels | 0.99 | -0.04 | -0.02 | -0.02 | -0.01 | -0.01 | -0.00 | -0.01 | -0.02 | -0.02 | -0.03 | -0.02 | 0.06 |
| Differences | 0.40 | 0.06 | 0.06 | 0.02 | -0.04 | 0.05 | 0.03 | -0.01 | 0.05 | -0.01 | -0.08 | -0.20 | 0.06 |

[a] *Note*: Throughout this table and section "correlation" is used for "autocorrelation" for convenience.

series $E$ are all zero, as it is a white noise series, and the estimated values are seen to be generally small in absolute value. However, a question arises in deciding what is "small." It is well known in statistical theory that if a population parameter has true value zero, then estimates of this parameter from a sample of finite size will be near zero but are unlikely to take exactly the value zero. The standard deviation of these estimates about the true parameter value is known as the standard error, and one would generally expect most of these estimates to be in the region from $-2 \times$ (standard error) to $+2 \times$ (standard error). In the present context, if the true correlation is zero, it is usual to expect that its estimate should be in the region $\pm 2/\sqrt{n}$, where $n$ is the sample size. Thus, for series $E$–$G$ $n$ is 200 and $2/\sqrt{n} = 0.14$, so estimates should lie in the region from $-0.14$ to $0.14$. Other standard errors, using this same formula, are shown in Table 3.3, although it should be pointed out that the formula is, at best, rather approximate.

The correlations for series $E$ are all seen to be in the region $\pm 0.14$, although that for lag 1 is only just in this region. Thus, the estimates agree with the true zero values. In this instance, the partial correlations are of no interest as all the required information, which tells about how the series should be identified, is in the correlations.

For an MA(1) series, such as $F$, all autocorrelations are zero except for that at lag 1, and the estimated correlations are seen to have exactly this pattern. Thus, an MA(1) model is easily identified. The MA(1) model

$$x_t = \varepsilon_t + b\varepsilon_{t-1}$$

has first autocorrelation equal to $b/(1 + b^2)$. The estimated autocorrelation with lag 1 is 0.42, and this formula gives an estimate for $b$ of 0.565, which compares well with the true value of 0.5 used to actually generate the series. Apart from the correlation at lag 1, all of the others are small and in the region $\pm 0.14$, or at least very nearly so. The value of $-0.15$ at lag 5 is just outside this region but is not really large enough to alter the identification of an MA(1) model, which is simple compared to an alternative model, such as MA(5). Once more, the partial correlogram is not relevant as it is not needed for model identification.

Series $G$ is AR(1) and the theoretical value of its autocorrelation of lag $k$ is $(0.5)^k$, so that the theoretical sequence is 0.5, 0.25, 0.125, 0.0625, and the rest very small (Fig. 3.5). The estimated values (Fig. 3.6) follow this pattern fairly well, although by no means exactly. The partial correlations are particularly designed to help identify autoregressive models. For an AR(1) model, the partial autocorrelations should be small except for lag 1 and the estimated values show exactly this pattern, so the correct model is easily identified. The coefficient of an AR(1) model is estimated by the autocorrelation of lag 1, which in this case is 0.58, and this value compares well with the true parameter value of 0.5.

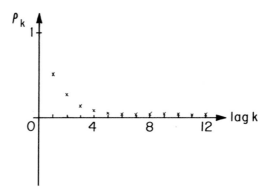

**Fig. 3.5**   Theoretical correlogram AR(1) series $G$.

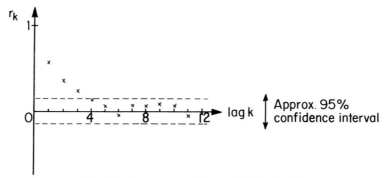

**Fig. 3.6**   Estimated correlogram AR(1) series $G$.

Series $H$ is AR(2) of form

$$x_t = 0.7x_{t-1} + 0.2x_{t-2} + \varepsilon_t. \tag{24}$$

The correlogram for the series, denoted by "levels" in Table 3.3, is seen to be smooth and to decline rather slowly as lag increases. From the rules given earlier in this chapter, autocorrelation values suggest that the differenced series be considered. Suppose we do that and look at the correlogram and partial correlation of the differences, which are also shown in Table 3.3. Both of these sets of numbers have a significant value at lag 1 and small values at all of the other lags shown. This suggests that the difference series could either be AR(1) or MA(1).[4] Suppose that the first of these is chosen; then the

[4] It is easy to show that the AR(1) model $x_t = ax_{t-1} + \varepsilon_t$ and the MA(1) model $x_t = \varepsilon_t + a\varepsilon_{t-1}$ have correlograms and partial correlograms very similar in appearance if $a$ is fairly small, say 0.3 or less.

identified and estimated model would be

$$x_t - x_{t-1} = -0.23(x_{t-1} - x_{t-2}) + \varepsilon_t, \qquad (25)$$

as the first autocorrelation of the differenced series is $-0.23$. Rearranging the terms in this expression gives

$$x_t = 0.77x_{t-1} + 0.23x_{t-2} + \varepsilon_t, \qquad (26)$$

which is seen to be quite similar to the true model of series $H$. Alternatively, one could say that the correlogram dies out sufficiently fast for differencing not to be required. If we now look at the partial correlogram for levels, the first two values look significant, being outside the range $\pm 0.12$, and all other values are small, suggesting identification of an AR(2) model, which would be correct.

If we try to estimate the AR(2) model

$$x_t = a_{21}x_{t-1} + a_{22}x_{t-2} + \varepsilon_t, \qquad (27)$$

it will be recalled that the partial autocorrelation with lag 2 is an estimate of $a_{22}$, so that this estimate is 0.19, which is very near the true value of 0.2. It will also be recalled from Section 3.6 that, if $r_k$ is the $k$th autocorrelation, then for the AR(2) model one has the equation

$$r_1 - a_{21} - a_{22}r_1 = 0.$$

Using $r_1 = 0.90$, from Table 3.3, and the estimate of $a_{22}$ just achieved, one finds the estimate of $a_{21}$ to be 0.73, which is again near the true value of 0.7. Thus, the alternative identified and estimated model is

$$x_t = 0.73x_{t-1} + 019x_t + \varepsilon_t. \qquad (28)$$

With the information given in Table 3.3 for series $H$, it is difficult to decide which of the two models (26) or (28) should be preferred. In practice, it quite frequently happens that one cannot satisfactorily decide between two alternative models. It will generally be true to say that for short-term forecasting, say one or two steps, it will make little difference which model is selected, but for longer-term horizons the models could produce substantially different forecasts. For example, the one-step forecasts are 0.512 using (28) and 0.542 using (26), the two-step forecasts are 0.503 using (28) and 0.574 from (26), but the ten-step forecasts are 0.24 by (28) and 0.68 by (26). There are a number of ways of deciding which model one prefers, if a choice is necessary, but the safest way is to choose the model that forecasts the better out of sample, using medium or long-term forecasts.

Turning now to series $J$, this is a series that does need differencing, and the correlogram for levels shows this quite clearly as it is both smooth and declines very slowly. The fact that the first autocorrelation of 0.98 is so near 1 confirms that differencing is required. Looking at the correlogram for the differenced series, only the first value is of any real significance, suggesting that MA(1) should be identified, as is correct. Recalling series $F$, the estimated model for the differenced series has parameter 0.545, i.e.,

$$x_t - x_{t-1} = \varepsilon_t + 0.545\varepsilon_t,$$

whereas the true parameter value is 0.6. Thus, the identification and estimation appear to be satisfactory.

Data from real economic series, such as series $K$, the index of production, do not always allow such easy identification. The smoothness of the correlogram and the very high value for the first autocorrelation certainly suggest that the differenced series should be examined. The correlogram of the differences, taking values 0.40, 0.21, 0.15, 0.11 for the first four lags, declines as one would expect an AR model to do. The partial correlogram has a clearly significant value at lag 1 but other values are generally small, so that an AR(1) model for the differenced series is identified. The estimated model is

$$x_t - x_{t-1} = 0.4(x_{t-1} - x_{t-2}) + \varepsilon_t,$$

and no other model is suggested by the values in the table. There is, however, a significant value of $-0.19$ for the lag 12 autocorrelation of the differenced series. The data used have been seasonally adjusted, that is, a seasonal component has been removed by a technique similar to those discussed in the next chapter. It is quite frequently observed that the purely automatic techniques extract too much, in a sense, and so impose a negative autocorrelation at lag 12 with monthly data. For most forecasting purposes this problem adds little time structure and does not require a more complicated model to be constructed, as such a model would produce forecasts very little different from those of the simpler model.

## QUESTIONS

1. The following are 20 values from a white noise series $\varepsilon_t$, $t = 1, \ldots, 20$:
   $-7.5, -7.1, -4.7, 5.0, -8.9, -7.9, -8.9, 5.1, 6.9, -3.5, -1.4, -7.6,$
   $-3.3, 1.4, -4.2, -4.6, -8.5, 3.5, 0.0, 7.0.$
   Form the two series $x_t$ and $y_t$ by

   $$x_t = 0.9x_{t-1} + \varepsilon_t \qquad \text{and} \qquad y_t = \varepsilon_t + 0.9\varepsilon_{t-1},$$

   for $t = 2, \ldots, 20$, assuming $x_1 = 2$. Plot $\varepsilon_t$, $x_t$, and $y_t$ against $t$. By examining the theoretical values of $\rho_1$, the first autocorrelation, discuss which model should produce the smoothest series.

**2.** Show that for the MA(1) model $x_t = \varepsilon_t + b\varepsilon_{b-1}$, $\rho_1 = b/(1 + b^2)$, and hence $\rho_1 \leq \frac{1}{2}$.

**3.** During a severe drought in Southern California there was a worry that exceptionally low rainfall years were inclined to occur in groups. Annual total rainfall data was gathered for San Diego for 100 years. The estimated autocorrelations for this series were

$$r_1 = -0.50, \quad r_2 = 0.14, \quad r_3 = 0.12, \quad r_4 = 0.20, \quad \text{and} \quad r_5 = 0.06.$$

How would you interpret these figures?

**4.** Suppose the recent observed values of the series $Z_t$ are

| $t$ | 1 | 2 | 3 | 4 | 5 |
|-----|----|----|----|----|----|
| $Z_t$ | $-2$ | 0 | 6 | 4 | 16. |

A statistician suggests that $Z_t$ is generated *either* by

$$Z_t = 0.5Z_{t-1} + \varepsilon_t$$

or by

$$Z_t = \eta_t + 0.5\eta_{t-1},$$

where $\varepsilon_t$ and $\eta_t$ are taken to be white noise series with zero means. Provide forecasts for $Z_6$ and $Z_7$ using both models, assuming $\eta_0 = 0$. Discuss (nonnumerically, nonmathematically) how you might decide which was the better model for forecasting purposes by repeating the above exercise for many values of $t$.

**5.** Suppose that a long sample of $x_t$ gives the following estimates of autocorrelations (i.e., of $\mathrm{corr}(x_t, x_{t-k}) = \rho_k$):

| $k$ | 0 | 1 | 2 | 3 | 4 | 5 | 6 |
|-----|----|--------|-------|-------|--------|----|----|
| Estimate of $\rho_k$ | 1 | 0.3448 | 0.002 | 0.001 | $-0.001$ | 0 | 0. |

Suggest a possible model for $x_t$. Supposing that your one-step forecast error at time $t = 6$ was $-0.36$ and $x_7 = 1$, forecast $x_8$.

**6.** A statistician claims to have fitted both an MA(1) model and an AR(1) model to some annual factory accident data with a mean removed, denoted $x_t$. The two models he provides are

$$x_t = \varepsilon_t + 0.5\varepsilon_{t-1} \quad \text{and} \quad x_t = x_{t-1} + \varepsilon_t,$$

where $\varepsilon_t$ is supposed to represent white noise. Why might you be surprised that he is unable to distinguish between these two models?

Given the following observations from the $x_t$ series

| $t$ | 1 | 2 | 3 | 4 | 5 | 6 | 7 | 8 |
|-----|---|---|---|---|---|---|---|---|
| $x_t$ | $-4$ | 0 | $-1$ | 5 | $-1$ | $-4$ | 3 | 2, |

form one- and two-step forecasts during each of the years $t = 1$ to $t = 6$ using both of the models, and compare the relative forecasting abilities of the models. (Assume $\varepsilon_0 = 0$.)

7.  If $x_t$ is generated by

$$x_t = \varepsilon_t + 0.3\varepsilon_{t-1} + 0.4\varepsilon_{t-2},$$

where $\varepsilon_t$ is zero-mean white noise with variance 2, prove $\text{var}(x_t) = 2.5$ and has first autocorrelation $\rho_1 = 0.336$. If $e_{n,2}$ is the two-step forecast error using the optimum forecast based on this model, find the variance of $e_{n,2}$.

8.  Suppose you observe the time series

| $t$ | 0 | 1 | 2 | 3 | 4 | 5 | 6 | 7 | 8 | 9 | 10 |
|-----|---|---|---|---|---|---|---|---|---|---|----|
| $x_t$ | $-6$ | 4 | 6 | $-2$ | 2 | 0 | $-4$ | 4 | 2 | $-4$ | $-2$. |

Statistician A states that he believes the series to be generated by the AR(1) model

$$x_t = 0.5x_{t-1} + \varepsilon_t,$$

but statistician B believes the true model is

$$x_t = \varepsilon_t + 0.5\varepsilon_{t-1},$$

where $\varepsilon_t$ is zero-mean white noise in each case. Given that $\varepsilon_0 = 4$, find the one-step optimum forecasts $f_{n,1}$ for each $n$ from 0 to 9 from both alternative models. Given your results, which model do you prefer and comment briefly on its quality.

9.  (more difficult)   The series $x_t$ and $y_t$ obey the MA(1) models

$$x_t = \varepsilon_t + 0.4\varepsilon_{t-1} \qquad \text{and} \qquad y_t = e_t + 0.8e_{t-1},$$

where $\varepsilon_t$, $e_t$ are independent, zero-mean white noises. $z_t$ is the sum of $x_t$ and $y_t$, so that

$$z_t = x_t + y_t.$$

If the variance of $x_t$ is 3.32, that of $y_t$ is 4.92 and, of course, the variance of $z_t$ is the sum of these, i.e., 8.24, show that $z_t$ obeys the model

$$z_t = \eta_t + 0.48\eta_{t-1},$$

where $\eta_t$ is white noise.

If you forecast $z_{n+1}$, using the information set $I_n : z_{n-j}$, $j \geq 0$, what is the variance of the forecast error? If now you forecast $z_{n+1}$, using the information set $I_n' : x_{n-j}$, $y_{n-j}$, $j \geq 0$, what will be the forecast error variance? Intuitively, why should you expect the second of these variances to be smaller than the first?

10. Explain why the mixed ARMA model can be expected to arise frequently in practice.

## FURTHER READINGS

Anderson, O. (1976). *Time Series Analysis and Forecasting: The Box–Jenkins Approach*, London: Butterworth.

Yet a more elementary account than Nelson's, with useful worked examples.

Box, G. E. P., and G. M. Jenkins (1970). *Time Series Analysis, Forecasting and Control*, San Francisco: Holden Day.

The original account of ARIMA modeling, very detailed and with plenty of examples.

Granger, C. W. J., and P. Newbold (1976). *Forecasting Economic Time Series*, Chapters 1 and 3, New York: Academic Press.

Nelson, C. R. (1973). *Applied Time Series Analysis for Managerial Forecasting*, San Francisco: Holden Day.

An account of ARIMA modeling more elementary than Box and Jenkins's.

# 4

# Further Aspects of
# Time Series Forecasting

An unsophisticated forecaster uses statistics as a drunken man uses lamp-posts—
for support rather than for illumination.

after Andrew Lang

## 4.1 CYCLES AND THE SEASONAL
## COMPONENT

When statisticians first turned their attention to time series to any appreciable extent, in the late nineteenth century, it was immediately obvious that most series were too smooth to be white noise, so an appropriate class of models was sought to explain this smoothness. It so happened that most of the rather limited number of series that were then available and of any worthwhile length contained cyclical components. These are parts of the series that consist of some shape that is continually repeated with little variation in a periodic and fairly regular fashion. An example was the monthly price of wheat, which would generally be lowest directly after the harvest, because of a plentiful supply, but would then be inclined to increase as the available supply was reduced until the next harvest started the cycle off again. Agricultural prices provided many of the time series then available and they all contained this twelve-month, or seasonal, cycle. Other series that were analyzed that contained, or appeared to contain, cycles were the varying light intensity of a pair of rotating stars, annual death rates, and a sunspot series. The mortality data contained long swings of fairly constant deviation because some disease would sweep the country causing high deaths and would be inclined to leave the young and healthy as survivors, who could fend off the effects of other possible epidemics until they also became older and vulnerable, when a new disease would appear and raise the death rate once again. The sunspot series arises from the fact that if one looks at the surface of the sun, it will usually contain dark spots, which are areas of relative coolness. It seems that every eleven years or so the sun suffers a serious case of acne and the proportion of the sun's disk that is covered by the spots increases dramatically. Since the mid-eighteenth century, an observatory in Switzerland has been recording monthly a measure of the number of sunspots, for reasons of their own and presumably at considerable risk to the astronomer's eyesight, thus providing one of the longest, but least useful, time series available for analysis. The fact that the sunspot measure reaches a peak roughly every eleven years, for reasons that are still not completely understood, leads to a cycle in the data. An appropriate model for all of these series might seem to be

$$x_t = A \cos(\omega t + \theta) + \varepsilon_t, \tag{1}$$

where $\varepsilon_t$ is a white noise series and the first term is a purely periodic component with amplitude $A$ and frequency $\omega$ (corresponding to period $2\pi/\omega$), and $\theta$ is the phase value. When such models were fitted to the series, a worthwhile fit was usually obtained, but the estimated residuals were frequently observed to still be too smooth to be white noise. As previously the smoothness had been attributed to the presence of a cycle, it was natural to extend model (1) to include several cosine, cyclical terms, of possibly unknown periods. Some very sophisticated techniques were developed to identify these cyclical components, but by the 1930s analysts were becoming dissatisfied with models involving cycles. The ARMA models, discussed in the previous chapter, were therefore developed. These were found to provide satisfactory explanations of the fluctuations in most series and to involve fewer parameters than the numerous cycles that previous techniques were "finding." With the important exception of the seasonal cycle, most academic time series analysts now strongly discount the usefulness of searches for cycles in most economic and business series. This view is not universally held, as is shown by the existence of groups such as The Society for the Investigation of Recurring Events or journals such as *Cycles*. It is possible that occasionally a true cycle is to be found in some data, for whatever reason, and if this occurs, it is essential to identify this cycle and use it to help forecast future values of the series. Such cycles are more likely to be found in physical series such as found in oceanography, geophisics, or chemical engineering rather than in economics or business series.

   The one very clear exception to these remarks is the seasonal, or annual, cycle which is found very frequently in economic data. Examples of series containing strong seasonal components are those concerned with production, sales, inventories, personal income and expenditure, government receipts and expenditures, profits, unemployment rates, imports, and exports. Thus, for example, unemployment figures are highest during the winter months, when construction workers may be laid off, most vacation resorts are shut down and many high school and college graduates may still be looking for their first full-time job. The main causes of the seasonal swings are the timing of public holidays, such as Christmas and Easter, of school vacations, and of the payment of company dividends, the choice of when a tax year or accounting period ends, and of course, the effects of weather. Figure 4.3 (Section 4.5) shows an example of a seasonal series.

There are many ways of dealing with the seasonal component of an economic series, but they all basically aim to produce a series that appears to be nonseasonal. This can either be done directly by filtering,[1] or indirectly by estimating the seasonal component and then subtracting this estimate from the series. However, some of the proposed methods of seasonal adjustment are not really suitable in a forecasting framework as they are designed only to remove a seasonal component from a set of historical data and, in doing this, some of the most recent pieces of data are lost. As these pieces of data are the most important when forecasting, such methods are inappropriate.

The seasonal problem would not be difficult if the seasonal component consisted of a regular shape that reoccurred regularly every 12 months. If this were so, then a twelve-month difference would totally remove the component. That is, if

$$x_t = S(t) + z_t,$$

where $x_t$ is the observed series, $S(t)$ is a perfectly regular seasonal component such that $S(t) = S(t - 12)$ and $z_t$ is the remaining, nonseasonal component, then

$$y_t^{(12)} = x_t - x_{t-12}$$
$$= S(t) - S(t - 12) + z_t - z_{t-12}$$
$$= z_t - z_{t-12},$$

and $y_t^{(12)}$ has no seasonal component. However a consequence of this procedure is that if a time series model is fitted to the differenced series, such as an AR($p$) or ARMA($p'$, $q'$), the orders of these models, $p$ or $p' + q'$, will probably be very large. Box and Jenkins have extended their model-building approach, as described in the previous chapter, to include seasonal series. The method is based on the use of a twelve-month difference and the fitting

---

[1] If a series $y_t$ is formed from another series $x_t$ by a formula of the form $y_t = \sum_j d_j x_{t-j}$, then $y_t$ is said to be a filtered version of $x_t$. Thus, a moving average is a filtered white noise.

of particular high-order models to the resulting series, but the details are too complicated for this text. The method has been successfully applied to series that do not have a constant seasonal pattern but rather slowly evolve through time. Once the full seasonal model has been achieved, forecasts are made from it in exactly the same way as from the models discussed in the previous chapter. Thus, for example, if $y_t$ is the twelve-month difference

$$y_t = x_t - x_{t-12}$$

and the model fitted to $y_t$ is

$$y_t = 0.6y_{t-1} + 0.2y_{t-12} + 0.3y_{t-13} + \varepsilon_t,$$

then, using the rules outlined in Chapter 3, the one-step forecasts will be

$$f_{n,1}^{(y)} = 0.6y_n + 0.2y_{n-11} + 0.3y_{n-12},$$

$$f_{n,1}^{(x)} = f_{n,1}^{(y)} + x_{n-11},$$

$$f_{n,2}^{(y)} = 0.6f_{n,1}^{(y)} + 0.2y_{n-10} + 0.3y_{n-11},$$

$$f_{n,2}^{(x)} = f_{n,2}^{(y)} + x_{n-10},$$

$$\vdots$$

An alternative, and rather easier approach, is to first estimate the seasonal component. A convenient way of doing this is to put the available data into tabular form as shown in Table 4.1, where the data $x_t$ are assumed to be recorded monthly, with the first value $x_1$ occurring in a January and the most recent observation in a December. Thus, all January values are found in the first column, all the February values in the second column, and so forth. One way of estimating the seasonal is to form the average of each column, $\bar{x}_J$, $\bar{x}_F, \ldots, \bar{x}_D$. A plot of these averages against the months shows the estimated seasonal pattern, as in Fig. 4.1.

To illustrate the results of this method in practice, Table 4.2 shows

**TABLE 4.1**

| Jan. | Feb. | March | $\cdots$ | Nov. | Dec. |
|------|------|-------|------|------|------|
| $x_1$ | $x_2$ | $x_3$ | | $x_{11}$ | $x_{12}$ |
| $x_{13}$ | $x_{14}$ | $x_{15}$ | | $x_{23}$ | $x_{24}$ |
| $x_{25}$ | $x_{26}$ | $x_{27}$ | | $x_{35}$ | $x_{36}$ |
| $\vdots$ | $\vdots$ | $\vdots$ | | $\vdots$ | $\vdots$ |
| $x_{n-11}$ | $x_{n-10}$ | $x_{n-9}$ | | $x_{n-1}$ | $x_n$ |
| $\bar{x}_J$ | $\bar{x}_F$ | $\bar{x}_M$ | | $\bar{x}_N$ | $\bar{x}_D$ |

**Fig. 4.1**  Seasonal pattern.

**TABLE 4.2**
*Seasonal Sales[a]*

|                       | DJ  | FM  | AM  | JJ  | AS  | ON  |
|-----------------------|-----|-----|-----|-----|-----|-----|
| Cake mix              | 89  | 100 | 110 | 94  | 94  | 105 |
| Carbonated soft drinks| 92  | 87  | 99  | 117 | 114 | 91  |
| Frozen dinners        | 100 | 107 | 106 | 91  | 90  | 106 |
| Canned dog food       | 101 | 96  | 98  | 99  | 102 | 104 |
| Acne remedies         | 98  | 94  | 89  | 100 | 119 | 104 |
| Deodorants            | 87  | 96  | 106 | 110 | 108 | 93  |
| Throat lozenges       | 143 | 115 | 73  | 58  | 86  | 124 |

[a] Figures taken from *The Nielsen Researcher*, No. 1 (1976).

average U.S. sales of various supermarket and drug store items for pairs of months. The figures have been adjusted so that the bimonthly average is 100. DJ denotes December and January, FM February and March, and so forth.

The causes of seasonal sales fluctuating due to temperature is obvious, but the swings in acne remedy sales are less clear cut. Provided several year's data is available and the seasonal component changes little from year to year, this estimate will be a good one. To remove the seasonal component from the data, the values in each column have the column average subtracted from them, so that the resulting series $y_t$ is given by

$$y_1 = x_1 - \bar{x}_J, \qquad y_2 = x_2 - \bar{x}_F, \qquad y_3 = x_3 - \bar{x}_M, \qquad \text{etc.}$$

Suppose a time-series model, such as an autoregressive model, is then fitted to the $y_t$ values and forecasts of future $y$ values are constructed. Forecasts of the $x$'s are made by adding the appropriate month average to these $y$

forecasts. Thus, for example, if $x_t$ is recorded in a December, then the forecasts for the subsequent January, February, and March values are

$$f_{n,1}^{(x)} = f_{n,1}^{(y)} + \bar{x}_J, \qquad f_{n,2}^{(x)} = f_{n,2}^{(y)} + \bar{x}_F, \qquad f_{n,3}^{(x)} = f_{n,3}^{(y)} + \bar{x}_M, \qquad \text{etc.}$$

If the seasonal pattern is changing through time, but in a slow fashion, the procedure just outlined will not be appropriate, as the monthly averages include data values which include a seasonal shape that no longer occurs. To get around this problem, the monthly averages could be taken over just a few recent years, say the last 5 years. As new data become available, the most distant value is replaced by the new one when forming the average. An alternative method of estimating a changing seasonal is to form

(current January average) $= \alpha$(Previous January average)

$+ (1 - \alpha)$(most recent January figure),

where $\alpha$ is some parameter to be chosen by the analyst. A typical value for $\alpha$ would be 0.7, a value larger than this is appropriate if the seasonal is thought to change very little, and a smaller value for $\alpha$ should be used if the seasonal cycle is thought to be changing rapidly. This iterative procedure is started by taking the first monthly average equal to the first monthly value of $x_t$.

To illustrate the first of these methods of estimating a changing seasonal pattern and using it for forecasting, consider the data shown in Table 4.3A.

TABLE 4.3A

*Original Data* $(x_t)$

|  |  |  | Year | Jan. | Feb. | March | $\cdots$ | Nov. | Dec. |
|---|---|---|---|---|---|---|---|---|---|
| First average period | Second average period |  | 1 | 18 | 15 | 10 |  | 10 | 20 |
|  |  |  | 2 | 19 | 16 | 11 |  | 14 | 19 |
|  |  |  | 3 | 22 | 18 | 9 |  | 12 | 20 |
|  |  |  | 4 | 20 | 17 | 12 |  | 14 | 22 |
|  |  |  | 5 | 18 | 18 | 11 |  | 15 | 18 |
|  |  |  | 6 | 21 | 16 | 12 |  | 13 | 16 |
| 5th year average |  |  |  | 19.4 | 16.8 | 10.6 |  | 14.4 | 19.8 |
| 6th year average |  |  |  | 20 | 17 | 11 |  | 14 | 19 |

Although there is no evidence of a changing seasonal shape, suppose that averages over the last five years are used. In January of year 5, the most recent five January figures are 18, 19, 22, 20, and 18, with an average of 19.4, so the seasonally adjusted figure is $18 - 19.4 = -1.4$. In January of year 6, the most recent January figures are 19, 22, 20, 18, and 21, with average

20, so the adjusted figure is $21 - 20 = 1$. The other averages are shown in Table 4.3A and the adjusted values for years 5 and 6 are in Table 4.3B.

**TABLE 4.3B**

*Adjusted Data, Recent Years $(y_t)$*

| Year | Jan. | Feb. | March | $\cdots$ | Nov. | Dec. |
|------|------|------|-------|----------|------|------|
| 5 | −1.4 | 1.2 | 0.4 | | 0.6 | −1.8 |
| 6 | 1 | −1 | 1 | | −1 | −3 |

Suppose now that for the whole set of adjusted data an AR(1) model is found to be appropriate, of the form

$$y_t = 0.7y_{t-1} + \varepsilon_t.$$

The forecasts of $y_t$ for January and February of year 7 are then

$$f_{n,1}^{(y)} = 0.7(-3) = -2.1, \qquad f_{n,2}^{(y)} = (0.7)^2(-3) = -1.47,$$

with the forecasts made in December of year 6 using the rules for forecasting an AR(1) model given in Chapter 3. The corresponding forecasts for the original $x_t$ series are

January of year 7

$$f_{n,1}^{(x)} = -2.1 + 20 = 18.9, \qquad f_{n,2}^{(x)} = -1.47 + 17 = 15.53.$$

The method of seasonal adjustment used by the U.S. government is based on the five-year average method just outlined, although a number of further sophistications are added. The current method used by the U.S. Department of Commerce is known officially as the "X-11 variant of the census method II seasonal adjustment program," but is usually called just X-11. Not only does it allow for the possibility of there being a changing seasonal shape, but the effect of untypical figures, or outliers, is automatically allowed for, as is the variation in the number of working days or trading days from one month to another.[2] An example of the use of X-11 will be found in Section 4.5.

The methods of seasonal adjustment described in this section and virtually all of those used by governments are autoadjustment methods; that is, the values of a series are used to adjust this series. More advanced methods

---

[2] A complete description of X-11 may be found in Technical Paper No. 15, "The X-11 variant . . . ," published by the U.S. Dept. of Commerce, Bureau of the Census in 1967.

would ask what is causing the seasonal variation and use values, from the causal series, such as temperature, in the adjustment process. These techniques are much more costly as more sophisticated analysis is required and frequently insufficient data is available for the causal variables. Problems with modeling interrelationships among series will be discussed in Chapter 5.

The question of how to best deal with a seasonal element in a series is one of the oldest, most difficult and most studied aspects of analyzing an economic time series. Very sophisticated approaches are possible and attitudes towards the question are still developing. It should be noted that most of the macroeconomic series that contain a seasonal are published by government statistical offices in a seasonally adjusted component form. The adjusted series usually are free of a seasonal component, but the adjustment procedure can occasionally induce other undesirable properties in the series which make model building more difficult. When available, most forecasters prefer to work with unadjusted series.

### Exercise

Using the above figures and model for the adjusted series $y_t$, show that forecasts of $x_t$ for January and February of year 6 made in December of year 5 are 18.14 and 15.92 respectively.

## 4.2  LOW-COST TIME SERIES FORECASTING METHODS

The whole process of analyzing a time series, from worrying about trends and seasonal patterns to identifying, estimating, and diagnostic checking a time series model, is likely to be a lengthy and costly one. The main costs involved are for the use of complicated computer programs plus that of the time of a, one hopes, competent statistician who has to look at various diagrams and draw on his experience to make essential decisions. If this is all done properly, then the available information in the information set being used, the past and present of the series to be forecast, is efficiently squeezed out and a relatively successful forecasting formula is attained, at least in the short run. However, there exist forecasting situations where either the required expertise is not available to use this approach or the cost of the whole procedure is too great. A small firm, for example, may want to forecast sales for several brands in each of ten sales areas.

An obvious way of reducing costs is to use a technique that provides forecasts without the necessity of employing an expensive specialized statistician. It is not difficult to decide whether or not to use a differenced series to remove or reduce a trend, and also to use a simple seasonal adjustment method such as those outlined in the previous section. In fact, these aspects of the analysis can be completely automated by using a computer program provided with suitable criteria to apply if decisions have to be made. The complete identification of models is more difficult to automate, but various methods have been devised to choose and fit autoregressive models which are capable of producing good, if not completely optimum forecasts. One of these methods, known as stepwise autoregressive series, proceeds as follows (assuming $x_t$ does not need differencing and has no seasonal component):

(i)   All models of the form

$$x_t = \alpha_{1k} x_{t-k} + \varepsilon_t^{(1)}$$

are fitted, for $k = 1, 2, \ldots, K$, and choose the one that fits best, so that $\mathrm{var}(\varepsilon_t^{(1)})$ is a minimum.

(ii)   Fit all models of the form

$$x_t = \alpha_{2j} x_{t-j} + \alpha_{2m} x_{t-m} + \varepsilon_t^{(2)},$$

$j, m = $ all $1, 2, \ldots, K$ and choose the one that fits best.

(iii)   Fit all models of the form

$$x_t = \alpha_{3r} x_{t-r} + \alpha_{3s} x_{t-s} + {}_{3q} x_{t-q} + \varepsilon_t^{(3)}$$

and choose the best, etc.

Thus, in the first stage the best equation involving a single lagged $x_t$ is found (the lag need not be 1), in the next stage, the best equation involving a pair of lagged $x$'s is found (the lags need not necessarily include that used in the first stage, but will usually do so), and so forth. A criterion can be given which tells the computer to stop when the addition of further variables does not significantly improve the fit of the equation. The result is an autoregressive series of possibly a high order but with many zero coefficients such as

$$x_t = 0.4 x_{t-3} + 0.1 x_{t-5} + 0.2 x_{t-8} + \varepsilon_t.$$

Many computers have programs available to form such a stepwise autoregressive model, and once the model is obtained, forecasts are made from it in the usual way. Although such a method is often quite successful, it is still fairly sophisticated and costly to find the model and to form forecasts from it. On some occasions, even lower cost methods of forecasting are required.

Consider, for example, a company that manufactures very complicated pieces of machinery, such as an aeroengine. Each engine may contain 100,000 separate and distinct parts. To allow for servicing and repairs of the engines, the company will have to keep spares of each of the parts in at least one place in the world, and maybe in several places. If an insufficient inventory of parts is maintained, customers who have purchased the engines may find that these expensive pieces of machinery are remaining idle for long periods, whilst special parts are manufactured, which could lead to them buying alternate makes of engines sometime in the future. However, the manufacturing company will find it very expensive tying up large amounts of capital in over-large inventories of spare parts. Inventory theory provides fairly simple formulas to be applied by the company to help decide how many spares of each part to keep available, but these formulas require forecasts of demand for each part over some prescribed time period, say the next three months. The company could certainly monitor demand for each part for a period but is unlikely to be willing, or able, to analyze each of the resulting 100,000 time series and find or use sophisticated forecasting techniques for each. What is required is a really low cost method that does have *some* forecasting ability.

A number of simple so-called *adaptive* or exponentially weighted moving average methods (EWMA) methods have been developed specifically for such situations. They are based on quite a different philosophy about what is the most important aspect of a time series than those encountered so far. Suppose that the series to be forecast $x_t$ fluctuates around some unknown mean $m$. Then if an estimate of $m$ can be obtained, denoted by $\hat{m}$, a not totally hopeless forecast for all future values of the series would be $\hat{m}$, i.e., $f_{n,h} = \hat{m}$, all $h \geq 1$. Now suppose that occasionally some unknown outside influence changes the value of $m$, so that before the influence $x_t$ fluctuates about $m_1$ but after it $x_t$ lies around a different value $m_2$. A technique is required to estimate the *current* mean, or level value, for the series and the forecast is made that all future values will be equal to this current mean. Figure 4.2 shows the underlying idea.

Denote the current mean by $\bar{x}_t$; then one method of estimating this

*Fig.4.2*   Series with changing mean.

quantity is by the iterative equation

$$\bar{x}_t = \alpha x_t + (1 - \alpha)\bar{x}_{t-1}, \tag{2}$$

where $\alpha$ is a parameter in the region 0–1, and the sequence $\bar{x}_t$ is started by taking $\bar{x}_1 = x_1$. By continual substitution, it is found that (2) may be written

$$\bar{x}_t = \alpha x_t + \alpha(1 - \alpha)x_{t-1} + \alpha(1 - \alpha)^2 x_{t-2} + \alpha(1 - \alpha)^3 x_{t-3} + \cdots, \tag{3}$$

so that apart from the $\alpha$ that is in all of the terms $\bar{x}_t$ is seen to give weight 1 to the current $x_t$, $(1 - \alpha)$ to the previous $x_t$, $(1 - \alpha)^2$ to the $x_t$ before that, and so forth. Because $1 - \alpha$ lies between 0 and 1, $\bar{x}_t$ is seen to give less weight to more distant $x_t$ values. The big advantage in forming (2) to estimate $\bar{x}_t$ rather than (3) is its considerable simplicity, particularly when run on a computer, as only the values $\alpha$, $\bar{x}_{t-1}$, and $x_t$ need be stored in the computer's memory. The quantity $\alpha$ is called the smoothing constant. It can either be estimated from past data, although at considerable computing cost, or a value can simply be guessed at, depending on how variable the series is about a mean and how often one believes the current mean value really changes. If the mean level is thought to change value frequently, a value of $\alpha$ near one is appropriate, but if the series is volatile about a fairly constant mean, a value of $\alpha$ near zero is better. A simple rule that has been suggested is to take $\alpha$ equal to one of 0.7, 0.5, or 0.3 on purely subjective grounds. Once $\bar{x}_n$ is obtained, all forecasts are put equal to this value, i.e.,

$$f_{n,h} = \bar{x}_n.$$

The simplicity and underlying philosophy of this approach is appealing, and it is much used in industry, possibly also because of its low cost of operation. In practice, the forecasts produced are usually far from optimal but are generally by no means valueless. In terms of cost effectiveness, such methods have much to recommend them.

It is fairly natural to ask if they can be improved to a worthwhile extent whilst retaining their main characteristics. Many improvements have been suggested, particularly to take into account observable trends or seasonality. For example, Holt (1957) and Winters (1960) have suggested that the main features of a time series can be captured by considering a linear trend, with changing parameter values, plus a changing seasonal series. To estimate all of the components, the following three equations are used:

$$\bar{x}_t = \alpha(x_t - S_{t-12}) + (1 - \alpha)(\bar{x}_{t-1} + T_{t-1}),$$
$$T_t = \beta(\bar{x}_t - x_{t-1}) + (1 - \beta)T_{t-1},$$
$$S_t = \gamma(x_t - \bar{x}_t) + (1 - \gamma)S_{t-12},$$

where $\bar{x}_t$ represents the current level for the series, $T_t$ is the current slope of the straight-line trend and $S_t$ is the current estimate of the seasonal, assuming monthly data. Then

$$f_{n,h} = \bar{x}_n + hT_n + S_{n+h-12},$$

for $h = 1, 2, \ldots, 12$. For $h$ between 13 and 24, the last term is replaced by $S_{n+h-24}$, and so forth. If the parameters $\alpha$, $\beta$, and $\gamma$ are merely selected by the forecaster rather than estimated from the data, the forecasting procedure is purely automatic and makes little demands on a computer or its memory. In this case some simplicity is lost but not too much and doubtless rather better forecasts can result. Other, more sophisticated, generalizations have also been suggested, but most become too complicated for the technique still to be characterized as low cost, so the only clear-cut gain over the modeling techniques described in the previous chapter is lost. As will be seen in Chapter 8 these low-cost techniques do have a role to play in a forecasting strategy.

## 4.3   WHICH METHOD TO USE

In this and the previous chapter three quite different time series methods of forecasting have been discussed based on:

(i)   the ARIMA or Box–Jenkins modeling procedure, which typically requires a number of critical decisions to be made at the identification stage by a well-trained statistician,

(ii)   the stepwise autoregressive model, and

(iii)   the adaptive or EWMA models.

Once any of these models have been determined, the production of forecasts is usually quite easy. Given an actual forecasting situation, which method should be used? The decision has to depend on how much time and money one is able to spend, on how important it is to get as good a forecast as possible and on how much data is available. The last two methods listed above are typically cheaper, use less data, and produce rather poorer forecasts than the first method. If one has virtually no data, then the adaptive method is the only one available, the stepwise autoregressive method can be used with 30 or more pieces of data, whereas it is recommended that Box–Jenkins modeling be not attempted unless 60 or so data points are available. The ARIMA modeling methods are expensive because of the necessary intervention of a (probably) highly paid statistician at the identification decision-making stage, but as automatic modeling procedures, by which a computer makes decisions by applying various comprehensive criteria, become more widely available this particular expense will decline. There will still be a relatively considerable computing cost for ARIMA models compared to adaptive.

The question of how to measure the relative quality of the methods is discussed in Chapter 8, where the possibility of obtaining improved forecasts by combining different methods is also mentioned.

## 4.4 PROPERTIES OF OPTIMUM FORECASTS

Whenever an optimum forecast is produced from a proper information set,[3] the resulting forecast errors are found to have certain useful properties. The most important of these properties are the following:

(i) The $h$-step forecast errors $e_{n,h}$, when plotted against $n$, obey an MA($h - 1$) model. In particular, the one-step errors $e_{n,1}$ will be white noise. The relevance of this latter result is that if the errors produced by some forecasting procedure are not white noise, then it is not an optimum procedure. This should be clear, as if the $e_{n,1}$ are not white noise, then they will be at least partially forecastable from past errors. Thus the original forecasts can be improved by adding to them these forecasts of the errors.

(ii) The variance of $e_{n,h}$, when plotted against $h$, will generally be a increasing curve, and, as $h$ gets large enough, this value gets close to the variance of $x_t$, the series being forecast. An alternative way of stating this property is that generally the further ahead one forecasts, the less well one does. Also, if one tries to forecast very far ahead, the information set ceases to contain anything of relevance, so that for $n$ fixed and increasing $h$, $f_{n,h}$ tends to the mean of $x_t$, and $e_{n,h}$ and $x_{n+h}$ have equal variances. The forecast errors occur because of the occurrence of unforeseeable events. The further ahead one forecasts the more opportunity there is for such events to occur and to accumulate, which is why the variance of the errors increases as $h$ increases.

The proof of these results will be given just for the information set $I_n$: $x_{n-j}$, $j \geq 0$, but they do hold true for larger information sets containing the past and present of $x_t$ and of other series. If $x_t$ is a stationary series with zero mean and no deterministic or perfectly forecastable components, such as a linear trend or a pure cycle, then according to Wold's theorem, it can always be represented by a moving average model of the form

$$x_t = \sum_{j=0}^{m} c_j \varepsilon_{t-j}, \qquad c_0 = 1,$$

where $m$ may be infinite. In particular, any ARMA($p, q$) model can be so

---

[3] That is, an information containing all past values of the series being forecast plus those of any other variables used to make the forecast.

represented. Assume that the $c_j$ values are known; then $x_{n+h}$ will be generated by

$$x_{n+h} = \sum_{j=0}^{h-1} c_j \varepsilon_{n+h-j} + \sum_{j=h}^{m} c_j \varepsilon_{n+h-j}.$$

All of the components in the second of these terms are potentially knowable at time $n$, and so this second component can be equated with $f_{n,h}$. (In practice, with only a finite amount of data, this will only be true approximately, but generally such details can be safely ignored.) Thus, the $h$-step error will be

$$e_{n,h} = \sum_{j=0}^{h-1} c_j \varepsilon_{n+h-j}$$

and in particular, the one-step error is just $\varepsilon_{n+1}$. It is immediately obvious that $e_{n,h}$ is MA($h - 1$) and has variance

$$\text{var}(e_{n,h}) = \left( \sum_{j=0}^{h-1} c_j^2 \right) \sigma_\varepsilon^2,$$

so that, for example,

$$\text{var}(e_{n,h}) - \text{var}(e_{n,h-1}) = c_{h-1}^2 \sigma_\varepsilon^2,$$

which cannot be negative. It follows that the sequence of these variances will generally increase as $h$ increases.

A further use for these results is to provide confidence intervals around the point forecasts $f_{n,h}$. If the residuals are normally distributed or nearly so, the approximate 95% confidence forecast interval is $f_{n,h} \pm 1.96\sqrt{\text{var}(e_{n,h})}$, where $\text{var}(e_{n,h})$ is given above. To evaluate this quantity the $c_j$ values are required. There are various ways of finding these values, but one of the easiest is just to substitute for $x_t$ into an ARMA model and get iterative equations for the $c_j$'s. For example, suppose one has the AR(2) model

$$x_t - a_1 x_{t-1} - a_2 x_{t-2} = \varepsilon_t,$$

which becomes

$$\sum_{j=0}^{m} c_j \varepsilon_{t-j} - a_1 \sum_{j=0}^{m} c_j \varepsilon_{t-1-j} - a_2 \sum_{j=0}^{m} c_j \varepsilon_{t-2-j} = \varepsilon_t.$$

Gathering up terms, this gives

$$(c_0 - 1)\varepsilon_t + (c_1 - a_1 c_0)\varepsilon_{t-1} + (c_2 - a_1 c_1 - a_2 c_0)\varepsilon_{t-2}$$
$$+ (c_3 - a_1 c_2 - a_2 c_1)\varepsilon_{t-3} + \cdots = 0.$$

This equation must hold true for any set of $\varepsilon_t$ values, and for this to be true, every coefficient must be identically zero. Remembering that $c_0 = 1$, this gives

$$c_1 = a_1, \qquad c_2 = a_1 c_1 + a_2, \qquad c_3 = a_1 c_2 + a_2 c_1, \qquad \text{etc.}$$

These equations are easily solved iteratively. A similar procedure can be used for any ARMA($p, q$) model, although for large p the sequence of equations can become quite complicated. The only other quantity required to form var$(e_{n,h})$ is $\sigma_\varepsilon^2$, which can be estimated as the variance of the residuals from the fitted ARMA model. The resulting confidence bands wfll be rather approximate and experience suggests that they are often optimistically narrow.

All of the methods and results in this section also apply to series generated by ARIMA models, but are better applied to the data after differentiating.

To give a specific example of the preceding theory, suppose that an ARMA(1, 1) model has been fitted to some data of the form

$$x_t - 0.6 x_{t-1} = \varepsilon_t + 0.3 \varepsilon_{t-1}, \qquad \hat{\sigma}_\varepsilon^2 = 0.42.$$

Substituting

$$x_t = \sum_{j=0}^{m} c_j \varepsilon_{t-j}, \qquad c_0 = 1,$$

and similarly for $x_{t-1}$ into the model and gathering terms gives

$$(c_0 - 1)\varepsilon_t + (c_1 - 0.6 c_0 - 0.3)\varepsilon_{t-1} + (c_2 - 0.6 c_1)\varepsilon_{t-2}$$
$$+ (c_3 - 0.6 c_2)\varepsilon_{t-3} + \cdots = 0,$$

so that

$$c_1 = 0.9,$$
$$c_2 = 0.6 c_1 = 0.54,$$
$$c_3 = 0.6 c_2 = 0.324,$$
$$c_4 = 0.6 c_3 = 0.194,$$
$$c_5 = 0.6 c_4 = 0.117,$$
$$\vdots$$

Then using the theory,

$$e_{n,1} = \varepsilon_{n+1},$$

$$e_{n,2} = \varepsilon_{n+2} + 0.9\varepsilon_{n+1},$$

$$e_{n,3} = \varepsilon_{n+4} + 0.9\varepsilon_{n+3} + 0.54\varepsilon_{n+2} + 0.324\varepsilon_{n+3},$$

$$\vdots$$

and

$$\text{var}(e_{n,1}) = \sigma_\varepsilon^2 = 0.42,$$

$$\text{var}(e_{n,2}) = \sigma_\varepsilon^2(1 + (0.9)^2) = 0.76,$$

$$\text{var}(e_{n,3}) = \sigma_\varepsilon^2(1 + (0.9)^2 + (0.54)^2) = 0.88,$$

$$\text{var}(e_{n,4}) = \sigma_\varepsilon^2(1 + (0.9)^2 + (0.54)^2 + (0.324)^2) = 0.927,$$

$$\text{var}(e_{n,5}) = \text{var}(e_{n,4}) + \sigma_\varepsilon^2(0.194)^2 = 0.942,$$

$$\text{var}(e_{n,6}) = \text{var}(e_{n,5}) + \sigma_\varepsilon^2(0.117)^2 = 0.948,$$

$$\vdots$$

From the form of the model, it can be shown that the theoretical variance of $x_t$ is 0.952.

For this model, the optimum forecasts are

$$f_{n,1} = 0.6x_n + 0.3(x_n - f_{n-1,1}), \quad \text{and} \quad f_{n,h} = (0.6)^{h-1}x_{n,1}, \quad h > 1.$$

Thus, if $x_t = 10$, $f_{n-1,1} = 8$, the approximate 95% confidence intervals are (using 2 in place of the correct 1.96)

$$h = 1: \quad 6.6 \pm 2\sqrt{0.42}, \quad \text{i.e.,} \quad 5.30 \text{ to } 7.90,$$

$$h = 2: \quad 3.6 \pm 2\sqrt{0.76}, \quad \text{i.e.,} \quad 2.22 \text{ to } 5.70,$$

$$h = 3: \quad 2.16 \pm 2\sqrt{0.88}, \quad \text{i.e.,} \quad 0.50 \text{ to } 4.46,$$

$$h = 4: \quad 1.23 \pm 2\sqrt{0.927}, \quad \text{i.e.,} \quad -0.50 \text{ to } 3.35,$$

$$h = 5: \quad 0.74 \pm 2\sqrt{0.942}, \quad \text{i.e.,} \quad -1.09 \text{ to } 2.79,$$

$$\vdots$$

## 4.5   NUMERICAL EXAMPLE OF SEASONAL SERIES

Tables 4.4 and 4.5 show the value of retail sales in the United States, in millions of dollars, for the period 1953–1964, both the original series and

**TABLE 4.4**

*U.S. Total Retail Sales in Millions of Dollars, Original Series*

| Year | Jan. | Feb. | Mar. | Apr. | May | Jun. | Jul. | Aug. | Sep. | Oct. | Nov. | Dec. | Total |
|------|------|------|------|------|------|------|------|------|------|------|------|------|-------|
| 1953 | 12903 | 12198 | 13711 | 14115 | 14520 | 14442 | 14250 | 14045 | 13952 | 14819 | 13828 | 16314 | 169097 |
| 1954 | 12213 | 11948 | 13576 | 14025 | 14116 | 14533 | 14259 | 13771 | 14012 | 14538 | 14401 | 17738 | 169130 |
| 1955 | 13147 | 12642 | 14609 | 15450 | 15333 | 15600 | 15261 | 15481 | 15765 | 15685 | 15751 | 19124 | 183848 |
| 1956 | 13727 | 13551 | 15527 | 15074 | 16109 | 16579 | 15382 | 16187 | 15582 | 16130 | 16493 | 19380 | 189721 |
| 1957 | 14741 | 14058 | 15945 | 16285 | 17205 | 17114 | 16864 | 17490 | 16373 | 16949 | 17133 | 19844 | 200001 |
| 1958 | 15286 | 13783 | 15464 | 16362 | 17364 | 16603 | 16596 | 17000 | 16326 | 17360 | 17039 | 21174 | 200357 |
| 1959 | 16225 | 14961 | 16967 | 17821 | 18600 | 18708 | 18332 | 18054 | 17570 | 19095 | 17635 | 21454 | 215422 |
| 1960 | 16312 | 15829 | 17632 | 18973 | 18548 | 18918 | 18066 | 18153 | 17848 | 18648 | 18385 | 22153 | 219465 |
| 1961 | 15803 | 15071 | 17714 | 17618 | 18532 | 18907 | 17922 | 18325 | 18158 | 18761 | 19224 | 22881 | 218916 |
| 1962 | 17007 | 16042 | 19193 | 19097 | 20226 | 20254 | 19138 | 19920 | 18863 | 20576 | 20911 | 24127 | 235354 |
| 1963 | 18261 | 17087 | 19653 | 20518 | 21228 | 20737 | 20540 | 21018 | 19267 | 21528 | 21494 | 25104 | 246435 |
| 1964 | 19154 | 18758 | 20502 | 21186 | 22508 | 22242 | 22145 | 21778 | 21313 | 22605 | 21720 | 27719 | 261630 |
| Avg. | 15398 | 14661 | 16708 | 17210 | 17857 | 17886 | 17396 | 17602 | 17086 | 18058 | 17834 | 21418 | |

## TABLE 4.5
U.S. Total Retail Sales in Millions of Dollars, Seasonally Adjusted Series

| Year | Jan. | Feb. | Mar. | Apr. | May | Jun. | Jul. | Aug. | Sep. | Oct. | Nov. | Dec. | Total |
|------|------|------|------|------|------|------|------|------|------|------|------|------|-------|
| 1953 | 14582 | 14212 | 13997 | 14101 | 14306 | 13974 | 14121 | 14003 | 14095 | 14609 | 13869 | 13414 | 169284 |
| 1954 | 13802 | 13921 | 13859 | 14011 | 13908 | 14062 | 14179 | 13709 | 14195 | 14355 | 14371 | 14596 | 168969 |
| 1955 | 14816 | 14724 | 14917 | 15492 | 15068 | 15098 | 15234 | 15373 | 16020 | 15507 | 15588 | 15792 | 183631 |
| 1956 | 15392 | 15802 | 15890 | 15192 | 15733 | 16025 | 15400 | 16028 | 15922 | 15950 | 16252 | 16070 | 189656 |
| 1957 | 16363 | 16446 | 16418 | 16471 | 16681 | 16557 | 16851 | 17316 | 16790 | 16706 | 16891 | 16488 | 199976 |
| 1958 | 16878 | 16189 | 15997 | 16530 | 16770 | 16035 | 16581 | 16874 | 16793 | 17038 | 16877 | 17519 | 200081 |
| 1959 | 17896 | 17644 | 17572 | 17941 | 18011 | 18060 | 18329 | 18003 | 18042 | 18659 | 17442 | 17692 | 215291 |
| 1960 | 18072 | 18733 | 18185 | 19061 | 18024 | 18241 | 18213 | 18144 | 18323 | 18168 | 18065 | 18229 | 219459 |
| 1961 | 17549 | 17903 | 18215 | 17680 | 18015 | 18281 | 18161 | 18288 | 18679 | 18236 | 18724 | 18905 | 218636 |
| 1962 | 18880 | 19072 | 19749 | 19181 | 19560 | 19665 | 19459 | 19796 | 19520 | 19960 | 20250 | 20014 | 235106 |
| 1963 | 20220 | 20300 | 20293 | 20602 | 20436 | 20237 | 20849 | 20815 | 20014 | 20856 | 20770 | 20900 | 246291 |
| 1964 | 21179 | 22247 | 21231 | 21284 | 21608 | 21758 | 22479 | 21568 | 22139 | 21899 | 20988 | 23077 | 261457 |
| Avg. | 17136 | 17266 | 17193 | 17295 | 17343 | 17333 | 17488 | 17493 | 17544 | 17662 | 17507 | 17725 | |

**Fig. 4.3**   U.S. retail sales.

**Fig. 4.4**   U.S. retail sales, seasonally adjusted.

also the series seasonally adjusted by the simplest version of X-11, as discussed in Section 4.1. These series are plotted in Figs. 4.3 and 4.4. As can be seen both from Fig. 4.3 and also from the monthly means, the original data contain a clear-cut seasonal variation, with lows in January and February and a high in December. The adjusted data is seen to contain little or no seasonal pattern.

### Exercise

With this data, why do you think it is better to use a method that uses monthly averages over five years rather than over the full twelve-year period? Is there any evidence that the seasonal has changed in *shape*, rather than merely in *level*?

Denote $\bar{x}_T$ as the average monthly value for the year $T$ (so that with the above data $\bar{x}_{1953} = 169097/12 = 14091$) and consider the following seasonal adjustment procedure:

(Adjusted January figure for year $T + 1$) = (original January figure for $T + 1$) − (original January figure for year $T − \bar{x}_T$),

and similarly for other months. Thus, January 1954 adjusted = $12213 − (12903 − 14091) = 13401$. Compare the adjusted figures using this method for year 1954 and 1964 with those from the X-11 method. Do you think this method of adjustment may have any advantages or disadvantages compared to X-11 and discuss its relationship with the twelve-month differencing method.

Use the low-cost forecasting methods discussed in Section 4.2 to forecast both the original and the adjusted retail sales figures for 1963 and 1964, the forecasts to be made in December 1962.

## QUESTIONS

1. A firm records sales over a quarter. It finds that an appropriate model seems to be:

$$\text{Sales in } t\text{th quarter} = (\text{seasonal}) + y_t.$$

The average quarterly values over the last six years are

|  | Average |
|---|---|
| 1st quarter | 136 |
| 2nd quarter | 271 |
| 3rd quarter | 482 |
| 4th quarter | 193 |

The estimated autocorrelations for the $y$ values over the same period are observed to be

| $k$ | 0 | 1 | 2 | 3 | 4 | 5 | 6 | 7 |
|---|---|---|---|---|---|---|---|---|
| $\rho_k$ | 1 | 0.8 | 0.66 | 0.50 | 0.40 | 0.33 | 0.25 | 0.20 |

and the average $y$ over the period is zero.
The company statistician suggests that an appropriate model for the $y$'s is

$$y_t = 0.8y_{t-1} + \varepsilon_t,$$

where $\varepsilon_t$ is zero-mean white noise. Do you agree with his suggestion (giving reason)?
Given that sales in the 4th quarter in 1974 are 213, forecast sales for each of the four quarters in 1975.
A director asks for a forecast of total sales in 1975. What forecast would you give?

2. For the quarterly, nonseasonal series $x_t$, whose first five values are

| $t$ | 1 | 2 | 3 | 4 | 5 |
|---|---|---|---|---|---|
| $x_t$ | 10 | $-5$ | 15 | 10 | $-10$, |

forecast $x_t$ for $t = 6$ and 7 using a simple, low-cost forecasting method.

**3.** If $I_n$ is some information set that includes the past and present of the series to be forecast $x_t$ and $f_{n,1}$ is the optimum forecast based on $I_n$, resulting in the error series $e_{n,1}$, why would you expect $e_{n,1}$ to be white noise?

**4.** An industrial forecaster decides to use the following low-cost model for predicting quarterly sales $(x_t)$:

$$\bar{x}_t = \alpha(x_t - S_{t-4}) + (1 - \alpha)\bar{x}_{t-1}, \qquad S_t = \gamma(x_t - x_{t-4}) + (1 - \gamma)S_{t-4},$$

where $\bar{x}_t$ estimates the current level of the sales series and $S_t$ estimates the seasonal component (with $S_{1+4k}$ occurring in the first quarter, $S_{2+4k}$ in the second quarter, etc., as $k = 0, 1, 2, \ldots$). The sales figures in 1974 and 1975 were

| Quarter | 1 | 2 | 3 | 4 |
|---------|----|----|----|----|
| 1974 | 20 | 18 | 16 | 20 |
| 1975 | 24 | 20 | 18 | 22 |

the values of $S_t$ in 1974 were

| Quarter | 1 | 2 | 3 | 4 |
|---------|---|---|----|---|
| $S_t$ | 8 | 0 | -4 | 4 |

and the value of $\bar{x}_t$ for the final quarter of 1974 was 16. If $\alpha = 0.5$, $\gamma = 0.5$, forecast sales for all four quarters of 1976 and 1977. Briefly discuss why this is unlikely to be an optimum forecast.

**5.** (i) Discuss the use of inexpensive (adaptive) methods of forecasting, including their advantages and disadvantages.

(ii) Three different models are being used to forecast the series $x_t$. They are (a) adaptive model,

$$\bar{x}_t = 0.7\bar{x}_{t-1} + 0.3x_t;$$

(b) AR(1),

$$x_t = 0.5x_{t-1} + \varepsilon_t + 20;$$

(c) MA(1),

$$x_t = e_t + 0.6e_{t-1} + 50;$$

where $e_t$ and $\varepsilon_t$ are taken to be zero-mean white noise. At time $t = 20$, the forecasts made by these models for $x_{21}$ are (a) 80, (b) 110, and (c) 90. At time $t = 21$, what forecasts of $x_{22}$ and $x_{23}$ do these models produce given that $x_{21} = 100$?

**6.** (i) Briefly discuss why ARMA models might well be expected to arise in practice when analyzing a single time series.

(ii)   A statistician working for the Central Bank in a small South American country wants to forecast money supply for the country. He only has monthly data of the seasonally adjusted series from July 1965 to February 1976 ready for the computer and figures for March and April 1976 in print. He wants to fit a simple time series model and is uncertain about whether to use an MA(1) or an AR(1) model. How would you advise him to decide on a model?

He puts the computer-available data onto his computer and obtains an estimate of 0.5 for $\rho_1$, the first-order serial correlation coefficient and 100 for the mean of the series. However, the machine loses the data whilst performing this calculation. The two remaining values for his series are 126 and 84 for March and April 1976 respectively.

Using the available information and both of the two simple models, obtain alternative forecasts for money supply in May and June 1976.

7.  In general, would you expect the plot of $f_{n,h}$ to look similar in shape to $x_{n+h}$ as $h$ increases and with $n$ fixed? If no, say why.

8.  An electrical utility company thinks that there is a weekly variation in the total daily demand for electricity. Figures, in some appropriate unit, for the first week of each of the last seven months were

| Month | Sat. | Sun. | Mon. | Tues. | Wed. | Thurs. | Fri. |
|-------|------|------|------|-------|------|--------|------|
| 1 | 4 | 9 | 8 | 7 | 8 | 10 | 6 |
| 2 | 8 | 6 | 6 | 10 | 6 | 8 | 4 |
| 3 | 6 | 5 | 10 | 8 | 10 | 4 | 9 |
| 4 | 5 | 4 | 4 | 6 | 5 | 6 | 3 |
| 5 | 7 | 7 | 9 | 11 | 7 | 7 | 5 |
| 6 | 2 | 3 | 5 | 5 | 9 | 5 | 7 |
| 7 | 3 | 8 | 7 | 9 | 11 | 9 | 8 |

Forecast daily sales for the next month. If you were now told that the data for the first week of month 6 was disturbed by a very violent storm bringing down power lines and disrupting service, how, if at all, would your forecast vary? Do your forecasts take into account the fact that electricity demand varies seasonally?

9.  If $x_t$ is AR(1) of the form

$$x_t = \alpha x_{t-1} + \varepsilon_t, \quad 0 < \alpha < 1,$$

$\varepsilon_t$ is zero-mean white noise and you use optimum forecasts one and two steps ahead, find the variances of the errors made, and prove that the two-step error variance is necessarily the larger of the two. State what time-series models these series of errors obey.

10. The number of working man-days lost due to strikes, $S_t$, are recorded quarterly by a large company. The average quarterly values over the five years 1970–1974 and 1971–1975 are

| Quarter | 1 | 2 | 3 | 4 |
|---|---|---|---|---|
| Average 1970–1974 | 83 | 96 | 41 | 102 |
| Average 1971–1975 | 80 | 91 | 40 | 94 |

and the actual values observed in 1974 and 1975 were:

| Quarter | 1 | 2 | 3 | 4 |
|---|---|---|---|---|
| Values 1974 | 85 | 100 | 44 | 105 |
| Values 1975 | 76 | 84 | 39 | 90 |

The company statistician observes that if the most recently available five-year quarterly averages are subtracted from the actual series, the resulting residuals $x_t$ obey the moving average model $x_t = \varepsilon_t + 0.5\varepsilon_{t-1}$. Using this procedure, the forecast of the actual series for the first quarter 1975 made in the fourth quarter of 1974 was 70. The statistician also notes that if the annual differences are formed, $y_t = S_t - S_{t-4}$, the resulting series obeys the AR(2) model

$$y_t = 0.6y_{t-1} + 0.2y_{t-2} + e_t.$$

Assuming that both $\varepsilon_t$ and $e_t$ are zero-mean white noise series, forecast the values of $S_t$ throughout 1976 using the alternative procedures.

## FURTHER READINGS

Gilchrist, W. (1976). *Statistical Forecasting*, London: Wiley.
  Sound detailed survey of several statistical forecasting methods.
Granger, C. W. J., and P. Newhold (1976). *Forecasting Economic Time Series*, Chapters 4 and 5, New York: Academic Press.
Holt, C. C. (1957). "Forecasting Seasonal and Trends by Exponentially Weighted Moving Averages," Office of Naval Research, Memorandum 52.
Winters, P. R. (1960). "Forecasting Sales by Exponentially Weighted Moving Averages," *Management Science* **6**, 324–342.

CHAPTER
# 5

# Regression Methods
# and Econometric Models

An economist is an expert who will know tomorrow why the things he predicted yesterday didn't happen today.

Evan Esar

## 5.1 RELATING VARIABLES

In the previous three chapters forecasts have been made by relating a variable to its own past, so that if a forecast is required of $x_{n+h}$, the information set considered is $I_n : x_{n-j}, j \geq 0$. It is now time to move to wider information sets, such as

$$I_n : x_{n-j}, y_{n-j}, z_{n-j}, \qquad j \geq 0,$$

so that the forecast of $x_{n+h}$ will be based on the past and present values not only of $x_t$ but also of other series $y_t$ and $z_t$. For example, a forecast of future unemployment could be based on past and present unemployment and also past and present production figures.

A linear relationship between a pair of random variables of the form

$$X = a + bY + \text{error} \tag{1}$$

is known as a regression of $X$ on $Y$. The formulation and estimation of regression relationships is a major topic in classical statistics and a complete account can be found in any statistics text. The parameters $a$ and $b$ are estimated using a least-squares criteria, as explained briefly in Chapter 2. The estimation technique is easily extended to the more complicated multiple regression case, where

$$X = a + bY + cZ + dW + \cdots + \text{error}, \tag{2}$$

although use of a computer is necessary to form these estimates. The variable being explained is called the dependent variable and the variables on the right-hand side of the equation are called the independent or explanatory variables. The main difficulty in forming such models, and then using them to forecast, is to decide what set of independent variables to use. Questions such as whether or not lagged values of the dependent variable should be included amongst the explanatory variables and what other economic time series are appropriate are very important and can make a considerable difference to the forecasting performance of the model.

In the next section, a particular example is considered in some detail to illustrate the difficulties in forming an appropriate forecasting model. The third section in this chapter then returns to discussion of the general case.

## 5.2   CAUSAL MODELS: AN EXAMPLE

Suppose that one is interested in forecasting the dividend that some corporation is going to declare next month. If the sequence of previous annual dividends is denoted by $D_t$, the methods of earlier chapters would involve building a model from this sequence and then using it to forecast. However, anyone at all versed in economics may well think that it would be worthwhile expanding the information set by trying to explain dividends in terms of company earnings, otherwise known as after-tax profits. It might be argued that the money paid out to shareholders in the form of dividends has to come from the earnings, denoted by $E_t$, and so it becomes appropriate to consider a relationship of the form

$$D_t = a + bE_t + e_t, \tag{3}$$

where in this and other equations to follow $e_t$ just represents some residual or "error" series with indeterminate properties. The coefficients $a$ and $b$ are chosen from the available data to give the "best" fit possible, using the classical least-squares regression technique. Suppose that $a$ and $b$ have been estimated and so can be taken as being known and that a forecast of $D_{n+1}$ at time $n$ is required. Equation (3) then gives

$$D_{n+1} = a + bE_{n+1} + e_{n+1}, \tag{4}$$

and so is immediately seen to be of little direct use for forecasting, as the future value of one variable has simply been expressed in terms of the future value of some other variable. An equation such as (3) can be called an *explanatory model*. These models can be used for forecasting purposes in two different ways. The first is to use them to provide *conditional forecasts*, that is, to forecast the value of $D_{n+1}$ given some specific value for $E_{n+1}$. For example, the company management may have announced earlier an expected earnings figure for the year and formula (4) may be used to forecast dividends conditional on the assumption that the expected earnings figure turns out to be the correct one. The formula can be used to provide a whole table of forecasts for $D_{n+1}$ for different $E_{n+1}$ values, using

$$\text{forecast of } D_{n+1} = a + bE_{n+1}, \tag{5}$$

although, as will be explained later, this may not be the optimal forecasting use of the model, as the forecastability of the error term is being ignored. If one has some prior set of beliefs about possible earnings figures, such as

$$
\begin{aligned}
E_{n+1} &= 1000 &&\text{with probability} \quad 0.2\\
&= 1100 &&\text{with probability} \quad 0.3\\
&= 1250 &&\text{with probability} \quad 0.2\\
&= 1350 &&\text{with probability} \quad 0.2\\
&= 1500 &&\text{with probability} \quad 0.1,
\end{aligned}
$$

then these beliefs can be transformed into a distribution for forecast dividends. For example, if $a = 100$, $b = 0.1$, direct substitution into (5) gives

$$
\begin{aligned}
D_{n+1} &= 200 &&\text{with probability} \quad 0.2\\
&= 210 &&\text{with probability} \quad 0.3\\
&= 225 &&\text{with probability} \quad 0.2\\
&= 235 &&\text{with probability} \quad 0.2\\
&= 250 &&\text{with probability} \quad 0.1.
\end{aligned}
$$

Conditional forecasting may also be relevant for control purposes, as will be explained later.

Explanatory models can also be used to provide forecasts of the variable being explained by linking it with forecasts of the explanatory variables. For example, a financial analyst who is familiar with the company and also other firms in the same industry may provide a forecast for earnings which could be converted into a forecast for dividends by using (4) in the form

$$\text{forecast of } D_{n+1} = a + b(\text{forecast of } E_{n+1}). \tag{6}$$

Any forecast for earnings can be used here, but obviously the better the forecast for earnings the better that for dividends. A remarkably simple but widely applicable and successful model is available for company earnings, of the form

$$E_t = m + E_{t-1} + \varepsilon_t, \tag{7}$$

where $\varepsilon_t$ is white noise. A variable generated by such a model is said to be a random walk with drift, and this property of company earnings has been described as "higgledy-piggledy growth." Accepting (7) as true and putting $t = n + 1$ give as a good forecast of earnings,

$$\text{forecast of } E_{n+1} = m + E_n, \tag{8}$$

and substituting into (6) gives

$$\text{forecast of } D_{n+1} = a + b(m + E_n). \tag{9}$$

Note that this forecast is strictly derived from the pair of relationships (4) and (7), but it could equally well have been reached by simply regressing $D_{n+1}$ on $E_n$, that is, by considering a model of the form

$$D_t = \alpha + \beta E_{t-1} + e_t'. \tag{10}$$

However, using the pair of relationships might be thought preferable since more use is then made of an economic theory, however naive. A model of the form (10) may be called a forecasting relationship, as it relates a variable to past values of some other variables.

The economic basis of the original model (3) relating current dividends to current earnings is a very simple-minded one. In practice, the dividend payment in any particular year need not come out of current earnings, but could come from reserves or from borrowed capital, although such a policy could not continue indefinitely. Management often appears to place a great deal of emphasis on stability of dividends, apparently believing that shareholders greatly appreciate this, and so empirical studies of actual dividend data find that a better explanatory model is

$$D_t = c + dD_{t-1} + fE_t + e_t. \tag{11}$$

A positive value of $d$ is almost inevitably found, and this ensures that the dividend sequence is less variable than if $d$ took the value zero. Combining (11) with the higgledy-piggledy earnings growth model gives the improved forecasting relationship

$$D_t = c' + dD_{t-1} + fE_{t-1} + e_t'. \tag{12}$$

For any particular company the coefficients $c'$, $d$, and $f$ could be estimated by the standard least-squares multiple regression procedure using past observed dividends and earnings figures, which are readily available in the financial literature for most large firms. The usual estimation procedures allow the coefficients of the model to take any values so that the model fits as well as possible. However, on occasion one might have a strong belief about the value that a coefficient should take, and if this belief is expressed in the form of a constraint, then a constrained least-squares estimating procedure is needed. For example, one might require that $d$ in (12) be positive. Computer programs are available on most machines that allow one to find estimates for the parameters that achieve the best possible fit, in terms of the lowest sum of squared errors, whilst obeying any constraints placed on the parameters. If the belief is correct, then generally a superior model, in terms of its forecasting ability, is achieved. What kind of belief should one have about the coefficient $f$ in (12)? One could certainly argue that management's aim is to please shareholders and so the larger earnings, the more dividends they will pay, implying $f$ should be positive. This belief could be imposed on the estimation procedure and a forecasting model obtained. However, if the belief is incorrect, the model so achieved will be inferior to one with no constraint on the sign of the coefficient $f$. That this belief could be wrong is suggested by the observation that fairly frequently a decline in earnings is accompanied by an increase in dividend. Why should this be? It seems to follow from an idea that the intrinsic value of a share, which might be equated with its price on the stock exchange, can be expressed by

$$P_t = gE_t + hD_t + e_t, \tag{13}$$

where $P_t$ is the current price and $e_t$ is some error series. If management believes that shareholders are more concerned with capital gains than with dividends, as may well be true due to inequalities in the tax rates, then a method of stabilizing prices if earnings should fall is to raise dividends simultaneously. It is thus seen that our earlier theory of how management should interrelate earnings and dividends may be wrong, and so any constraint placed on a forecasting model based on this theory may lead to a model that is incorrect.

Sometimes it seems as though one of the main preoccupations of upper-middle-class Americans is the prediction of stock market prices. If it were correct, Eq. (13) would seem to provide a method of predicting these prices, as substituting from (12) and (7) gives a forecasting model of the form

$$P_t = k + pE_{t-1} + qD_{t-1} + e_t'. \tag{14}$$

In fact, a popular method of share price prediction, known as the fundamentalist method, is based on this relationship or its generalization by adding further explanatory variables to the right-hand side. Unfortunately, considerable empirical testing has found no evidence that prices can be usefully forecast using this approach. To see why this occurs, (14) should be viewed in terms of forecasting models and information sets. In essence, this formula attempts to forecast $P_{n+1}$ from the information set $I_n: E_{n-j}, D_{n-j}$, $j \geq 0$, but there is no sensible reason why the past of the price series should be ignored. If the expanded information set $I_n': E_{n-j}, D_{n-j}, P_{n-j}, j \geq 0$, using past earnings, dividends, *and* prices is employed one might, for example, consider a model of the form

$$P_t = k + rE_{t-1} + sD_{t-1} + \omega P_{t-1} + e_t. \tag{15}$$

If this model is fitted to data, however, it is almost inevitably found that $r$ and $s$ are insignificantly different from zero, $\omega$ is near unity, $k$ is small, and the errors are white noise so that (15) effectively reduces to

$$P_t = P_{t-1} + \varepsilon_t, \tag{16}$$

where $\varepsilon_t$ is white noise, at least to a good degree of approximation. This is the well-known random walk hypothesis for stock market prices and essentially says that stock price changes are white noise and so cannot be forecast from their own past. As it is price changes that one needs to forecast in order to make money on the stock market, the model is not helpful in the search for ways of making a fortune. This is exactly what one should expect, as if a simple method of predicting stock prices existed it would not be published widely, for otherwise its value would soon be removed by overuse.

This discussion of dividends, earnings, and stock prices is a very brief summary of a few of the main empirical relationships that have been observed in this field. Further details and some references can be found in the book by Granger and Morgenstern (1970). The results have been presented in some detail as they do provide good examples of a number of important points concerning simple forecasting methods based on regression models. These points are reexamined in the following section.

## 5.3   CAUSAL MODELS: THE GENERAL CASE

It is very frequently the case that the value taken by a variable is at least partially determined by the values taken by other variables, either at the same time or in previous time periods. The quantity of some good sold in a day will probably depend on the price at which it is offered, for example, or the amount of electricity used by a household may depend both on the price of electricity and the income of the household. Models based on such ideas are often called causal models, although they are usually just observed, empirical relationships. The idea of causality is a difficult and subtle one, a proper discussion of which is beyond the scope of this text.

An explanatory model is then one that presents an equation explaining the value of the variable of interest in terms of present values of one or more other variables, and possibly also the past values of these variables. Equations (3) and (13) provide examples. By inserting plausible values of the explanatory variables, conditional forecasts are obtained directly. To achieve unconditional forecasts, further equations are required for each of the explanatory variables to provide forecasts for these variables. These forecast values for the explanatory or causal variables are then used to form a forecast for the variable of interest. Equations (7) and (9) provide examples. If $x_t$ is the series one wishes to forecast and $y_t$ and $z_t$ are possible explanatory series, then a further example of an explanatory model is

$$x_t = a + by_t + cz_{t-1} + dy_{t-1} + e_t. \tag{17}$$

To forecast one step ahead, write this as

$$x_{n+1} = a + by_{n+1} + cz_n + dy_n + e_{n+1}. \tag{18}$$

Another model is therefore required to provide a forecast for $y_{n+1}$ so that a forecast for $x_{n+1}$ can be constructed. To forecast two or more steps ahead, a further equation is required to provide forecasts for $z_{n+j}, j \geq 1$. Once the necessary models are obtained, it is obviously quite easy to construct forecasts; the main problem is to achieve the correct explanatory or forecasting model in the first place. The discussion of the dividends, earnings, and stock price example suggests the following two rules:

(i)   Do not rely too heavily on a theory that merely appears to be sensible and is not founded on a sound base or on comprehensive empirical testing; and

(ii)   there is little or no point in attempting to explain a variable just in terms of past values of *other* variables. It is almost always worth also including the past of the series being explained in the information set used to form a forecast. Equations (11) and (15) provide examples.

There are some circumstances where rule (ii) may seem not to apply, such as when the series being explained, $x_t$, is known to be made up of past and present values of the explanatory series $y_t$. For example, the number of people leaving a hospital in a week can only comprise patients who entered previously; the number of automobiles leaving the Lincoln Tunnel in a five-minute interval must be made up of automobiles that entered the tunnel in previous periods; after removing the effects of borrowing, the amount spent by a household in a period consists of money earned in earlier periods, and so forth. This last example is also true for corporations, but not for central governments, or at least they behave as though it is not true. These examples appear to lead to models of the form

$$x_t = ay_t + by_{t-1} + cy_{t-2} + \cdots + e_t \qquad (19)$$

and are called distributed lag models by economists. Although they may appear to be sensible, such models do not have a great deal to recommend them, as the output series $x_t$ may contain features that are not related to the input series $y_t$. For example, the income series $y_t$ for a family may be free of seasonal effects, but the spending series $x_t$ may have a strong seasonal component. Equally, there may be some congestion in the Lincoln Tunnel which will have a large effect on the output series but not affect the input series for a considerable period. In both cases, if a distributed lag model such as (19) is fitted to data, the error series will not be white noise. This has two effects. First, for technical reasons the estimates of the coefficients of the model obtained by a standard regression procedure may not be satisfactory, and second, the forecasts for $x_{n+1}$ have to be altered. For example, if the model fitted is

$$x_t = by_{t-1} + cy_{t-2} + e_t, \qquad (20)$$

then the forecast for $x_{n+1}$ made at time $n$ is

$$f_{n,1}^x = by_n + cy_{n-1} + \text{forecast of } e_{n+1}, \qquad (21)$$

where the forecast of $e_{n+1}$ is obtained by building a single-series model on past errors. It is possible that the need to forecast the error series exists in all of the models so discussed in this and the previous section wherever the time series properties of the error series were left indeterminate. If the coefficients of the model are known, or well estimated, then the sequence of past errors $e_t$ can be extracted and a single-series model found to fit this series, using the methods outlined in Chapter 3. Suppose, for example, that an AR(1) model seems appropriate, so that

$$e_t = \alpha e_{t-1} + \varepsilon_t, \qquad (22)$$

where $\varepsilon_t$ is white noise. The appropriate forecast of $e_{n+1}$ to insert into (21) is then $\alpha e_n$, which from (20) gives

$$\text{forecast of } e_{n+1} = \alpha[x_n - by_{n-1} + cy_{n-2}].$$

Substituting this into (21) shows that the best forecast of $x_{n+1}$ should involve $x_n$ as well as further lagged $y$'s. This then suggests that the original model would have been improved if it had used $x_{n-k}, k \geq 0$, in its information set. It is generally true to say that, if a model uses sufficient lagged values of the variable being explained as well as lagged explanatory variables, the resulting error series should be white noise.

The usual stages in forming a causal or regression model are as follows:

(i)   For the variable to be forecast, list likely explanatory or causal variables. The list should be based on some specific theory, if possible, but introspection is an acceptable source.

(ii)   Gather relevant data to be used to estimate and evaluate the model. Time series will be required for all of the variables involved, and the series should be as long as possible in time span, although very ancient data may not be relevant. Exactly what data to use has to be a judgment call, both for the time span and the time interval between observations, if data are available daily, weekly, monthly, etc. In practice, there may be little choice, as only a few years of monthly data, say, will be available.

(iii)   Propose a model of the following form (assuming $x_t$ is to be forecast and two explanatory variables $y_t$ and $z_t$ are being used):

$$x_t = \alpha_0 + \alpha_1 x_{t-1} + \alpha_2 x_{t-2} + \cdots + \alpha_k x_{t-k}$$
$$+ \beta_0 y_t + \beta_1 y_{t-1} + \cdots + \beta_p y_{t-p}$$
$$+ \gamma_0 z_t + \gamma_1 z_{t-1} + \cdots + \gamma_q z_{t-q} + e_t$$

and estimate it from the data, using ordinary least squares. If more than two explanatory variables are being used, then they should be added to the equation, both lagged and unlagged. The question of how many lags to use is a very difficult one, and it is doubtful if a satisfactory but simple method exists capable of answering it. If sufficient data are available, at least one lag for each variable may be recommended, but if the data contain a seasonal component, a value of $x_{t-12}$ should also be included. In practice, various alternative lagged models should be fitted to the data and the most satisfactory chosen, that is, the model which leads to the smallest sum of squared errors. There are some very sophisticated techniques available, generalizations of the single-series method or the Box–Jenkins procedures outlined in Chapter 3, but these methods lie outside the scope of this text.[1] One very important aspect of the model eventually chosen is that its error or residual series should be white noise. This can be checked by looking at the correlogram of the residuals of the model. The reasons for requiring the errors to be white noise is that if this is not so the estimation procedure can lead to unsatisfactory estimates, as will be further explained below, and also because the full forecasting possibilities are not being realized if the errors are themselves somewhat forecastable.

---

[1] Very much more sophisticated methods of modeling relationships between variables are discussed by Granger and Newbold (1977).

## 5.4  SOME PRACTICAL PROBLEMS

Once a regression equation has been obtained, it is not difficult to form forecasts from it, but unfortunately there are often several possible alternative formulations of the equation, and they do not necessarily produce similar forecasts. There are various diagnostic checks that can be applied to the model, and methods of comparing alternative models are available to help make a choice. This section considers such questions. It is necessarily rather technical and is not required reading for users of regression models, although it is important for those involved with constructing such models.

A convenient starting point is consideration of the statistics provided by most computer regression packages to help evaluate the quality of the model. Three types of statistics are usually given:

(i)  Attached to every estimated parameter in the model is a "$t$ value," though occasionally a "standard error" is provided instead. The usual rather inexact convention is to say that the parameter is significantly different from zero if the $t$ value is at least 2 in magnitude or if the estimated parameter is at least twice the standard error in magnitude. These interpretations are appropriate and correspond to using an approximate 95% confidence region, provided certain assumptions about the form of the model are correct. Unfortunately, as will be seen, these assumptions are often not correct, which makes interpretation of $t$ values very difficult.

(ii)  A value of $R^2$ or of $R_c^2$, which is $R^2$ corrected for degrees of freedom so that the number of explanatory variables used is accounted for, is almost always provided. These are interpreted as measures of the goodness of fit of the model and are defined by

$$R^2 = 1 - \frac{\text{(variance of error terms in model)}}{\text{(variance of variable explained by model)}}$$

and

$$R_c^2 = 1 - \frac{n}{n - k}(1 - R^2),$$

where $n$ is the sample size and $k$ the number of explanatory variables used. The general interpretation given to these quantities is that a model with a larger value is preferred to one with a smaller value.

(iii)  The Durbin–Watson $d$ statistic.  To a close approximation

$$d = 2(1 - r_1),$$

where $r_1$ is the estimated first-order autocorrelation for the residuals or errors in the model. Thus, if the errors are white noise, $d$ will approximately equal 2, but if the errors have a positive first autocorrelation, so that an above average error is inclined to be followed by another above average error, $d$ will be less than 2. If $d$ is far from the value 2, this indicates that the errors of the model have a strong time series structure, and are thus capable of being forecast from past errors using the methods discussed in Chapter 3.

Probably the most important of these three statistics is the last, the $d$ statistic. Many unsophisticated users of regression techniques are content to get a high $R^2$ value and ignore an unsatisfactory value for $d$, but this can lead to very poor models. It can be shown that if least-squares estimates of a regression model are formed when the errors are not white noise, then the $t$ values are overestimated in magnitude, so that parameters that are actually insignificant from zero may appear to be significant. In the extreme case, when $r_1$ for the error series is near 1, so that $d$ is very small, both theory and statistical experimentation have shown that spurious results not only can, but are very likely to occur. This is particularly likely if the levels of economic variables are used in the model. As was discussed in Chapter 3 such variables often need to be differenced to achieve stationarity. Using them in an indifferenced form can easily lead to spurious regressions, which can be distinguished by very low $d$ values even though the $R^2$ values may seem to be satisfactory or even rather high. If differenced data are used, the problem of non-white-noise errors will not totally disappear, but the effect is likely to be very much less important. For forecasting purposes, there is no preference for a model on levels rather than on changes, as forecasts are easily produced from either model, but there should be a strong preference for a model in whose structure and estimated parameters one can have some confidence.

The $R^2$ or $R_c^2$ values cannot be usefully interpreted in absolute terms. It is not correct, for instance, to say that a model with $R^2$ greater than 0.8 is satisfactory but that one with $R^2$ less than 0.3 is unsatisfactory. The value achieved for $R^2$ depends solely on how explainable one variable is in terms of another. $R^2$ can only be used to *rank* alternative models that are trying to explain the *same* dependent variable. For forecasting purposes the criterion one is most interested in when comparing different models is the variance of the error term, as this will be a guide to the variance of the forecast errors when the model is used to form forecasts. For example, if one has the pair of models

$$X_t = 18 + 0.64 Y_{t-1} + e_{1t}, \qquad R_c^2 = 0.86,$$

and

$$\Delta X_t = 0.23 \, \Delta Y_{t-1} + 0.13 \, \Delta Z_{t-1} + e_{2t}, \qquad R_c^2 = 0.22,$$

with $\mathrm{var}(e_{1t}) = 3.6$ and $\mathrm{var}(e_{2t}) = 1.3$, then the second model is more useful for forecasting, as its variance of error is smaller. The $R^2$ values are of no importance as the form of the dependent variable is not the same for the two models. In any case, the $d$ values for both models should also be considered, as one at least may indicate serial correlation in the errors. If such serial correlation is observed, improved methods of estimation for the parameters need to be employed. Descriptions of these more sophisticated estimation procedures can be found in the better econometrics texts.

One further problem that often occurs when economic data over a span of several years are used in forming a model is called heteroscedasticity. It is often noted that as the level of some economic variable, such as price or consumption, increases so does the variance of the errors of any model using this variable, even if the differenced form is used. Heteroscedasticity is a particularly strange word meaning unequal variance, and if a model is estimated for a situation in which the errors have this property, again somewhat unsatisfactory estimates of the parameters and, particularly, of the associated $t$ statistics, will usually occur. A frequently used strategy for at least reducing this problem is to build models on the logarithms of the data rather than on the raw data. This is a perfectly reasonable strategy, but it does have the unfortunate consequence that one ends up with a model that is capable of producing forecasts of the logarithm of a variable rather than of the variable itself, as is usually required. For example, denote the original variable to be forecast by $X_t$ and its logarithm by $x_t = \log X_t$. For simplicity, suppose that $Y_t$ is the only explanatory variable to be used and that $y_t = \log Y_t$. Further suppose that a model is selected and estimated of the form

$$ x_t = 0.2x_{t-1} + 0.4y_{t-1} + \varepsilon_t, $$

where $\varepsilon_t$ passes the usual tests for white noise and has variance $\sigma^2$. A one-step forecast of $x_{n+1}$ is then given by

$$ f_{n,1}^x = 0.2x_n + 0.4y_n, $$

but what is really required is a forecast of $X_{n+1}, f_{n,1}^X$. It is easily shown that a forecast of the form

$$ f_{n,1}^X = \exp f_{n,1}^x $$

is biased and that a better forecast is given by

$$ f_{nt\,1}^X = \exp(f_{n,1}^x + \tfrac{1}{2}\sigma^2). $$

The main point is that if transformations of the data are used in modeling, then great care has to be taken in unraveling this transformation when using the model to forecast.

It is hoped that this section will at least give an indication of the very real and important practical problems that arise when using regression models.

These problems are often ignored by unsophisticated users of such models and often result in unsatisfactory or suboptimal forecasts. A complete description of all aspects of these problems and the strategies to overcome them is well beyond the scope of this text. Descriptions can be found in the more advanced texts in econometrics and forecasting, but completely satisfactory solutions to all of the problems have not yet been discovered and advances are to be found in recent research literature.

## 5.5 ECONOMETRIC MODELS

Any economics textbook or course in macroeconomics emphasizes the considerable extent to which economic variables are interrelated. Production will depend on consumption and consumption on employment and employment on production, for example. Such feedback relationships, or relationships holding simultaneously for groups of variables, not only introduce particular problems of modeling but also suggest the existence of true, important relationships that can be utilized to produce improved forecasts in economics.

An example of a simple, simultaneous national income model is as follows:

$$C_t = a_1 + b_1 Y_t \qquad\qquad\qquad + e_{C_t}, \qquad (23\text{i})$$

$$I_t = a_2 \qquad + c_2 P_{t-1} \qquad\qquad + e_{I_t}, \qquad (23\text{ii})$$

$$T_t = \qquad\qquad\qquad d_3 \text{GNP}_t \qquad + e_{T_t}, \qquad (23\text{iii})$$

$$P_t = a_4 + b_4 Y_t \qquad\qquad + f_4 I_{t-1} + e_{P_t}, \qquad (23\text{iv})$$

$$\text{GNP}_t = C_t + I_t + G_t, \qquad (23\text{v})$$

$$Y_t = \text{GNP}_t - T_t, \qquad (23\text{vi})$$

where $C$ is consumption, $I$ investment, $Y$ disposable national income, GNP gross national product, $G$ government expenditure on goods and services, $T$ taxes, $P$ profits, and $e_{C_t}$, $e_{I_t}$, $e_{T_t}$, and $e_{P_t}$ are error terms.

The model consists of two different types of equations. The first four are called structural equations and involve parameters ($a_1$, $b_1$, etc.) that need to be determined. These equations arise from some economic theory and determine the four variables $C$, $I$, $T$, and $P$. Thus, for example, Eq. (23i) states that aggregate consumption is a linear function of national income and Eq. (23iii) has aggregate taxes as a fixed proportion of GNP, although both equations do not fit exactly and so contain error terms. The final two equations are identities and are simple definitions linking different variables.

An identity is known to hold exactly and thus has neither error term nor parameters to be estimated. It would be possible to substitute for the variables defined by the identities in the structural equations and thus reduce the total number of variables involved in the system, but there may then be some loss of interpretability.

The variables can also be subdivided into important classes. Variables $C_t$, $I_t$, $T_t$, and $P_t$ are called endogenous, which means that they are determined by structural equations in the system. Variables $P_{t-1}$ and $I_{t-1}$ are called predetermined because at time $t$ there is little or no doubt about their values. $G_t$ is an exogenous variable, meaning that its value at time $t$ is determined outside the system, presumably as a result of various government decisions. The two remaining variables $GNP_t$ and $Y_t$ are determined by identities and so are completely determined from the other variables. Because of the two identities, the set of endogenous variables can in fact be almost any four of the group $C$, $I$, $T$, $P$, GNP, and $Y$, provided the identities are obeyed.

The error terms will be taken to be white noises, for the moment. If one tries to use the structural equations to form forecasts, difficulties immediately arise because of the simultaneous nature of the system. For example, replacing $t$ by $n + 1$ in (23i) gives

$$C_{n+1} = a_1 + b_1 Y_{n+1} + e_{c, n+1},$$

and so a "forecast" for $C_{n+1}$ can be written

$$f_{n, 1}^C = a_1 + b_1 f_{n, 1}^Y,$$

but a forecast for $Y_{n+1}$ is required for this equation to be usable. The simultaneous form of the model also makes estimation of the parameters of the system difficult. However, econometric texts invariably include extensive discussions of this estimation problem, and it would be quite inappropriate to try to summarize this area here. In what follows, it will be assumed that good estimates of the parameters have been obtained so that attention can be focused on the use of the model for forecasting purposes.

A different formulation of the model is particularly useful for forecasting, known as the reduced form. A reduced form expresses each endogenous variable just in terms of exogenous and predetermined variables, plus error. Suppose the above model is to be used to provide a forecast for GNP. Adding the first two equations and using the identities, one gets

$$GNP_t - G_t = (a_1 + a_2) + b_1(GNP_t - T_t) + c_2 P_{t-1} + (e_{c_t} + e_{I_t}).$$

Substituting for $T_t$ from (23iii), rearranging, and dividing through by

$H \equiv 1 - b_1 + b_1 d_3$ gives

$$\text{GNP}_t = A + \frac{G_t}{H} + \frac{c_2 P_{t-1}}{H} + e_{G_t}, \tag{23vii}$$

where $A \equiv (a_1 + a_2)/H$ and $e_{G_t} = (e_{C_t} + e_{I_t} - b_1 e_{T_t})/H$.

The other endogenous variables can be expressed in similar ways. Equation (23ii), for $I_t$, is already in a reduced form, as it only involves the predetermined variable $P_{t-1}$ and substituting from (23vii) for $\text{GNP}_t$ into equation (23iii) immediately gives the reduced form equation for $T_t$. Finally, writing (23iv) as

$$P_t = a_4 + b_4(\text{GNP}_t - T_t) + f_4 I_{t-1} + e_{P_t}$$

and then substituting for $\text{GNP}_t$ from (23vii) and for $T_t$ from (23iii) gives the reduced form equation for $P_t$, which can be written

$$P_t = h_1 + h_2 G_t + h_3 P_{t-1} + h_4 I_{t-1} + e'_{P_t}, \tag{23viii}$$

where the parameters $h_1$, $h_2$, $h_3$, $h_4$ are all functions of the parameters of the structural equations and the error $e'_{P_t}$ is a linear function of the errors in the original set of equations.

From (23ii), which is a reduced form equation, a one-step forecast for $I_{n+1}$ is easily formed:

$$I_{n+1} = a_2 + c_2 P_n + e_{I, n+1}$$

and so

$$f^I_{n, 1} = a_2 + c_2 P_n$$

if $e_{I_t}$ is white noise, as has been assumed. The rule, as in previous chapters, is to write down the equation that you believe will determine the future value of the variable of interest and then to replace all explanatory variables by either their known values or by their optimum forecasts. To use (23vii) to forecast $\text{GNP}_{n+1}$, one has

$$\text{GNP}_{n+1} = A + \frac{G_{n+1}}{H} + \frac{c_2 P_n}{H} + e_{a, n+1},$$

and so

$$f^{\text{GNP}}_{n, 1} = A + \frac{G_{n+1}}{H} + \frac{c_2 P_n}{H} \tag{23ix}$$

The question immediately arises of how to forecast future government expenditure. If an economist is employed by a company and has no inside information about what are the government's intentions, he can take one of two alternative approaches. The first is to list a set of plausible values for $G_{n+1}$ and, for each of these values, to then use equation (23ix) to give *conditional* forecasts of GNP, as was discussed in the second section of this chapter when relating dividends to earnings. The alternative technique is to try to determine a model relating past government expenditure figures to other economic variables, such as unemployment levels, national income, or price changes. This model essentially completes the system by treating $G_t$ as though it were endogenous rather than exogenous. The resulting reduced form of this extended system will then have each exogenous variable in terms of just predetermined variables, so that forecasts are easily formed. This approach gives *unconditional* forecasts for the GNP. The only problem with this method is that it is difficult to take into account nonnumerical information, such as rumors one might have about government interactions. It is usual to use a model to forecast $G_{n+1}$ and then to alter this forecast subjectively if relevant extra information is available to the forecaster. The success or lack thereof of such adjustments clearly depends on the quality of the information being utilized and the abilities of the forecaster who tries to use it.

An economist employed by the government may use Eq. (23ix) in a quite different fashion. If the viewpoint is taken that the government has some considerable flexibility in the value that $G_{n+1}$ can take, since this value is determined by governmental decisions, Eq. (23ix) can be used as a control equation, with the value of $G_{n+1}$ chosen so that $f_{n,1}^{GNP}$ is at or near some target value for the GNP in the next period, as determined by those in control. Discussion of control theory would take us too far from the central theme of this chapter, but the importance of correct forecasting models for control purposes should be clear.

Due to the simultaneous nature of an econometric model, the information set being used to form a forecast can become substantial. The form taken by any individual structural equation may be quite simple, but this is because many of the variables in the information set are excluded from the equation, due to the constraints on the model imposed by the economic theory that is being referred to when the model is being specified. The main advantage of basing an econometric model on a specific economic theory is the resulting simplification in the structural form and a consequent saving in the number of parameters that need to be estimated. The reduced form may well involve many predetermined and exogenous variables and so not be simple in form. The difficult estimation problem with a set of structural equations can be circumvented by applying ordinary least squares to each individual equation of the reduced form. For example, the $h$'s in equation (23viii) could be estimated directly, rather than derived from the parameters of the structural equations, and the resulting equation used to form forecasts. However, if this is done for every reduced form equation, the total number of parameters to be estimated may become very large, and so suspect if the total amount of data available is not large. Further, any simplifications suggested by the economic theory will not have been utilized, and so the estimates may be less efficient than is achievable. If one has available a correct theory, or at least a good approximation to one, it is clearly better to base one's forecasts on this theory. The timing of high tides is an example of forecasts based on a sound theory.

On the other hand, a model based on an incorrect or incomplete theory will produce suboptimal forecasts. A problem with economic theories is that they are not obviously correct. There are often competing theories which econometricians have not been able to decide between, possible because neither theory is correct and many theories are insufficiently precise for a full-scale econometric model to be based upon them. In particular, few theories specify the lag structure of the variables entering into the model with an acceptable degree of precision. These effects often result in models having non-white-noise errors, plus many of the other problems discussed in the previous section. Because of this, a certain amount of experimental modeling is conducted with econometric models, particularly with the error terms.

The correct size of the model, that is, the number of equations that it should contain, is also a source of controversy. The larger the model, the more likely it is to capture all the important feedback loops in the economy, but the likelihood of misspecification also increases and estimation of the parameters of the model necessarily becomes more difficult. Some econometricians prefer a "small" model of only 20–30 structural equations, but models of 1000 or more equations are considered to be necessary by other experts. A worldwide model, linking individual country models with trade flows, has also been constructed and consists of several thousand equations. As one bad egg can spoil an omelette, there must be a worry with such large models that one poorly specified sector of the model may have bad effects throughout, unless special care is taken.

In practice, most of the really influential macroeconomic forecasts of developed economies are based on econometric models. It is also true that the forecasts produced by the model are not necessarily the forecasts issued by the model's constructors. If a forecast for some segment seems strange or out of line with other forecasts or the econometrician's own judgment, then it will probably be altered to look more reasonable. This application of "tender loving care" has been shown to result in improved forecasts and, to some extent, overcomes the most important misspecifications that inevitably occur when constructing a large-scale model.

It could be claimed that the construction of a really well specified model for the economy should be the ultimate goal of all statisticians concerned with economic data, as such a model would both result in the very best possible forecasts and also allow governments to efficiently control the economy. It is also clear that econometricians are a very long way from achieving this objective.

The question of how forecasts from econometric models can be evaluated and how well they perform in practice compared to alternative methods will be discussed in Chapter 8.

One practical problem that has arisen in recent years is the use of non-linear forms of the variables in the structural equations. For example, consumption may be explained by income and also the square root of income. Such transformations may well lead to improved structural equations, but the reduced form cannot always then be derived and so forecasting becomes more difficult. The usual practice is to "linearize" the model and then to find the corresponding reduced form, but this is probably a sub-optimal solution to the problem.

## 5.6  AN ACTUAL ECONOMETRIC MODEL

To further emphasize some of the more important points made in the previous section and also to introduce a little more reality, use will be made of an actual econometric model published by Pindyck (1973). A somewhat simplified version of this model is presented below. It is a quarterly model estimated for the period 1955-1–1974-4[2] and consists of nine equations plus three identities, relating nine endogenous variables plus three other quantities derived from them and two exogenous variables. These variables, and the notation used, are

    $C$      personal consumption
    $INR$  private investment—nonresidential
    $IR$   investment in residential buildings
    $IIN$  change in business inventories
    $G$     government purchases of goods and services

All of these variables are in billions of 1958 dollars.

    $R$     interest rate on U.S. Government three-month bills
    $RL$   interest rate on long-term U.S. Government bonds

---

[2] Here, and later in the section, 1974-2 or 74-2 will be used to denote the second quarter of 1974.

P       price level, the implicit price deflator for GNP
UR      unemployment rate, the ratio of total unemployed to the civilian
        labor force
W       hourly wage rate
M       money supply, currency plus demand deposits
I       $INR + IR + IIN$, investment
Y       $(1 - \tau)(C + I + G)$, disposable income, that is, the GNP reduced
        by application of the average tax rate $\tau$
$\tau$      tax rate, estimated to be 0.15
YP      potential, or full-capacity, disposable income

Exact definitions of these variables can be found in Pindyck's original publication. The endogenous variables, those which are determined by the model, are $C$, $INR$, $IR$, $IIN$, $R$, $RL$, $P$, $UR$, and $W$. $I$ and $Y$ are derived directly from these quantities by the two identities given above. $G$, $M$, and $YP$ are taken to be exogenous, that is, determined outside the model. The structural form of the estimated model is shown below. The coefficients obtained have been simplified and are all apparently significant, in that they have $t$ statistic values with magnitudes greater than 2. The errors to the equations are not shown, but are assumed to obey the AR(1) model

$$e_t = \rho e_{t-1} + \varepsilon_t,$$

where $\varepsilon_t$ is zero-mean white noise and the $\rho$ value is shown for each equation. The notation used is: $x_{-2}$ means a lag of two quarters and $\Delta x$ denotes a change, i.e., $x - x_{-1}$. The values of $R^2$ shown for each equation indicate the goodness of fit achieved, being the proportion of the variance of the dependent variable explained by the explanatory variables. The actual estimation technique used is called two-stage least squares with the Hildreth–Lu autoregressive transform.

$$C = 0.42Y - 2.4P - 0.28Y_{-1} + 8.2W_{-1} + 2.4P_{-1} + 0.76C_{-1} + 5.3,$$
$$R^2 = 0.9991, \quad \rho = -0.4, \quad (24\text{i})$$

$$INR = 0.16Y - 0.16Y_{-1} + 0.04\,\Delta Y_{-3} - 1.4\,\Delta RL_{-5} + 1.33INR_{-1}$$
$$- 0.34INR_{-2}. \quad R^2 = 0.718, \quad \rho = -0.34, \quad (24\text{ii})$$

$$IR = 0.01Y - 0.55(R_{-2} + R_{-3}) + 0.60IR_{-1} + 6.65,$$
$$R^2 = 0.992, \quad \rho = 0.7, \quad (24\text{iii})$$

$$IIN = 0.47Y - 0.6C - 0.46Y_{-2} + 0.6C_{-2} + 0.42IIN_{-1} - 2.46,$$
$$R^2 = 0.740, \quad \rho = 0.4, \quad (24\text{iv})$$

$$R = 0.04Y - 0.16M + 0.48P + 0.03Y^-_{\,1} + 0.16M_{-1} - 0.48P_{-1}$$
$$+ 0.37R_{-1} - 1.47, \quad R^2 = 0.883, \quad \rho = 0.4, \quad (24\text{v})$$

$$RL = 0.06R + 0.006Y - 0.006Y_{-2} + 0.87RL_{-1} + 0.31,$$
$$R^2 = 0.941, \quad \rho = 0.25, \quad \text{(24vi)}$$

$$P = -0.02Y + 6.3W_{-1} + 0.02(Y_{-1} - YP_{-1}) - 0.03IIN_{-2}$$
$$+ 0.80P_{-1}, \quad R^2 = 0.984, \quad \rho = 0.5, \quad \text{(24vii)}$$

$$UR = -0.00043Y + 0.00032Y_{-2} + 0.0024W_{-1} + 0.80UR_{-1} + 0.0065,$$
$$R^2 = 0.953, \quad \rho = 0.05, \quad \text{(24viii)}$$

$$W = 0.00012Y + 0.01P_{-3} + 0.001Y_{-1} - 0.83UR_{-4} + 0.63W_{-1}$$
$$- 0.685, \quad R^2 = 0.9992, \quad \rho = 0.02. \quad \text{(24ix)}$$

The model is seen to be of structural form as the equations contain the present values of other endogenous variables. In particular, it is noticeable that current $Y$ appears in each equation. To form forecasts of the exogenous variables it is clearly important to first form a forecast for $Y$. This is best achieved by finding the reduced form equation for $Y$. To obtain this, first add up the first four equations, which gives

$$C + I = 1.06Y - 2.6P - 0.6C + L_1,$$

where $L_1$ denotes the sum of all the constants and lagged terms in these equations. Substituting for $C$ from (24i) into the right-hand side gives

$$C + I = 0.81Y - 0.96P + L_2,$$

where $L_2$ consists of $L_1$ plus the lagged and constant components in (24i) multiplied by $-0.6$. Now, substituting for $P$ from (24vii) gives

$$C + I = 0.83Y + L_3,$$

where $L_3$ is $L_2$ plus the lagged and constant components in (24vii) multiplied by $-0.96$. Adding $G$ to both sides and using the definition of $Y$, with $\tau = 0.15$, gives

$$Y = 0.85(0.83Y + G + L_3),$$

which, on solving for $Y$, gives

$$Y = 2.93G + L_4,$$

where $L_4$ is $L_3$ multiplied by 2.93. Although $L_4$ is rather complicated, it consists only of components that are constants or lagged. Using this last equation to designate how $Y_{n+1}$ will be generated one has

$$Y_{n+1} = 2.93G_{n+1} + L_{4,n} + \text{error}$$

and, at time $n$, all of the components of $L_{4,n}$ are known. To forecast $Y_{n+1}$, a value for $G_{n+1}$ has to be decided upon. If a forecast of $G_{n+1}$ is used, then an unconditional forecast for $Y_{n+1}$ will result, but if a series of alternative values for $G_{n+1}$ are substituted into the equation, then the corresponding conditional forecasts are obtained. In the equation for $Y_{n+1}$, the error term is also somewhat forecastable from its components each of which are assumed to be AR(1). There is obviously some effort required to forecast $Y_{n+1}$, but it is worthwhile, since forecasts of all the other endogenous variables follow quickly. Using the forecast of $Y_{n+1}$ plus known values at time $n$ for other variables, forecasts of $INR$, $IR$, $P$, $UR$, and $W$ follow immediately from equations (24ii), (24iii), and (24vii)–(24ix) respectively. The forecasts of $Y_{n+1}$ and $P_{n+1}$, substituted into (24i) give a forecast for $C_{n+1}$. The forecasts of $Y_{n+1}$ and $C_{n+1}$ together with equation (24iv) give a forecast for $IIN_{n+1}$. To obtain a forecast for $R_{n+1}$, not only are forecasts of $Y_{n+1}$ and $P_{n+1}$ required for equation (24v) but also a value for future money supply $M_{n+1}$. Finally, equation (24vi) is used to forecast $RL_{n+1}$ and this will depend on the forecasts for $R_{n+1}$ and $Y_{n+1}$. It should be remembered that in each of the equations the errors are forecastable from previous error; the formula to be used is

$$(\text{forecast}) = \rho(\text{previous error})$$

using the usual AR(1) forecasting equation discussed in Chapter 3. It is also seen that all of the exogenous variable forecasts can be conditioned on future government expenditure and that the two interest rate series, $R$ and $RC$, will also be conditioned on future money supply. If forecasts more than one step ahead are determined from the model, a future value for potential disposable income will be required for Eq. (24vii) and so price $P$ and some other forecasts may be conditioned on this value.

The method by which this econometric model is used to produce forecasts is somewhat complicated but not inherently difficult. It should be noted, however, that the model used there as an example is considered a very small one. The models actually used to forecast the economy generally consist of from twenty to several hundred equations and do become very complicated to use without a computer.

The quality of the forecasts obtained is discussed in Chapter 8.

**Exercises**

1.  Using the expression

$$Y = 2.93G + L_4,$$

find the reduced form equations for $P$, $W$, $C$, $R$, and $RL$.

**2.**  Suppose that the following values are observed for the variables shown and at the times shown:

| | Quarter of 1960 | | | | | Quarter of 1960 | | | |
|---|---|---|---|---|---|---|---|---|---|
| | 1 | 2 | 3 | 4 | | 1 | 2 | 3 | 4 |
| *IIN* | 9.6 | 3.1 | | | *YP* | | 425 | 430 | |
| *P* | | 102 | | | *C* | | 320 | | |
| *W* | | 2.0 | | | *M* | | 140 | 142 | 145 |
| *Y* | | 419 | | | *R* | | 3.9 | | |

The table also shows "best-guess" forecasts for future money supply and *YP*, made by an economist during the second quarter of 1960. It is observed that when Eq. (24vii) is applied for 1960-2, the resulting error is 7, and similarly the errors for Eq. (24i) and (24v) are 26 and $-0.5$ respectively. From the model and his estimate of *G* for 1960-3 and -4, the economist predicts the value of *Y* to be 416.5 for 1960-3 and 412 for 1960-4. Use this information to forecast *P*, *C*, and *R* for 1960-3 and 1960-4.

## QUESTIONS

**1.**  Explain the main differences in approach between forecasts formed from econometric models and time series models. Outline any advantages or disadvantages the two methods possess.

**2.**  An econometrician fits the following multiplier–accelerator model to some data:

$$I_t = \alpha + \beta C_t + \text{error},$$

$$C_t = \delta I_t + \gamma I_{t-1} + \lambda G_t + \text{error},$$

where $I_t$ is investment in period $t$, $C_t$ consumption in period $t$, and $G_t$ government expenditure in period $t$.
The coefficients are estimated to be

$$\alpha = 0.03, \quad \beta = 0.8, \quad \delta = 0.5, \quad \gamma = 0.2, \quad \lambda = 0.5$$

and the errors can be taken to be white noise.
If $C_n = 1000$, $I_n = 500$, and $G_n = 300$, forecast $C_{n+1}$ and $I_{n+1}$
(a) using a conditional forecast, and
(b) using a forecast for $G_{n+1}$ of 350.

**3.**  A report by a market researcher states, "I have found the following relationship between total savings $S_t$ and advertising by savings banks $A_t$,

$$S_t = 487 + 0.3A_t + 0.2A_{t-1} + \text{error},$$

and this will be useful in helping forecast future savings." Comment on how a forecast would be made and also on its likely quality.

4. A company econometrician builds the following model for his company relating sales $S$ in a quarter, the wages $W$ paid to salespersons in that quarter, and national income $Y$:

$$S = 0.2W + 0.5S_{-1} + 0.02Y + e_S, \qquad R^2 = 0.76, \quad d = 1.9,$$
$$(3.1) \qquad (4.6) \qquad (2.2)$$

$$W = 82 + 0.3S + 0.01Y + e_W, \qquad R^2 = 0.82, \quad d = 0.9.$$
$$(3.1) \quad (4.0) \qquad (1.1)$$

Critically discuss the quality of this second equation. Explain how you would use this model to forecast next quarter's sales.

5. A statistician wrote the following report: "My task was to forecast demand for new single family houses in Salt Lake City. I had available annual data for the period 1947–1976. As clearly this demand is largely due to population increases, I ran the following two regressions:

$$(\text{total houses in region})_t = a + b(\text{total population})_t + e_t$$

and

$$(\text{new houses built})_t = c + d(\text{change in population}) + f_t.$$

The values for the coefficients were found to be

$$a = 10{,}526, \qquad b = 0.3, \qquad c = 122, \qquad d = 0.7.$$

The first equation had $R^2 = 0.62$ and $e_t$ had variance 269, and the second equation had $R^2 = 0.24$ and $f_t$ had variance 42. I then modeled the residual series and found that the following equations give good fits:

$$e_t = 0.9e_{t-1} + \varepsilon_t \qquad \text{and} \qquad f_t = 0.2f_{t-1} + \eta_t.$$

I noted that in the Salt Lake City region total population $P_t$ appeared to have a linear trend of the form

$$P_t = 4629 + 2000t,$$

where $t = 0$ occurs in 1900. The two models give different forecasts and I could not decide which ones to use."

Comment on his report. Using whichever model you think is the better, forecast new house sales in Salt Lake City for 1977, 1978, and 1985. Discuss how you would try to obtain superior forecasts.

## FURTHER READINGS

Granger, C. W. J., and Oskar Morgenstern (1970). *Predictability of Stock Market Prices*, Lexington, Massachusetts: Heath.

Discusses forecasting of stock prices, earnings and dividends and the random walk hypothesis.

Granger, C. W. J., and P. Newbold (1977). *Forecasting Economic Time Series*, Chapter 6, New York: Academic Press.

A critical account of regression and econometric methods.

Klein, L. R. (1971). *An Essay on the Theory of Economic Prediction*, Chicago: Markham.

A very sound account of the use of econometric models for forecasting.

Maddala, G. S. (1977). *Econometrics*, New York: McGraw-Hill.

Up-to-date textbook on econometrics.

Pindyck, R. (1973). *Optimal Planning for Economic Stabilization*, Amsterdam: North Holland Publ.

CHAPTER

# 6

# Survey Data:

# Anticipations and Expectations

If you can look into the seeds of time, and say which grain will grow and which will not, speak then unto me.

Shakespeare

## 6.1 OVERVIEW OF THE USE OF SURVEY DATA

Much of the value to be taken in the future by some economic variable may already have been determined by plans or commitments by the individual decision-making units of the economy. Examples are the following:

(i) A household may have decided to buy a new automobile in three months time and is already adjusting its spending plans to allow for this anticipated purchase. By aggregating up these anticipations over all households, part of the automobile sales that will occur in three months time will have been determined.

(ii) A company is planning to extend its factory in twelve months time and is already organizing the details of the construction and is also considering how to raise the necessary capital. Many major investments by firms require planning and long-term commitments have to be made. By asking companies about these plans, data on future investment can sometimes be obtained.

(iii) A firm knows that a new major piece of machinery will be delivered in two months time and that its arrival will affect the company's manpower requirements. The firm therefore has an anticipated change in employment levels.

A sensible way of gathering data that may well have a useful forecasting potential is to conduct a survey of households or firms and simply ask about their plans for future spending, manpower needs, or other resource requirements. Such surveys will provide what is called *anticipations data*.

This idea can be extended to asking opinions of individuals or firms about what they expect will happen either in the economy at large or in sectors that particularly affect them. It is possible, for instance, that consumers are particularly sensitive to clues that precede a substantial price change in an item they buy frequently. The consumers may therefore have an aggregate opinion about forthcoming price changes that is potentially useful. Surveys that ask opinions of essentially nonexpert forecasters provide what will be called *expectations data*. Even if the expectations of price changes are not very good forecasts of actual price changes, if consumers alter their expectations, they may consequently alter their consumption patterns. An expected large price increase may lead to panic buying of a commodity even though subsequent events show the expectation to be wrong. An indirect way of obtaining related data is to ask households or firms how contented they are with their present economic situation. It is possible that a happy group of consumers consistently behaves in a different fashion than an unhappy group. Data of this kind will be called *attitudinal*.

There is no reason why only forecasts by nonexperts should be considered when a large number of forecasts is being continually produced by professional forecasters in business, government, and universities. A survey of the opinions of these forecasters about the future value of some variable will give both a consensus opinion or expectation and also measures of the extent of disagreement to be found. For example, a panel of financial analysts, employed by large pension funds, banks and other financial institutions, could be asked each month for their opinions about future movements in the stock market. Presumably, the panel members will be able to apply more expertise and expend more time in weighing the various factors affecting the market than could the ordinary investor. They may also have access to relevant information not available to the general public, so that the combined opinion of this panel of experts could provide superior stock market forecasts. This type of data will be called *forecast survey data*.

A great deal of these types of survey data is collected, particularly anticipations and expectations data. But as collection costs are often high and the data is collected for commercial reasons, the results are sometimes not made public. A list issued in 1977, for example, mentions 88 different anticipations or expectations surveys in 33 countries. Of these surveys, 61 collected expectational data on business conditions, 41 were investment surveys, and 23 interviewed consumers on anticipations, expectations, or attitudes. Thirty of the surveys fell into more than one category. No attempt will be made in this book to survey the data that are available, as presumably any forecaster working in a particular industry, say, will be aware of survey data relevant to his field. However, a number of general points about how survey data can, or should, be utilized can be made and each of the main types are considered in the following sections. It is important to realize that survey data can either be used directly to form forecasts or it can be used simply to expand some information set. It is often in this second role that the main forecasting advantages of survey data can be realized.

## 6.2  ANTICIPATION DATA

Anticipations data consist of replies by a sample of companies, institutions, or individual households to questions put to them about their plans for some future period. For example, a sample of construction companies can be asked how many single-family housing units they plan to build in the next six months, or households can be asked how many new television sets they intend to buy in the next year. As will be seen, the usefulness of this data in improving forecasts is not always clear-cut. The least controversial and most obviously useful data relate to anticipations of investments by companies. Virtually all types of investment in plant and equipment takes several months planning or prior commitment, and for a large investment such as a new factory or production line, plans need to be made several years ahead. The two major U.S. surveys of anticipated investments by companies have quite different horizons, that organized by the Department of Commerce produces anticipations one and two quarters ahead, whereas the survey conducted by McGraw-Hill lists investment anticipations for one, two, three, and four years ahead. The firms approached in these surveys do appear to take them seriously, and the survey forms are often signed by high-ranking officers of the company. The data produced by the survey can either be considered as providing direct forecasts of future investments or as useful additional information to be added to a regression model, for instance. The evidence of empirical studies suggests that changes in aggregate company investment can be better forecast from changes in anticipations than from either econometric models not using anticipations or by simple time series models relating investments just to previous investments. It is thus seen that, in this case, anticipations data does have clear forecasting value.

The evidence is much less clear-cut for other anticipation survey data, for instance, those of housing starts or inventories. As these quantities involve more guesswork or forecasting and less prior commitment than investments, the poorer quality is perhaps to be expected. A more controversial type of

**TABLE 6.1**

| Answer in first survey | Percentage of this group making a consumer durable purchase in following twelve months |
|---|---|
| 1 or 2 | 24% |
| 3 or 4 | 27% |
| 5 or 6 | 39% |
| 7 or 8 | 43% |
| 9 or 10 | 46% |

data is the result of surveying households about their consumption plans. A great deal of this type of data is collected for commercial reasons and strong claims are made about its usefulness, although these claims are often based on regression studies using improper information sets. These studies usually concentrate on consumer durable goods, such as automobiles, refrigerators, freezers, and air conditioners, which often involve considerable expenditure and therefore possibly some planning. The earlier surveys simply asked one or more members of the houshold if they intended to buy a freezer, say, in the next six months or year; the only allowable answers were yes or no. Because there is obviously some uncertainty in the buying plans, more sophisticated answers are now possible, usually on a scale of 10 to 0, with 10 meaning practically certain, 6 interpreted as a probability of 0.6, or in words "good possibility," 3 as a probability of 0.3 or "some possibility," 1 as very slight possibility, and 0 as almost no chance, or a probability of 1 in 100, say. Follow-up surveys do indicate that the higher the score given by the household, the higher the chance of a purchase being made. For example, an English survey found the relationship shown in Table 6.1. However, the majority of households did not expect to make a purchase and so answered 0; in fact in this particular survey, nearly 92% of replies were zero. Of these households, only about 6% did in fact make a consumer durable purchase in the next twelve months. Although this is a small proportion, because this was such an important and large group, it was found that almost two-thirds of all purchases were made by those households who claimed they had no plans to make a purchase. The main reason given for this occurrence was that some appliance broke down unexpectedly and had to be replaced. This aspect of the data does make interpretation of consumer durable anticipation surveys difficult, particularly as replacement of a somewhat deficient automobile or appliance can be postponed in difficult economic times. In general, it does seem that these surveys do possibly have some value but should be interpreted and used carefully.

## 6.3 EXPECTATIONS AND ATTITUDES

In several countries, surveys of companies ask their expectations of new orders, employment, sales, and prices. In some cases, these seem to be little more than company forecasts of these quantities based on publically available information rather than true expectations using useful insider information. Although this type of data may have some forecasting potential, expectations elicited from households about the national economy are much less obviously useful. For example, the Gallup Poll asked cross sections of over 1000 persons aged 18 and over, "Will economic conditions get better or worse during the next six months?" at different dates. The replies did vary considerably, with about 15% saying "better" and 70% "worse" during 1974 and about 50% "better" and 25% "worse" in early 1976. Whether such figures have any extra forecasting information over other publically available data is doubtful. It was fairly obvious during 1974 that the economy was on a decline because of the oil crisis, whereas all indications were much better in 1976. Although there are few convincing reasons for expecting the general public to be better at forecasting the economy, their attitudes as to how they see the future could affect their behavior, such as making decisions on how much to put aside as savings. The probable inability of the general public to produce useful forecasts is reflected in the known inability of house-persons to estimate inflation during the previous six or twelve months. The general estimate is often widly exaggerated, reflecting the movement of the most variable priced item rather than an index or average value.

A more careful attempt to measure household attitudes about what the future is likely to bring has been conducted by the Survey Research Center at the University of Michigan, which regularly produces an "index of consumer sentiment." The index is based on the answers to five questions, which in 1970 took the following form:

(i) "We are interested in how people are getting along financially these days. Would you say that you and your family are better off or worse off financially than you were a year ago?"

(ii) "Now looking ahead, do you think that a year from now you people will be better off financially, or worse off, or just about the same as now?"

(iii) "Now turning to business conditions in the country as a whole, do you think that during the next twelve months we'll have good times financially, or bad times, or what?"

(iv) "Looking ahead, which would you say is more likely, that in the country as a whole we'll have continuous good times during the next five years or so, or that we will have periods of widespread unemployment or depression, or what?" and

(v) "About the big things people buy for their homes—such as furniture, house furnishings, refrigerator, stove, television, and things like that—for people in general, do you think now is a good or bad time to buy major household items?"

For each question the percentage of answers that are unfavorable is subtracted from the percentage giving favorable or optimistic answers. These relative scores are then added to the number 100. The index can swing quite dramatically, taking a value near 95 for 1959–1968, with a peak of over 100 in 1965, dropping to 75 in mid-1970, increasing back to 95 in mid-1972, and thereafter declining steadily to about 55 in 1974, possibly due to Watergate and the unusual inflation in 1974. The index is widely quoted in the media, but its actual value is certainly controversial. The Michigan group views its index as having clear relevance to consumer spending, but the plot of this variable against the index does not suggest any simple relationship. The prediction of turning points in the economy is an important problem and is discussed in the next chapter. The data produced by the attitudinal surveys are not consistently found useful for making such predictions. However, there is some evidence that the Index of Consumer Sentiment is of some use as a turning point indicator, and particularly the answers to questions (ii) amd (v).

Once more, the expectations and attitudinal data might be relevant for improving forecasts when added to some other information set but are less clearly useful if used by itself.

## 6.4  SURVEY OF FORECASTERS

Rather than use forecasts made by the public, who are not experts in this field, would it not be better to survey those who do claim to be experts? Two prestigious institutions, the American Statistical Association and the National Bureau of Economic Research, do collaborate to produce such a quarterly survey in the United States. Similar surveys do exist in a few other countries, although they are not always conducted so regularly. A postal questionnaire is used, but the response rate is not particularly high, with often only about 50 people replying. Of these about 40% come from manufacturing and banking or other financial institutions, with the other major groups coming from consulting or research companies and the academic world. Forecasts are requested for a number of important economic variables, including gross national product, inflation, industrial production,

**TABLE 6.2**

| Percent change | Distribution | Percent change | Distribution |
|---|---|---|---|
| 9% or more | 3.8 | 5.0–5.9 | 26.1 |
| 8.0–8.9 | 4.0 | 4.0–4.9 | 9.8 |
| 7.0–7.9 | 13.7 | less than 4% | 8.1 |
| 6.0–6.9 | 34.5 | | |

unemployment rate, corporate profits, and new housing starts for each of the next four or five quarters. The forecasts are made both in terms of actual values and also percentage changes. The survey not only provides interesting average forecasts, but, for a few variables, the extent of agreement or disagreement between forecasters is indicated. For example, in December 1973, the forecasters produced the distribution of forecasts shown in Table 6.2 for inflation rates during 1974. Thus, the median forecast was for between 6.0% and 6.9% inflation and 90% of the forecasters suggested a value between 4% and 9%, which is quite wide. The actual inflation rate was just over 9%. In 1974, 70% of the forecasters predicted an inflation of 8%–10% in 1975 and the actual inflation was 9.4%. Further, 90% of the forecasters named a value from between 7% and 11%. It seems that there was more agreement in 1975 than in 1974, and the forecast was better in this second year. No sophisticated evaluation of the sequence of forecasts produced by the survey has been published, but some unpublished work suggests that the forecasts are better than those produced by a single-series model of the type discussed earlier in Chapter 3. The survey also produces information on the techniques that the forecasters are employing and also on the kind of broad assumptions they are using. During the period 1968–1973, 54% of the respondents named an informal GNP model as their most important technique and 22% named an econometric model, although this percentage was increasing through time. For their second most important method, 35% named leading indicators, which are discussed in Chapter 7, 23% named econometric models, 22% anticipation surveys, and 16% informal GNP models. For the third most important method, the majority named leading indicators and anticipation surveys.

   These surveys do appear to produce useful forecasts even though the various forecasts are combined totally uncritically. It is interesting to contemplate if superior forecasts would be produced if greater weight were given to those forecasters who had performed particularly well in recent periods and the obvious turkeys were given little weight. The possible advantages of combining forecasts is discussed in Chapter 8.

## QUESTIONS

1.  A survey of college football head coaches asked what record, in terms of number of wins and losses, they predicted for their teams in the coming season. Would you classify this as expectations or anticipations data? Would you expect the forecasts to be of good quality?

2.  It is important, when selecting a career during college, to find a field that will both have ample openings when you graduate and also one that is not too popular with your fellow graduates. Discuss how you would survey potential employers or career counselors to get an impression of the demand side of the job market for different kinds of jobs and also how you would survey undergraduates to help forecast the supply side.

3.  Give your own answers to the questions used by the University of Michigan Survey Research Center to construct its index of consumer sentiment. Discuss any problems you encounter in giving answers.

4.  Suppose that you want to construct an *index of political sentiment* to be applied separately to politicians of each of the major parties to gauge their feelings about the upcoming elections. Suggest three questions that you would ask and outline how an index would be formed.

## FURTHER READINGS

Cohen, Morris (1976). "Surveys and Forecasting," in *Methods and Techniques of Business Forecasting* (W. F. Butler, R. A. Kavesh, and R. B. Platt, eds.), Englewood Cliffs, New Jersey: Prentice-Hall.
    A constructively critical discussion of various actual survey data sources.
Rippe, R. D., and M. Wilkinson (1976). "Forecasting Accuracy of the McGraw-Hill Anticipatory Data," *Journal of the American Statistical Association* **69** (December), 849–858.
    Presents results of an empirical investigation.

# 7

# Leading Indicators

A good forecaster is not smarter than everyone else, he merely has his ignorance better organized.

## 7.1 SWINGS IN THE ECONOMY

Even the most casual observer of the economy will be aware that progress is typically not along a smooth curve, but is rather the accumulations of periods of relative decline and advance. Since 1950 there has been a tendency for the wealth of the nation, as measured by gross national product (GNP), to increase, but the actual slope of the curve can vary from about 10% per year down to zero, and there have been some pairs of years for which wealth has actually gone down, during 1974 and 1975, for instance. Prior to 1940 the swings in the economy were much more severe. Some examples of swings are shown in Fig. 7.1, which uses GNP in real terms as a measure of the state of the economy.

It is vital for both government economists and businessmen to determine and predict the turning points of these long-term swings in the economy. The government may want to use policies to reverse a trend, particularly a decline, and management, when making investment decisions, needs to know if the economy will be expanding or contracting over the next couple of years. There are a number of reasons why it is difficult to decide whether or not a turning point has occurred. The GNP series does not consist only of trend plus long swings, but also includes much shorter swings of lesser amplitude which obscure the picture. The data also contain measurement errors and inevitably appear some weeks, or even months, after the date that they

***Fig. 7.1***  GNP per capita (1929 dollars), 1919–1955.

apply to. It is not too difficult to decide on a sensible month when it can be said that a turning point occurred, given data both before *and* after this point, but it is extremely difficult to pick a turning point given data before it but none, or virtually none, after it. The reader should try covering the components of Fig. 7.2 immediately after the indicated turning points and ask if the existence of the turning point is then obvious with the data available.

Because so many decision makers view turning points as being of considerable importance, special attention has been given to producing forecasts of when these turns will occur. One fairly obvious way to proceed is to try to find sectors in the economy that lead the rest, so that an observed turning point in these sectors suggests that the whole economy will soon turn. Individual economists are inclined to have their own favorite leading indicators. For example, some may want to look at the sales of the special paper used to make blueprints, as it is argued that firms have to order this paper in order to make plans for future investments, and so orders will increase when firms intend to invest. Other favorites are sales by large retail firms, such as Sears Roebuck in Chicago, or sales figures from the automobile industry. The main advantages of such series is their immediate availability and ease of interpretation. Monetary statistics are also much used, such as the inflow and outflow of New York mutual savings banks or the relationship between demand deposits and currency in circulation, all of which are published both quickly and frequently. Many company economists merely watch some of their own company's results, such as the percentage of cancellations relative to new orders, or they ask their own sales force for impressions about change in the marketplace. Some of the most used, and probably least useful, indicators are derived from the stock market. These favorite indicators may well produce useful forecasts on some occasions but are not necessarily reliable. As turning points may occur only every two or three years, on average, the casual observations of an individual economist may not allow sufficient evaluation in the typical length of a career for definite conclusions about their usefulness to be determined. What is needed is a more systematic approach, and this is discussed in the following section.

First, however, consideration has to be given to how the state of the economy should be measured and how turning points in historical data can be determined. There is clearly no ideal measure of the state of the economy, simply because all sectors are not affected in the same way. Near a turning point, for example, some sectors will be expanding whereas other parts will be in decline, which is the whole point of the leading indicator approach. The most obvious measure to use is the aggregate known as the gross national product, which is the total value of all goods and services produced in the economy over some period of time, and is, by definition, equal to gross national income. Although this is certainly the best understood measure of the state of the economy, it does have the disadvantage that it is complicated and costly to estimate, so that its value is only available on a quarterly time period for most advanced countries, such as the United States and Britain. Because a more frequently available measure is desirable, it has become more usual to use the index of industrial production, which is published monthly. Empirical studies suggest that this index and GNP do move very closely together, although the index of industrial production does ignore the important agricultural and service parts of the economy.

To decide on the location of a turning point in the economy in a historical series, a group of expert economists might be assembled and, from plots against time of GNP, the index of industrial production, and possibly a few other closely correlated, coincident aggregate series, a consensus opinion about the precise month in which the turn occurred might be reached after some discussion. In the United States, the National Bureau for Economic Research, which originated most of the work on leading indicators and is much concerned with business cycle research, has been responsible for dating the turning points, and these *reference dates* are needed for evaluation of indicators. The precise dating of a turn is sometimes difficult and the actual choice may seem arbitrary, especially after the initial estimates of the index of production have been updated. Figure 7.2 shows both GNP and the production index for the period 1955–1979 with the National Bureau's reference dates.

The figure also suggests that there has been a change in the character of business cycle swings since the 1940s. In the earlier period there were severe declines in aggregate personal income in some years, as the figures in Table 7.1 illustrate. Thus, GNP per capita in real terms was approximately the same in 1919, 1922, 1931, and 1935. Since the 1940s this measure of national income had less clear-cut swings, partly due to institutional changes designed to dampen out the oscillations in the economy and partly due to better control techniques by the central government. Although these changes do not

*Fig. 7.2*   GNP and industrial production, 1955–1979 (P, peak; T, trough).

**TABLE 7.1**

| GNP ($1929) Per Capita | | GNP ($1929) Per Capita | |
|---|---|---|---|
| 1919 | $710 | 1930 | $772 |
| 1920 | 688 | 1931 | 721 |
| 1921 | 660 | 1932 | 611 |
| 1922 | 689 | 1933 | 590 |
| 1923 | 766 | 1934 | 639 |
| 1924 | 775 | 1935 | 718 |
| 1925 | 781 | 1936 | 787 |
| 1926 | 821 | 1937 | 846 |
| 1927 | 817 | 1938 | 784 |
| 1928 | 817 | 1939 | 847 |
| 1929 | 857 | 1940 | 916 |

guarantee a steady growth in wealth, as the combination of a sudden change in oil prices and poor crops in the mid-1970s showed, there is now the presumption that the amplitude of the business cycle has been reduced and a fairly steady growth can be achieved. This has meant that turning points in GNP, say, occur less frequently and are more difficult to define. For this reason an alternative measure has been used in recent years, the difference between actual production and "potential" production for the economy if it were working at full capacity. Thus turning points are effectively sought in changes in the growth rate rather than in the absolute level of national wealth. Although this change has important practical implications, it is not crucial to the basic underlying ideas of the leading indicator forecasting strategy, which are described in the next section.

## 7.2   THE SEARCH FOR INDICATORS

One of the earliest attempts at using leading indicators was the system devised before World War I that became known as the Harvard ABC curves. The A curve consisted of a stock price index, representing speculation, the B curve used the dollar volume of checks drawn on bank deposits, representing business activity, and the C curve consisted of the rate of interest. Empirical studies had suggested that around turning points in the economy the three curves were inclined to move in sequence, with stock prices first, then bank debits, and finally interest rates. The economic theory underlying this selection of variables is that increasing interest rates lead to a decline in economic prospects and hence of stock prices, which causes a reduction in investment and so a recession in business. This recession leads to a reduction in interest rates which improves business prospects, thus raising stock prices and consequently generating an expansion of economic activity. This particular system came to grief in the tremendous depression of 1929, largely due to the fact that the stock market proved to be an unreliable leading indicator, but also because of poor interpretation by economists at that time.

Before the economy had fully recovered from the post-1929 Great Depression, a sharp recession occurred in 1937–1938, and this event caused Henry Morgenthau, Jr., the Secretary of the Treasury, in the fall of 1937 to approach the National Bureau of Economic Research and ask them to devise a system of indicators to help signal when the recession was nearing an end. Under the leadership of Wesley C. Mitchell and Arthur F. Burns, the National Bureau selected a number of series, using both observed empirical behavior and theories of the business cycle, that promised to be fairly reliable indicators of business activity. This list was presented to Morgenthau in late 1937 and published in 1938. Three classes of indicators were proposed—

leading, coincident, and lagging—and this system of classification is still used by the National Bureau, although the economic variables used have changed in subsequent years.

The economic theory of the causes of business cycles that Mitchell and Burns proposed can be briefly summarized as follows:

(i) After a period of expansion, some parts of business begin to meet bottlenecks when trying to further expand production, such as shortages in raw materials, specialized labor, spare parts, or capital. When this occurs, businessmen become more cautious and reduce demand for capital goods, such as machinery and equipment. They may also reduce inventories, thus causing production slowdowns, and profits can become more uncertain. There could also be reductions in overtime and hours of work and the closing down of marginal activities at the same time.

(ii) Although some parts of the economy may be showing evidence of the end of the growth phase of the business cycle, other parts will still be carried along by the considerable momentum in the economy, so that current employment and production may continue to rise, perhaps to all time highs. However, eventually the decisions to reduce investment begin to affect production and employment and the downturn is experienced generally.

(iii) During the ensuing depression, production bottlenecks vanish, costs may decline and profit prospects improve, and the forces that lead to a new expansion gradually gain importance, sometimes helped by government policy decisions affecting government expenditure and interest rates. Thus, the economy begins an upturn and the cycle will eventually start to repeat itself once more.

It should be emphasized that this is a very simplified version of the Mitchell–Burns theory and that this is not the only theory available. Nevertheless, it does provide a framework to search for leading indicators, as well as coincident and lagging ones. Originally, series were simply stated to be leading, lagging, or roughly coincident. In 1966, 72 indicators had been selected by the National Bureau, of which 36 were leading indicators, 25 were classified as coincident, and 11 labeled as lagging. However, a revised list issued in 1977 considered the timing at peaks and troughs separately. Table 7.2 shows these various indicator series, now numbered 111, classified under different economic headings. It is seen that quite a few series are considered to be leading at peaks and lagging at troughs, particularly some of the employment and unemployment series, together with such diverse series as unfilled manufacturing orders in the durable goods industries, bank borrowing from the Federal Reserve, and materials and supplies, stocks in hand and on order.

The leading indicator series are those that might be expected to turn before the aggregate economy, so if some of these series are observed to make an apparent turn, this could suggest that a turning point for the whole economy is about to occur. The "roughly coincident" indicators turn at about the same time as the aggregate economy measures, but will sometimes be series whose figures are released quickly after the date to which they relate. Thus, if many of these coincident indicators appear to be changing in direction, this is taken to be evidence that a turn has already occurred in the economy. The lagging indicators are series that react slowly to changes of direction in the main part of the economy. Thus, if changes are observed in these lagging series, it becomes fairly certain that a turning point has occurred in the recent past. The lagging series are thus used mainly to confirm what the other indicators have been suggesting, if the system works properly.

The large number of indicators mentioned in Table 7.2 presents almost an excess of information when trying to predict a turning point, and so it is natural to try to distill out the most relevant information and form averages or indices, as are used in Figure 7.3. In fact, the indices used in that figure involved twelve leading indicators, four coincident ones, and six lagging indicators. They are not just simple averages, however, for various weights and adjustments are used, one hopes, to increase both the value and the interpretability of these composite indices. To decide which variables to use in an index, the National Bureau has assigned scores to every indicator within a range of 0–100 under each of six headings in (i) economic significance, (ii) statistical adequacy, (iii) historical conformity to business cycles, (iv) cyclical timing record, (v) smoothness, and (vi) promptness of publication. Some examples of the scores assigned in 1967 are given in Table 7.3.

The scores are rather arbitrary and are based more on opinion than on any sophisticated empirical analysis. The average scores are used to weight the various indicators when forming an index, those with highest scores being given the highest weight. However, before this is done, two other adjustments are made. The first inverts any series that moves in an opposite direction to the major economic measures, an example of which is unemployment. The second adjustment divides each series by a measure of its average or usual amplitude or variability, so that the variability of all of these amplititude adjusted series is comparable. Finally, the leading group is also subject to a further adjustment, designed to make its long-run trend the same as that of the index of coincident series. This reverse trend adjustment is likely to make leads more uniform and is designed to improve the cyclical comparability among the leading, coincident, and lagging indices by removing most of the differences in long-run trend. However, the basic timing remains the same, with the leading index typically moving first, the coincident index next, and the lagging index last. In the more recent classification of indicators introduced in 1977, the components of the leading index are said to be leading at both peaks and troughs. Similarly, the series used in the coincident and lagging indices are consistently coincident and lagging, respectively.

**TABLE 7.2**

*Cross Classification of Cyclical Indicators by Economic Process and Cyclical Timing[a]*

*A. Timing at Business Cycle Peaks*

| Economic process / Cyclical timing | I. Employment and unemployment (18 series) | II. Production and income (10 series) | III. Consumption, trade, orders, and deliveries (13 series) | IV. Fixed capital investment (18 series) | V. Inventories and inventory investment (9 series) | VI. Prices, costs, and profits (17 series) | VII. Money and credit (26 series) |
|---|---|---|---|---|---|---|---|
| Leading (L) indicators (62 series) | Marginal employment adjustments (6 series) Job vacancies (2 series) Comprehensive employment (1 series) Comprehensive unemployment (3 series) | Capacity utilization (2 series) | New and unfilled orders and deliveries (6 series) Consumption (2 series) | Formation of business enterprises (2 series) Business investment commitments (5 series) Residential construction (3 series) | Inventory investment (4 series) Inventories on hand and on order (1 series) | Stock prices (1 series) Commodity prices (1 series) Profits and profit margins (7 series) Cash flows (2 series) | Money flows (3 series) Real money supply (2 series) Credit flows (4 series) Credit difficulties (2 series) Bank reserves (2 series) Interest rates (1 series) |
| Roughly coincident (C) indicators (23 series) | Comprehensive employment (1 series) | Comprehensive output and real income (4 series) Industrial production (4 series) | Consumption and trade (4 series) | Backlog of investment commitments (1 series) Business investment expenditures (5 series) | | | Velocity of money (2 series) Interest rates (2 series) |
| Lagging (Lg) indicators (18 series) | Duration of unemployment (2 series) | | | Business investment expenditures (1 series) | Inventories on hand and on order (4 series) | Unit labor costs and labor share (4 series) | Interest rates (4 series) Outstanding debt (3 series) |
| Timing unclassified (U) (8 series) | Comprehensive employment (3 series) | | Trade (1 series) | Business investment commitments (1 series) | | Commodity prices (1 series) Profit share (1 series) | Interest rates (1 series) |

*B. Timing at Business Cycle Troughs*

| Timing | | | | | | | |
|---|---|---|---|---|---|---|---|
| Leading (L) indicators (47 series) | Marginal employment adjustments (3 series) | Industrial production (1 series) | New and unfilled orders and deliveries (5 series); Consumption and trade (4 series) | Formation of business enterprises (2 series); Business investment commitments (4 series); Residential construction (3 series) | Inventory investment (4 series) | Stock prices (1 series); Commodity prices (2 series); Profits and profit margins (6 series); Cash flows (2 series) | Money flows (2 series); Real money supply (2 series); Credit flows (4 series); Credit difficulties (2 series) |
| Roughly coincident (C) indicators (23 series) | Marginal employment adjustments (2 series); Comprehensive employment (4 series) | Comprehensive output and real income (4 series); Industrial production (3 series); Capacity utilization (2 series) | Consumption and trade (3 series) | Business investment commitments (1 series) | | Profits (2 series) | Money flow (1 series); Velocity of money (1 series) |
| Lagging (Lg) indicators (40 series) | Marginal employment adjustments (1 series); Job vacancies (2 series); Comprehensive employment (1 series); Comprehensive and duration of unemployment (5 series) | | Unfilled orders (1 series) | Business investment commitments (2 series); Business investment expenditures (6 series) | Inventories on hand and on order (5 series) | Unit labor costs and labor share (4 series) | Velocity of money (1 series); Bank reserves (1 series); Interest rates (8 series); Outstanding debt (3 series) |
| Timing unclassified (U) (1 series) | | | | | | | Bank reserves (1 series) |

[a] From *Business Conditions Conditions Digest*, Washington, D.C.: U.S. Govt. Printing Office, March 1977.

**TABLE 7.3**

| | Criteria | | | | | | |
|---|---|---|---|---|---|---|---|
| | (i) | (ii) | (iii) | (iv) | (v) | (vi) | Average |
| *Leading indicators* | | | | | | | |
| 1. Average work week | 50 | 65 | 81 | 66 | 60 | 80 | 66 |
| (production workers, manufacturing) | | | | | | | |
| 6. new orders | 75 | 72 | 88 | 84 | 60 | 80 | 78 |
| (durable goods, industry) | | | | | | | |
| 19. stock prices, 500 stocks | 75 | 74 | 77 | 87 | 80 | 100 | 81 |
| *Coincident indicators* | | | | | | | |
| 41. employment (not agricultural) | 75 | 61 | 90 | 87 | 100 | 80 | 81 |
| 43. unemployment (inverted) | 75 | 63 | 96 | 60 | 80 | 80 | 75 |
| 205. GNP, in constant dollars | 75 | 75 | 91 | 58 | 80 | 50 | 73 |
| 52. personal income | 75 | 73 | 81 | 43 | 100 | 80 | 74 |
| *Lagging indicators* | | | | | | | |
| 71. inventories | 75 | 67 | 75 | 66 | 100 | 40 | 71 |
| 67. bank rate, short-term business loans | 50 | 55 | 82 | 47 | 80 | 25 | 57 |

One further group of indicators has been constructed to help understand current and prospective business conditions, the so-called *diffusion indices*. If some group of firms is considered, the diffusion index for employment shows the percentage of those firms that display an increase in employment in this month compared to the previous month. A diffusion index can be constructed showing the percentage of companies, industries, or geographic areas which are experiencing rises in some relevant variable over a month or a quarter. They can be used to indicate how widespread a recession or recovery is and whether it is continuing to spread. Diffusion indices that are considered to be leading indicators include average workweek, new orders, profits, and stock prices, whilst roughly coincident diffusion indices include employment, industrial production, wholesale prices, and sales of retail stores. In practice, these indices are extremely variable when monthly changes are considered and are still very variable and difficult to interpret if six- or nine-month changes are considered. Their use is only recommended for those experienced in all other aspects of indicators and their interpretation.

All of the main U.S. indicators and the various indices are presented, both in numerical and in an extremely convenient diagrammatic form, in the publication *Business Conditions Digest*, which is produced monthly by the U.S. Department of Commerce. They are also available for some other countries, such as Britain, Canada, and Japan, and are likely to become available in other countries in the near future. There is clearly a lot of interest in leading indicators and a great deal of money and effort is expended on their collection, construction, and publication. What now has to be asked is whether all this effort is worthwhile and if indicators are a useful forecasting tool.

## 7.3 EVALUATION OF INDICATORS

To a statistician, the problem of evaluating the effectiveness of leading indicators and measuring the extent of any lead is at first sight a straight-forward one. If the index of industrial production is used as the ideal coincident indicator, there are a variety of statistical techniques of varying sophistication which can be used to test if some other time series on the average leads industrial production. These techniques include a number of versions of regression analysis and the use of cross correlations and spectral methods. When these methods have been applied, statisticians have often discovered that the National Bureau's leading indicators do lead, but often by a lesser extent than suggested by the National Bureau analysis and not in a consistent fashion. Thus, for example, a stock market index might be observed to lead the aggregate economy by a couple of months on average, but in practice it leads about 60% of the time and lags during the remaining 40%, say. This kind of behavior makes interpretation of indicators extremely difficult. However, it can be argued that these kinds of statistical analysis are virtually irrelevant to evaluate the National Bureau's approach. This is because these statistical methods investigate the average lead over *all* points in time, whereas the National Bureau is only concerned about leads just prior to a turning point in the economy and does not concern itself with the interim periods. Thus it might be argued that proper methods of evaluation should concentrate just on turning points in the indicator series. To do this, however, one immediately runs into the problem of how to identify when the series displays such a point. To use an entirely subjective method could lead to biases in the analysis, but there is no entirely satisfactory objective or mechanical method. One method of proceding, although not ideal, is to record an upturn if the predictor series has been above a previous low for a specified number of months. Similarly, a downturn is said to have occurred if the series has been below a previous high for a set number of months. Thus, with a "two months up or down" criterion, a series must be below (above) its previous peak (trough) for two months before a prediction of a turn is said to occur. Consider, for example, the following constructed series and its plot, where $P$ indicate a peak, $T$ a trough.

The local peak at $t = 2$ is designated to be a downturn under both the one- and two-month criteria, as the values of $x_t$ at $t = 3$ and 4 are both lower than at $t = 2$, but it is not a peak under three- or four-month criteria as $x_5$ is larger than $x_2$. However, $t = 5$ is a peak under all four criteria and $t = 8$ is a trough under one-, two- and three-month criteria, since the next three $x$ values are all larger than $x_8$.

| $t$ | 1 | 2 | 3 | 4 | 5 | 6 | 7 | 8 | 9 | 10 | 11 | 12 |
|-----|---|---|---|---|---|---|---|---|---|----|----|----|
| $x_t$ | 5 | 6 | 5 | 5 | 7 | 5 | 4 | 3 | 4 | 5 | 4 | 3 |

| Criterion | | | | |
|-----------|---|---|---|---|
| 1 month | $P$ | $P$ | $T$ | $P$ |
| 2 month | $P$ | $P$ | $T$ | $P$ |
| 3 month | — | $P$ | $T$ | — |
| 4 month | — | $P$ | — | — |

Stekler and Schepsman (1973) used these criteria to choose turning points in the index of leading indicators (ILI) constructed from twelve indicators, as discussed above, to see how well it predicts turning points in the index of industrial production (IIP), which is used as the economy-wide measure or main coincident indicator. Using a one month up-or-down criterion, the turning points in the ILI can be compared with the turning points in the index of industrial production corresponding to the National Bureau reference dates, as shown in Table 7.4.

Although this table appears to indicate that the index of leading indicators is a useful predictive device, Table 7.5 shows its basic limitation in that it does

**TABLE 7.4**

| Date of turn in ILI | | Date of true turn in IIP | | Lead months |
|---------------------|------|--------------------------|------|-------------|
| Peaks | | | | |
| July | 1948 | June | 1948 | 1 |
| July | 1953 | January | 1953 | 6 |
| February | 1957 | November | 1956 | 3 |
| January | 1960 | January | 1960 | 0 |
| July | 1969 | September | 1969 | −2 |
| | | Average | | 1.6 |
| Troughs | | | | |
| October | 1969 | May | 1949 | 5 |
| April | 1952 | November | 1953 | 5 |
| April | 1958 | February | 1958 | 2 |
| February | 1961 | December | 1960 | 2 |
| November | 1970 | May | 1970 | 6 |
| | | Average | | 4.0 |

**TABLE 7.5**

*True and False Turns, Period 1948–1970*

| Criterion<br><br>No. of<br>months<br>up or<br>down | Peak | | | Trough | | |
|---|---|---|---|---|---|---|
| | Av. lead | No. of<br>true<br>turns | No. of<br>false<br>turns | Av. lead | No. of<br>true<br>turns | No. of<br>false<br>turns |
| 1 | 1.6 | 5 | 24 | 4.0 | 5 | 9 |
| 2 | 0.6 | 5 | 15 | 3.0 | 5 | 3 |
| 3 | −0.4 | 5 | 9 | 2.0 | 5 | 2 |
| 4 | −1.4 | 5 | 5 | 1.0 | 5 | 1 |
| 5 | −2.4 | 5 | 3 | 0.0 | 5 | 0 |

produce many false signals. It is seen that as a more stringent criterion is applied to identify a turn fewer false turns appear, but as one has to wait longer until the criterion can be applied, any lead will have been lost, on average. The existence of false signals is not a property only of the criterion used here, but will probably occur with any other method of choosing turning points amongst recent time periods. One further problem of practical significance is that the index of leading indicators is usually published at least a month after the index of industrial production, both relating to the same data, so any lead advantage is further reduced.

Other studies have also found similar problems with leading indicators in practice. Hymans (1973), for example, not only observed the false turns with the NBER index of leading indicators but also suggested that many of the twelve components of this index did not help its performance and that the weights used by the National Bureau were far from optimal. He went on to suggest a possibly superior index.

The National Bureau does not have a complete monopoly in the United States on the production of leading indicators, as they concentrate just on forecasting turns in business activity. The Federal Researve Board tried to develop a sensitive price index that can be used to forecast changes in price levels in the economy, but Yeats (1973) found that this index had virtually no predictive content for prices, although it was a useful leading indicator for business activity!

The evidence is thus accumulating that the leading indicator methodology as presently developed is not without its problems. This is unfortunate, as it is basically an obviously good idea and a great deal of effort has gone into producing the indicators. It can be argued that the evaluation and selection methods used by the National Bureau have not been sufficiently sophisticated and that superior indices and other ways of distilling the relevant information undoubtedly contained in the indicators could be devised. Until this is done, the present methods will continue to have a real place in forecasting a very important aspect of the economy. As the following example shows, they are not without value.

## 7.4   THE 1974–1975 DEPRESSION

The worldwide depression during 1974 and 1975 was one of the most severe since World War II. Figure 7.3 and Table 7.6 show a selection of six U.S. indicators:

(i)   The index of industrial production, which will be used in this illustration as the reference series, measuring the level of the aggregate economy. The series was remarkably level throughout virtually all of 1974, and it was not clear until early 1975 that a downturn had occurred by late 1974. The behavior of this series in 1974 shows how difficult it is to pinpoint the precise point at which a downturn occurred. By fall 1975, it was clear that an upturn had occurred in about April 1975.

(ii)   The composite index of twelve leading indicators, reverse trend adjusted (i.e., adjusted so that the trend in this series is similar to that of the index of coincident indicators). The series is seen to be trending down from March 1974, and so by mid-1974 evidence was accumulating that a downward turning point for the total economy was likely to occur. By the end of 1974, this evidence was overwhelming, so the leading indicator composite index did provide a correct forecast of a downturn before it became clear from the index of industrial production. From a low point in February 1975, the composite index consistently trends upward, suggesting that the upturn was about to occur in the economy, so that a correct prediction again was made.

(iii)   The composite index of four coincident indicators. The behavior of this series is very similar to the index of industrial production, as one would expect.

(iv)   The composite index of six lagging indicators. The lagging property of this index is clearly seen as there is no evidence of a downturn until February 1975 (which is almost when the upturn occurs in the rest of the economy), and there is no clear indication of an upturn up to the end of 1975. The extent of the lag in this composite index is so large that its usefulness is doubtful.

(v)   The fifth series is a particular, individual leading indicator, layoff rate in manufacturing industries, per 100 employees. This variable records just the percentage of employees that are removed from employment,

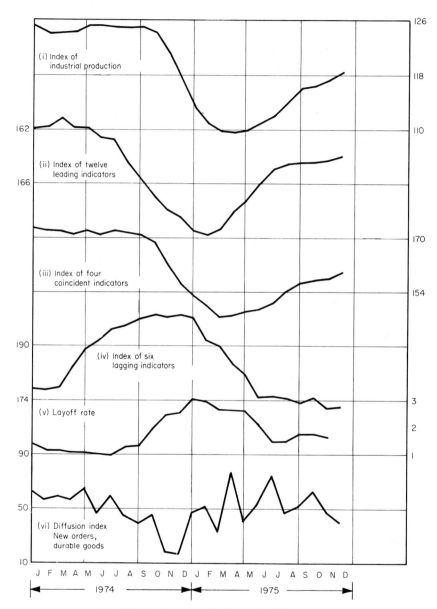

*Fig. 7.3* Performance of indicators in 1974 and 1975.

**TABLE 7.6**

*Selection of Indicators for 1974 and 1975*[a]

| | (i)<br>Index of<br>industrial<br>production | (ii)<br>Index of<br>12 leading<br>indicators<br>(reverse<br>trend<br>adjusted) | (iii)<br>Index of 4<br>coincident<br>indicators | (iv)<br>Index of 6<br>lagging<br>indicators | (v)<br>Layoff<br>rate in<br>manufacturing<br>per 100 | (vii)<br>Diffusion<br>index, new<br>durable<br>orders |
|---|---|---|---|---|---|---|
| 1974 Jan. | 125.4 | 162.5 | 173.7 | 177.7 | 1.4 | 65.7 |
| Feb. | 124.6 | 163.2 | 172.6 | 177.6 | 1.2 | 57.1 |
| Mar. | 124.7 | 166.0 | 172.2 | 178.7 | 1.2 | 60.0 |
| April | 124.9 | 163.4 | 171.8 | 184.0 | 1.1 | 57.1 |
| May | 125.7 | 163.0 | 172.5 | 189.4 | 1.1 | 65.7 |
| June | 125.8 | 160.0 | 171.6 | 192.3 | 1.1 | 47.1 |
| July | 125.5 | 159.1 | 172.4 | 195.5 | 1.0 | 60.0 |
| Aug. | 125.2 | 153.1 | 171.9 | 196.7 | 1.3 | 45.7 |
| Sept. | 125.6 | 147.7 | 171.0 | 198.3 | 1.4 | 40.0 |
| Oct. | 124.8 | 142.5 | 169.0 | 199.5 | 2.0 | 45.7 |
| Nov. | 121.7 | 138.7 | 162.8 | 198.9 | 2.5 | 18.6 |
| Dec. | 117.4 | 136.3 | 156.4 | 199.5 | 2.6 | 17.1 |
| 1975 Jan. | 113.7 | 132.2 | 152.7 | 198.5 | 3.1 | 48.6 |
| Feb. | 111.2 | 131.7 | 149.8 | 192.0 | 3.0 | 51.4 |
| Mar. | 110.0 | 133.3 | 147.2 | 189.9 | 2.7 | 34.3 |
| April | 109.9 | 138.0 | 147.5 | 185.5 | 2.6 | 77.1 |
| May | 110.1 | 141.5 | 148.4 | 182.0 | 2.6 | 42.9 |
| June | 111.1 | 146.4 | 148.9 | 175.3 | 2.1 | 54.3 |
| July | 112.2 | 150.5 | 151.1 | 175.7 | 1.5 | 74.3 |
| Aug. | 114.2 | 152.1 | 154.3 | 174.8 | 1.5 | 47.1 |
| Sept. | 116.2 | 152.5 | 156.7 | 173.6 | 1.7 | 51.4 |
| Oct. | 116.7 | 152.5 | 157.8 | 174.7 | 1.7 | 62.9 |
| Nov. | 117.3 | 153.2 | 158.1 | 171.8 | 1.6 | 47.1 |
| Dec. | 118.5 | 154.4 | 159.7 | 172.0 | 1.3 | 40.0 |

[a] Taken from the January 1976, issue of *Business Conditions Digest*, Washington, D.C.: U.S. Govt. Printing Office. Some of the figures are provisional.

ignoring the number of workers that may gain jobs in the same period. Some studies have found this indicator to be a consistent, long-lead one. It obviously has to be inverted to be used as an indicator of the main economy. By October or November 1974, a clear upturn had occurred in layoff rate, not only from the trend but also from the sizes of the numbers involved, indicating that a downturn will be occurring. Thus, a useful prediction was made. By July, 1975, a clear downturn is observed to have occurred in layoff rate, providing a somewhat earlier indication of an upturn in the economy than found in the index of industrial production. However, this individual indicator provides less successful predictions than does the composite index of leading indicators over the example time period.

(vi)  The final series illustrated is a leading indicator diffusion series, based on the value of manufacturer's new orders for the durable goods industries. The diffusion index represents the proportion of cases that new orders increase over a one-month span for a sample of 35 durable goods industries. The figures in 1974 show how unstable a one-month diffusion index can be, but the values strongly indicate a downturn in November and December 1974, and also an upturn in April 1975. Thus, this diffusion index does appear to contain some useful predictive information about the timing of economy-wide turning points, but interpretation is made difficult by what seems to be the inherent variability of diffusion indices.

In general, it is seen that in January 1976 the leading indicators do seem to have been useful in predicting turning points during the previous two years, although the extent of the leads is not impressive. In interpreting these results it should be noted that by the time sufficient GNP data had become available it was clear that in 1976 the index of industrial production had turned down about three months later than did GNP.

## QUESTIONS

1.  The board of directors of a company manufacturing consumer non-durable goods receives a forecast that the economy will very soon experience a downturn. Discuss how this could affect decisions made by the board. How different would your answer have been if the forecast had been of an upturn? Would your answers have been different if the company manufactured an investment good such as heavy machinery? If not, why not?

2.  List the properties that a good leading indicator should possess. Do you think that any of the following series would be good indicators of anything?
    (a)  the number of requests per week for Sears catalogs,
    (b)  the number of speeding tickets issued per week in Dallas, or
    (c)  the number of firms going bankrupt in a month in California.

3.  The small Caribbean island of Tabasco has two sources of income, tourists from the United States and sales of capsicum berries. The berries are all exported to Mexico, where they are made into a somewhat edible concoction, half of which is exported to the United States and the rest used in Mexico. Suggest three leading indicators, a coincident indicator, and a lagging indicator for the Tabasco economy.

**4.** An enthusiastic investor states that he has observed that the number of children born to local stockbrokers in a month is a good leading indicator of the Dow Jones stock market price index. Briefly describe how you would try to evaluate the truth of this claim and also the quality of this potential leading indicator.

**5.** Discuss how you would investigate the usefulness of the U.S. leading indicators for forecasting turning points in the Mexican and Canadian economies.

**6.** The dictator of a Caribbean island wants you to predict the effect on inflation in his country of the introduction of controls on money supply. Unfortunately, he has read an elementary forecasting book and suggests that you use either the method of leading indicators or Box–Jenkins ARIMA modeling. How would you try to persuade him that these techniques are inappropriate but that a small econometric model would probably do a better job. Discuss how this econometric model would actually be used to suggest an appropriate control policy for money.

## FURTHER READINGS

Hymans, Saul H. (1973). "On the Use of Leading Indicators to Predict Cyclical Turning Points," Brookings Papers on Econometric Activity, No. 2, pp. 339–384.

Moore, G. H. (1975). "The Analysis of Economic Indicators," *Scientific American* **232** (January), 17–23.
    Excellent, but uncritical, general account.

Shiskin, J., and L. H. Lampart (1976). "Indicator Forecasting," in *Methods and Techniques of Business Forecasting* (W. F. Butler, R. A. Kavesh, and R. B. Platt, ed.), Englewood Cliffs, New Jersey: Prentice Hall.
    Much more detailed account.

Stekler, O., and M. Schepsman (1973). "Forecasting with an Index of Leading Series," *Journal of the American Statistical Association* **68**, 291–295.

Yeats, A. J. (1973). "An Evaluation of the Predictive Ability of the FRB Sensitive Price Index," *Journal of the American Statistical Association* **36**, 782–789.

CHAPTER

# 8

# Evaluation and Combination
# of Forecasts

A. Did you know that some people can foretell the future?
B. I knew you were going to say that.

## 8.1 EVALUATING AN INDIVIDUAL
## FORECASTING METHOD

At first sight the problem of how to evaluate the quality of a set of fore-casts might seem to be a simple, straightforward one. Suppose that a sequence of one-step forecasts $f_{n,1}$ of the series values $x_{n+1}$ is available over some period, giving the set of data $f_{n,1}, x_{n+1}, n = 1, 2, \ldots, N$, say. As $f_{n,1}$ is, in a sense, an *estimate* of $x_{n+1}$, an apparently sensible method of establishing how good an estimate is to plot both $f_{n,1}$ and $x_{n+1}$ against $n$. It might be thought that if the $f_{n,1}$ are good forecasts, then the two plots should look similar. This plot is much used in books and articles involving forecasting, but in fact it is by no means as easy to interpret as the literature implies. There is no convincing reason why the two plots should be similar, as the shapes depend on the forecastability of the series $x_t$. As an extreme example, sup-pose that $x_t$ is a white noise series, with zero mean; then $x_{n+1}$ will be this white noise and so will have a very irregular plot, whereas $f_{n,1} = 0$ for all $n$ and so will look completely different. Generally, the time series properties of $f_{n,1}$ will not be the same as those of $x_{n+1}$, the series being forecast, as can be seen both by the white noise example or by considering the case where $x_t$ is generated by an MA(1) model, so that

$$x_{n+1} = \varepsilon_{n+1} + b\varepsilon_n.$$

153

The optimum forecast in this case was shown in Chapter 3 to be

$$f_{n,1} = b\varepsilon_n,$$

so that a plot of $f_{n,1}$ against $n$ will be that of white noise. Thus, again, the plots of the forecasts and the series to be forecast will look quite different.

A further reason why the two plots look different is seen by considering the variances of the two series. Writing

$$x_{n+1} = f_{n,1} + e_{n,1}, \tag{1}$$

where $e_{n,1}$ is the one-step forecast error; it was shown in Chapter 4 that if $f_{n,1}$ was an optimal forecast, according to some proper information set, then $e_{n,1}$ will be a zero-mean white noise series that is uncorrelated with $f_{n,1}$. If the errors $e_{n,1}$ were not white noise, they could be partly forecast from their own past, which is itself a function of past and present $x$'s and $f$'s and thus of the information set used to form the forecasts, which is contradictory. The zero correlation between the forecasts and errors may be thought to be sensible as the forecasts are based on the information set $I_n$, whereas the errors consist of events that cannot be forecast from $I_n$ (at least in a linear fashion). It follows that

$$\mathrm{var}(x_{n+1}) = \mathrm{var}(f_{n,1}) + \mathrm{var}(e_{n,1}).$$

Since virtually all series met in economics and business are such that they can never be consistently forecast without error, it follows that

$$\mathrm{var}(e_{n,1}) > 0,$$

so

$$\mathrm{var}(x_{n+1}) > \mathrm{var}(f_{n,1}).$$

Thus, the two series will have different variances and the plots against time will not be similar. If $x_t$ is a stationary series, that is, if it is trend free or has been sufficiently differenced according to the rules given in Chapter 3, then a reasonable measure of its forecastability relative to an information set $I_n$ is given by

$$R^2 = \frac{\mathrm{var}(f_{n,1})}{\mathrm{var}(x_{n+1})} \equiv 1 - \frac{\mathrm{var}(e_{n,1})}{\mathrm{var}(x_{n+1})},$$

where $f_{n,1}$ is the optimal forecast derived from $f_n$. For series that cannot be forecast, such as white noise, $R^2$ will be zero, but for all other series $R^2$ will lie between zero and unity. Only if a series can be forecast without error will $R^2 = 1$, and this is very unlikely to be true for any economic series. If a series is not stationary, such as a random walk, then a value of $R^2$ very near 1 can be obtained, but this situation was specifically excluded from the above definition. The reason for the exclusion is that the theoretical variance for such series is infinite, so that if the second of the two equivalent definitions of $R^2$ given above is used and the variance of the errors is finite, a value $R^2 = 1$ results, even though $x_t$ cannot be perfectly forecast. It should be clear that if the forecasts $f_{n,1}$ are given by some technique, and the components of the ratio

$$\frac{\mathrm{var}(f_{n,1})}{\mathrm{var}(x_{n+1})}$$

are estimated from the available data, then one cannot look at the resulting value and state that the forecasts are "good" or not, as there is no satisfactory or unsatisfactory level of the ratio. The possible value of the ratio depends on the degree of forecastability of the series. Some series are highly forecastable, whereas others cannot be forecast at all.

From (1), and the properties of $f_{n,1}$ and $e_{n,1}$, it follows that, if from an observed set of forecasts and of the series being forecast a regression of the form

$$x_{n+1} = \alpha + \beta f_{n,1} + \text{residual}$$

is calculated, then an optimal forecast will give $\alpha = 0, \beta = 1$ and the residuals will be white noise. If a regression obtained from an actual set of forecasts does not display these properties, then it follows that the forecasts can easily be improved. For example, if $\alpha$ is not zero, it can mean that the forecasts are consistently biased, in which case the addition of an appropriate constant to each forecast will remove this problem. Unfortunately, the regression results are of limited use as, with a wide enough information set being available, various alternative techniques can produce the correct values of $\alpha$ and $\beta$ and also a white noise residual. The correct way to choose the best amongst alternatives is discussed in the next section.

There is no really useful procedure for evaluating an individual forecasting technique, as any evaluation cannot be separated from the degree of forecastability of the series being predicted. As the *I Ching* says, "The best of hunters finds no game in an empty field." However, if the one-step forecast errors $e_{n,1}$ are *not* white noise, then the forecast is clearly suboptimal and can be improved simply by modelling these errors.

It should be emphasized that to evaluate an individual forecaster or a technique a whole sequence of forecasts is required. It is virtually impossible to evaluate the quality of a single forecast about some unique event. Even when evaluating a sequence of forecasts it is important to insure that they are collected in controlled circumstances. As an example of the difficulty of evaluation in a noncontrolled situation, suppose a confidence trickster gets the names of 1000 individuals who all subscribe to an investment journal. To 500 he writes a letter recommending that they buy a particular stock as he forecasts that it will rise in price over the next month. To the other 500 he recommends they sell short this same stock because he expects the price to fall. If actually the price does fall, he writes letters only to this last 500, half of the new letters recommending that they buy some stock and the other half that they sell short. Again, 250 people will have received a "correct forecast." After other further rounds there will exist about 30 people who have received five correct predictions in a row and they may well be prepared to pay substantially to receive further "forecasts." Their evaluation problem is a difficult one and perhaps heavy weight should be given to one's prior beliefs about the probability of being given such consistently good advice about the stock market and why anyone with such apparent abilities should be willing to sell the forecasts rather than utilizing them directly.

## 8.2   EVALUATING A GROUP OF FORECASTING METHODS

It should be clear from the preceding chapters that there is usually not just a single forecasting method available for consideration but rather a variety of alternative methods. These methods may have different cost characteristics and depend on different information sets or on alternative philosophies about how to proceed. Suppose for the moment that just two forecasting methods are being considered, giving one-step forecasts $f_{n,1}^{(1)}$ and $f_{n,1}^{(2)}$ with corresponding one-step forecast errors

$$e_{n,1}^{(1)} = x_{n+1} - f_{n,1}^{(1)}$$

and

$$e_{n,2}^{(2)} = x_{n+1} - f_{n,1}^{(2)}$$

An obvious question to ask is which method is superior? This question was already answered in Chapter 1 when discussing cost functions. If the cost of making an error of size $e$ is $C(e)$, then the preferable method is that which minimizes the average cost. Thus, if the cost is proportional to $e^2$, then the appropriate procedure is to form the sum of squared errors

$$SSE = \sum_{t=1}^{n} (e_{t,1})^2$$

or, equivalently, the mean square error

$$MSE = \frac{1}{n} SSE$$

and then to choose the method that produces the smaller value for these quantities over the data period being used for evaluation. It is strongly advised that this evaluation period be different from that used to form any model from which forecasts are produced. If several forecasts are available, the value of SSE should be found from the forecast errors of each method, and the best individual method is then that which produces the smallest sum of errors. It is thus possible to *rank* alternative forecasting methods, although one is not able to say if the best of these available methods is the best of all possible methods, unless the SSE for the evaluation period happens to be zero, which is extremely unlikely.

The more statistically sophisticated forecasters will not want to just order a pair of methods but would also like to test if one method is significantly superior to the other. Suppose that the forecasts produce unbiased errors, so that the means of $e_{n,1}^{(1)}$ and $e_{n,1}^{(2)}$ are both not significantly different from zero. It is not correct to use the usual $F$ test to see if the SSE's are significantly different, as generally one would expect the two sets of errors to be correlated. A way around this problem is to form the two series

$$P_n = e_{n,1}^{(1)} + e_{n,1}^{(2)}$$

and

$$Q_n = e_{n,1}^{(1)} - e_{n,1}^{(2)}$$

and then to test for any correlation between $P_n$ and $Q_n$, using any standard test for zero correlation, such as the $t$ test, Fisher's $z$ test, or even a rank correlation test. It can be shown that if any significant correlation is found, then this implies a significant difference in SSE values.

SSE values can be used to rank a group of alternative forecasts of the same variable. Any other statistic makes no sense if the models have been estimated using a least-squares criterion. However, the ranking does not have very much operational significance. In particular, it does not imply that only the top method should henceforth be used and all the other methods ignored. As will be shown in the next two sections, the lower-ranked methods may contain important information that can be utilized to improve the "best" method.

## 8.3 THE COMBINATION OF FORECASTS

Table 8.1 shows one-step forecast errors of total airline passenger miles, measured monthly, for the months of 1953 by two alternative forecasting methods; the first a Box–Jenkins model as discussed in Chapter 3 and the other an adaptive model similar to those discussed in Chapter 4. The original aim of the table was to illustrate the superiority of the Box–Jenkins approach.

**TABLE 8.1**

*Forecast Errors of Passenger Miles Flown, 1953*

| Month | Box–Jenkins | Adaptive | Combined forecast | Month | Box–Jenkins | Adaptive | Combined forecast |
|-------|-------------|----------|-------------------|-------|-------------|----------|-------------------|
| Jan.   | −3  | 1   | −1    | Aug.  | 2   | −16 | −7    |
| Feb.   | −10 | 18  | −2    | Sept. | −11 | −12 | −11.5 |
| March  | 24  | 18  | 21    | Oct.  | −10 | −9  | −9.5  |
| April  | 22  | 18  | 20    | Nov.  | −12 | −12 | −12   |
| May    | −9  | 3   | −3    | Dec.  | −7  | −13 | −10   |
| June   | −22 | −17 | −19.5 | MSE   | 188 | 196 | 150   |
| July   | 10  | −24 | −7    |       |     |     |       |

The scale involved in the table or the details of the forecasting methods are of no relevance in this example. The values of the mean square error (MSE) do suggest that the Box–Jenkins forecasts are better, on the average, than the forecasts from the model. This is equally true if data for the whole period 1951–1960 are used, with MSE values of 177.7 for the adaptive and 148.6 for the Box–Jenkins method. The final column in the table shows the errors from a simple combined forecast, where

$$\text{(combined forecast)} = \tfrac{1}{2}(\text{Box–Jenkins} + \text{adaptive forecasts}).$$

The errors from this combined forecast are simply the average of the errors from the two constituents. For 1953, the MSE for the combined is seen to be less than for the two original forecasts, and this holds true for the whole period 1951–1960, when the combined had MSE 130.2. Thus, a very simple method of combining has provided a set of forecasts that on average is superior to both constituent forecasts.

The approach can obviously be generalized, and hopefully improved, by considering more flexible weighting schemes. Suppose that $f_n$ and $g_n$ are both one-step forecasts of $x_{n+1}$, using different approaches, with resulting errors $ef_n$, $eg_n$. Further suppose that the forecasts have no consistent biases, so that the error series have zero means. A combined forecast given by

$$C_n = kf_n + (1 - k)g_n \qquad (2)$$

will necessarily be unbiased, and the resulting forecast error will be

$$ec_n = x_{n+1} - C_n = kef_n + (1 - k)eg_n. \qquad (3)$$

The value of $k$ is of our choice and it may be possible to choose so that the variance of the combined forcast's error $ec_n$ is smaller than either of the variances of the other two error series. Note that as means are assumed to be zero, variances and mean squared errors will be identical. The variance of $ec_n$ is given by

$$\text{var}(ec) = k^2 \,\text{var}(ef) + (1 - k)^2 \,\text{var}(eg) + 2k(1 - k) \,\text{cov}(ef, eg), \quad (4)$$

where $\text{cov}(ef, eg)$ is the covariance between the error series $ef_n$ and $eg_n$. A little calculus will show that $\text{var}(ec)$ is minimized by taking

$$k = \frac{\text{var}(eg) - \text{cov}(ef, eg)}{\text{var}(eg) + \text{var}(ef) - 2\,\text{cov}(ef, eg)}. \quad (5)$$

In the case when $ef_n$ and $eg_n$ are uncorrelated, this formula reduces to

$$k = \frac{\text{var}(eg)}{\text{var}(eg) + \text{var}(ef)}. \quad (6)$$

If the first of these formulas for $k$, (5) is inserted into the formula for $\text{var}(ec)$, (4), then the resulting variance for the combined forecast error will generally be smaller than both of the variances of $ef_n$ and $eg_n$ and is never more than the smaller of these two variances. Thus, in theory, a combined forecast will usually be superior to either constituent and can never be worse than the better of the constituents. This means that one should never lose by combining and will usually gain. Unfortunately, a formula such as (5) cannot be used to find the combining weight $k$, for the variances and covariances required are never known. They can, of course, be estimated from past forecast errors if these are available. However, it is not clear how many past errors should be used, as the forecasters who are producing the forecasts being combined may be changing in ability, at least relatively. For instance, $f_n$ may come from a simple regression model which is applied automatically, whereas the forecasts $g_n$ could come from an econometrician who is continually updating and improving his model as well as applying subjective corrections and learning from past mistakes. It would be reasonable to expect that the econometrician's forecasts should be given increasing weights through time as his forecasting ability improves relative to $f_n$. Another problem with applying (5) directly is that often only a few previous forecast errors are available, and so it is very difficult to get a satisfactory estimate for the covariance term. To circumvent these problems, a time-varying weight $k_n$ can be used, given by

$$k_{n+1} = \sum_{t=n-m}^{n} (eg_t)^2 \Bigg/ \sum_{t=n-m}^{n} [(eg_t)^2 + (ef_t)^2]. \quad (7)$$

Thus, formula (6) is used and the variances are estimated over just the last $m$ error terms. An appropriate value for $m$ would be 12, although this is a rather arbitrary choice, and if less than twelve previous errors are available, the sums are just over those errors that are known. An appropriate starting up value for $k_n$ where no previous forecasts have been made is obviously $k_1 = \frac{1}{2}$.

For example, using the data in the above table, with $m = 12$, the two forecasts for January 1954 would use weight

$$k_{13} = \frac{196}{188 + 196} = 0.51$$

and so

$$C_{13} = 0.51(\text{Box–Jenkins}) + 0.49(\text{Adaptive}).$$

The weight $k_{14}$ for February 1954 would be calculated by dropping the errors for January 1953 and adding those for January 1954 into the formula (7). The weights $k_n$ are seen to be proper weights in that they only depend on information available at the time the combined forecast is made. They are also seen to be necessarily positive, which is not necessarily a good thing, although it does imply the belief that both forecasts have something positive to contribute to the combination. There do exist alternative methods of forming the weights which do allow these weights to go outside the range $(0, 1)$. Occasionally giving one of the forecasts a negative weight does appear to produce a superior combination, but if the constituent forecasts have been prepared at all carefully and are based on some relevant data, only non-negative weights should be appropriate.

To gain an improved forecast by using this combination technique is usually worth considering as it is easy to do, is often successful, and at the very least removes the necessity of deciding which of a pair of forecasts is preferred. These are very pragmatic reasons, but if the combination is successful, there are some further implications. The reason a combined forecast may be preferable is that neither constituent forecast is using all of the data in the available information set in an optimum fashion. Thus, success of combination suggests that a more general model should be attempted, including the better features of the models underlying the constituent forecasts. This also suggests that combining forecasts will be particularly successful when using constituents based on quite different philosophies, such as those using a time series Box–Jenkins model and a regression model. It is also possible to insert nonnumerical information into one's forecasts by using such a combination. If an economist produces a sequence of forecasts based on whatever information he decides to use, including rumours or gut feelings about the situation, these can be combined with forecasts based on a standard data analysis. If the nonnumerical data have any consistent predictive value, the economist's forecasts should obtain a positive weight.

A final use of combining forecasts is to help evaluate forecasts based on a wide information set, such as those derived from an econometric model. The wide-based forecasts should be better than those using a subset of the information set. For example, a forecast based on a regression model using the past and present of series including that being forecast should be better than a single-series forecast, such as one from a Box–Jenkins model. As one information is a subset of the other, the wider-based forecast should not merely have a lower mean squared error, but, if combined with the other forecast, should have a weight very near 1, provided a long enough series of errors is available and weights based on (5) are used. This is a very strong condition to be used when evaluating forecasts from an econometric model.

The combining technique can be generalized to the combination of more than two forecasts, of the form

$$C_n = k_{1,n} f_{1,n} + k_{2,n} f_{2,n} + \cdots + k_{p,n} f_{p,n}.$$

If $e_{j,n}$ are the errors from the $j$th forecast $f_{j,n}$, with the notation

$$A_{j,n} = \left[ \sum_{t=n-m}^{n} (e_{j,t})^2 \right]^{-1},$$

$$B_n = A_{1,n} + A_{2,n} + \cdots + A_{p,n},$$

then a simple method of estimating the $j$th weight is to use

$$k_{j,n} = \frac{A_{j,n}}{B_n}.$$

However, it is better to discard any really bad forecasts, that is, those with particularly small $A$ values, as quickly as possible and then to apply the above procedure to combine the remainder.

The potential benefits to be gained from combining forecasts will be discussed in the following section.

## 8.4 HOW WELL DO THE METHODS WORK?

As has been seen in this and the previous chapter, there is a variety of methods for producing point forecasts. In fact, there are also many others that have not been discussed, although a few more are mentioned in Chapter 12. There naturally have been many studies that have tried to evaluate the relative success of the competing methods. It is not easy to summarize the results of these studies, as different sets of data have been used with differing groups of forecasting methods and no clear-cut consensus of conclusions has been achieved. Some of the studies have difficulties with their interpretation because improper procedures have been used, such as using information, like the future values of some series, that a real forecaster could not possibly have available. Some studies have used models estimated by a least-squares criterion and then have tried to evaluate forecasts from these models using a different criterion, which is obviously a dubious procedure.

There is a number of general rules that the theory presented in earlier chapters suggests are at least plausible:

(i)   The further ahead you forecast, the less well you do;

(ii)   the bigger the information set, the better the forecast, provided that the extra information is relevant;

(iii)   the more data analysis conducted, the better the forecast; and

(iv)   if two forecasts based on quite different approaches are combined, the result will often be better than the constituents.

On occasion these rules clash. For example, if one has the choice of forecasts from 1000- or a 50-equation econometric model, the larger model will be based on a larger information set but the smaller model will generally have been more carefully constructed, analyzed, and evaluated. It is often found that for key economic variables the smaller model produces superior forecasts but, of course, if one wants a forecast of a variable that is not in the smaller model, it is necessary to turn to the bigger model.

At this time there has been no comprehensive study comparing forecasts from a variety of different methods on many economic series. Only small group comparisons exist between several econometric models and AR(4) models, or between a single econometric model and ARIMA forecasts, or between regression equations using anticipations data and an econometric model not using these data, or between three different time series methodologies, for example. In attempting to summarize the results from these studies, which are not always in agreement, or even consistent, it is difficult to remain totally objective and not to reflect one's own preferences. However, it can be said that the results do generally support each of the above rules, at least to some extent. It is usually difficult to forecast further ahead, sophisticated data analysis does often produce somewhat superior forecasts, and combining often improves matters. On the other hand, it is frequently difficult to improve forecasts significantly based on a proper, but small information set by adding further information. To illustrate some of these conclusions, the results obtained by Granger and Newbold (1976) when applying three time series methods to 106 economic series can be quoted. The three methods were the Box–Jenkins ARIMA models discussed in Chapter 3 and the stepwise autoregressive and adaptive or expo-

**TABLE 8.2**

| $h$ | 1 | 2 | 4 | 6 | 8 |
|---|---|---|---|---|---|
| B–J versus Adapt. | 73 | 64 | 58 | 57 | 58 |
| B–J versus S–A | 68 | 70 | 62 | 61 | 63 |
| Adapt. versus S–A | 48 | 50 | 57 | 56 | 59 |

nentially weighted moving average methods described in Chapter 4. These methods are denoted B–J, S–A, and Adapt., respectively. All use the same information set, just the past and present of the series being forecast, and the second two are purely automatic, with any analysis being conducted by a computer, whereas the first requires the decision making abilities of a trained statistician. Some of the results obtained from making just pairwise comparisons are shown in Table 8.2, which gives the percentage of occasions that the first-named method outperforms the second for various forecast horizons $h$.

It is seen that the method involving the most analysis, B–J, outperforms the two automatic techniques for one-step forecasts and generally has a mean squared error about 15%–20% smaller, but that the advantage dissipates somewhat as longer horizons are considered. There is little to choose between the other two techniques for small $h$ values but the adaptive method does rather better for higher $h$ values. Using the notation $C(A, B)$ for the combination of methods $A$ and $B$, Table 8.3 shows how well the various combinations performed in pairwise comparisons for one-step forecasts, the number being the percentage the first named method outperforms the second. The combinations shown in this table used m = 12.

In an earlier study, Cooper (1972) compared the forecasts for 33 economic variables from seven of the most prestigious econometric models with those from fitted AR(4) models. The series were recorded quarterly. Comparing mean squared one-step forecast errors, the autoregressive models beat all

**TABLE 8.3**

| | Percentage first method wins |
|---|---|
| $C$(B–J, Adapt.) versus B–J | 56 |
| $C$(B–J, S–A) versus B–J | 55 |
| $C$(Adapt., S–A) versus Adapt. | 69 |
| $C$(Adapt., S–A) versus S–A | 76 |
| $C$(Adapt., S–A) versus B–J | 46 |
| $C$(Adapt., S–A, B–J) versus B–J | 63 |

of the econometric models for over half the series. The best individual
econometric model beat all the other forecasts on seven occasions. Although
these results show something of the power of single-series methods of forecasting, they do have to be interpreted with some caution. First, the results
given were for one-step ahead forecasts, but when looking further ahead
the econometric models perform much better. Secondly, Cooper did use
the forecasts just as produced by the models and without the subjective
corrections usually made by econometricians and which generally improve
matters. Finally, it can be said that econometric models have certainly improved since the Cooper study, partly because of the appearance of such
results, by better model specifications. Nevertheless, forecast-produced
ARIMA models are not at all easy to beat for most economic variables.

There is not a great deal of experience with the combination of time series
and econometric forecast in the published literature, but what is available
does suggest that combining often produces a forecast superior to both
components.

It is not possible to give a definite answer to a question such as, "What is
the best forecasting method?" In any particular forecasting situation, some
methods may be excluded either because of insufficient data or because the
cost is too high. If there are no such limitations, it is still not possible to give
a simple answer. All methods are based on simplifying assumptions about
the true world, and one method will produce a good approximation to the
truth on some occasions, a different method in other occasions. For macroeconomic variables, it should be expected that the Box–Jenkins ARIMA
models and econometric models should be superior to most simple alternatives. For microeconomic variables, ARIMA and carefully constructed
causal regression models should generally be the best. However, one of the
advantages of combining techniques is that it is not necessary to make a
definite choice between alternative methods, as both can be retained and
given a weight determined by recent performance.

The question of which methods to use is considered further in Chapter 12.

## QUESTIONS

1. A retired engineer has been attempting to forecast the local index of
   production for the past five years. He is under the impression that he
   is doing better than a forecast produced by the local newspaper but is
   unsure how to evaluate his forecasts. What advice would you give him?

2. To try to evaluate the quality of his forecasting technique, a statistician
   suggests using the correlation between the forecasts $f_{n,1}$ and the quan-

tity being forecast $x_{n+1}$. Explain why this is not likely to be a useful method of evaluation.

3. A large company that manufacturers frozen peas as well as many other products makes two sets of forecasts of the price of fresh peas, one set by statisticians in the Head Office and the other by market researchers in a subsidiary company's offices. There is need for a company forecast, so each quarter the two groups of forecasters meet, discuss their differences, and try to reach a compromise figure. These discussions are often acrimonious. Discuss how you might try to sell the idea of producing combinations of forecasts to the head statistician of the company.

4. A group of large oil firms provide anticipations of oil price changes over the following six months. A regression study finds

(actual change) = 5.0 + 1.0(anticipated change) + (residual),

where the residual series appears to be white noise. Over the last five periods the forecast errors [(error) = (actual change) − (forecast change)] from the anticipation data and an autoregressive model were those given by the following tabulation:

|  | | Period | | | |
|---|---|---|---|---|---|
| Errors | 1 | 2 | 3 | 4 | 5 |
| Anticipation | 8 | −1 | 9 | 1 | 2 |
| Autoregressive | −1 | 3 | 1 | −2 | 2 |

Suggest an appropriate method of combining the two forecasts made for the next period.

5. If $X_t$ is a trend-free series with no seasonal component, $f_{n,h}$ and $g_{n,h}$ are two forecasts made at time $n$ of $X_{n+h}$, and

$$C_{n,h} = k_{n,h}f_{n,h} + (1 - k_{n,h})g_{n,h}$$

is a combined forecast, where the $k$'s are chosen from past $h$-step errors, then if both $f_{n,h}$ and $g_{n,h}$ have the same mean (average) value as $X_{n+h}$, show why you would expect $k_{n,h}$ to tend to the value $\frac{1}{2}$ as $h$ becomes large.

## FURTHER READINGS

Armstrong, J. Scott (1978). *Long-Range Forecasting, from Crystal Ball to Computer*, New York: Wiley.

Cooper, R. L. (1972). In *Econometric Models of Cyclical Behavior* (B. Hickman, ed.), New York: Columbia Univ. Press.

Granger, C. W. J., and P. Newbold (1976). *Forecasting Economic Time Series*, Chapter 8, New York: Academic Press.

CHAPTER

# 9

# Population Forecasting

My interest is in the future because I am going to spend the rest of my life there.
C. F. Kettering

## 9.1 STATING THE PROBLEM

Virtually everyone is aware of the dramatic increases in world population that have occurred in the past 100 years or so. World population has increased from well under half a billion (i.e., 500 million) to around four billion in less than 1000 years, with the most spectacular increases happening since 1800. The figure is confidently expected to reach over six billion by the year 2000, a year which is always accorded special attention for purely numerological reasons. In this chapter we shall be solely concerned with the problem of how such forecast population figures are produced. No attention will be paid, in any direct fashion, to the question of how population might be controlled, although this is obviously a question of overwhelming and immediate importance. Virtually no one opposes the view that there now exist sufficient human beings for any conceivable purpose, although some nationalist politicians apparently feel that the mix could be improved. Many dramatic statistics can be quoted in an attempt to bring home the extent of the population problem. For example,

(i)   the population of the world at the time of the birth of Christ was probably less than the present population of the United States and Mexico;
(ii)   there are more scientists alive at this moment than the total of all who have died in the past; or

(iii)  it is expected that world population will have grown from two billion in 1930 to over six billion by 2000.

Such figures should make it clear why it is important and necessary to produce reliable forecasts not only of the population of the world or of separate geographic regions but also of how the population will be divided between different age groups. For governments, such forecasts are required in order to plan food and energy requirements and to organize long-run services, such as the size of universities and schools and even road construction. For firms, the forecasts are relevant to long-term investments in power stations or steel plants, to research into alternative raw materials and products, and possibly to decisions on whether or not to introduce brands aimed at specific age groups. The forecasts are essentially long run, over a decade or more, because significant changes generally do not occur over shorter intervals.

Population figures are often somewhat more easily interpreted and assimilated by considering changes or growth rates. At the start of the 1970s, the world population was growing at a rate of about 65 million people a year, which is almost 180,000 per day. Thus, in 4 days the world adds as many people as now live in San Diego, in 62 days as many as live in Australia, in 81 days the whole New York metropolitan area, all of France in 270 days, and all of Africa in just over 4 years.

A population is said to have a growth rate of 5% if for every 100 people alive at the start of the year there are 105 alive at the end. It can be shown that if a population has a growth rate of $g\%$ and this continues every year, then the population will double in $69/g$ years. Some figures for 1970 and 1976

**TABLE 9.1**

| | Population (millions) | | Growth rate | | No. of years to double | |
|---|---|---|---|---|---|---|
| | 1970 | 1976 | 1970 | 1976 | 1970 | 1976 |
| World | 3632 | 4281 | 2.0 | 2.2 | 35 | 31 |
| Africa | 344 | 432 | 2.6 | 2.8 | 27 | 25 |
| Asia | 2056 | 2476 | 2.3 | 2.5 | 31 | 28 |
| Kuwait | 0.7 | 1.1 | 8.3 | 6.1 | 9 | 11 |
| Japan | 103.5 | 112 | 1.1 | 1.1 | 63 | 63 |
| India | 555 | 652.7 | 2.6 | 2.6 | 27 | 27 |
| North America (U.S.) | 205 | 245.3 | 1.0 | 1.3 | 70 | 53 |
| Mid-America (including Mexico) | 67 | 80.3 | 3.4 | 2.6 | 21 | 26 |
| Europe | 462 | 476 | 0.8 | 0.6 | 88 | 115 |
| Britain | — | 56 | — | 0.0 | — | never |

on growth rates are given in Table 9.1. If the 1970 figures hold up, then from 1970 to 2000 the population of India will increase from 555 million to 1171 million, that of Kuwait from 0.7 million to 3.0 million, and that of Europe from 462 million to 620 million. Of course, it can be argued that these growth rates will not continue, that death rates will not continue to fall in Europe, that people will be rational and induce lower birth rates, that Malthusian effects will limit population in India due to shortages of food and space, and that the boom in the Kuwait population is due to a high rate of immigration caused by oil wealth and will not be allowed to continue. Such speculations certainly suggest factors that will affect population sizes and need to be carefully considered when forecasting. It is nevertheless true that rather good forecasts have been achieved in recent decades in most countries by simply fitting an exponential curve to past figures and then using this curve to extrapolate into the future. One would certainly expect more sophisticated, causal models to provide better forecasts, and these are considered in the next section.

As the population of the United States will be used as an example in later sections, it is perhaps worthwhile at this point to give some actual figures based on U.S. census figures (Table 9.2).

**TABLE 9.2**

| Year | U.S. population (millions) | Year | U.S. population (millions) |
|------|---------------------------|------|---------------------------|
| 1790 | 4 | 1890 | 63 |
| 1800 | 5 | 1900 | 76 |
| 1810 | 7 | 1910 | 92 |
| 1820 | 10 | 1920 | 106 |
| 1830 | 13 | 1930 | 123 |
| 1840 | 17 | 1940 | 132 |
| 1850 | 23 | 1950 | 151 |
| 1860 | 31 | 1960 | 179 |
| 1870 | 38 | 1970 | 203 |
| 1880 | 50 | 1976 | 222 |

## 9.2 POPULATION EXTRAPOLATION

The problems considered in this section are of the form: how many twelve-year-old children will be requiring education in 10 years time? Clearly, answers to such questions are of vital importance to school directors or supervisors. A problem of this form will be called one of extrapolation, rather than forecasting, because all the children involved are already alive, so that future births need not be considered. This makes the problem much easier, for the required extrapolation is

Number of children = (Number of 2-year-old children now alive)
      × (survival rate over next 10 years)
      + (net immigration).

Suppose, for the moment, that the last term is small and can be ignored and let $N_2$ denote the number of 2-year-olds now alive and $P_x$ the probability of a person aged $x$ living to age $x + 1$. The answer to the above problem can then be stated as

$$\text{Number} = N_2 P_2 P_3 P_4 P_5 P_6 P_7 P_8 P_9 P_{10} P_{11}.$$

$N_2$ can certainly be taken as known, from birth registration figures, and death rates for children in their first 2 years. Values for $P_2$, $P_3$ etc. can be estimated from the experience of the previous *cohorts* of children. For example, $P_2$ is estimated by looking at the children who were aged 2 *last* year and asking how many survived the year and so are now aged 3. Similarly, $P_3$ is estimated by looking at the cohort of children who were aged 3 last year and observing how many survived to become aged 4 now, and so forth. Merely by looking at available data, all of the constituents of the extrapolation formula can be estimated and so a forecast obtained. There would be equally little problem in providing forecasts of segments of the population, such as boys or girls, for different races or regions, provided that suitable data have been collected in recent years. However, in some cases, some care may have to be taken with the net immigration component.

Denoting by $N$ the total number alive and by $N_x$ the number of people alive aged $x$, so that

$$N = \sum_x N_x,$$

then the number expected to be alive next year is

$$\sum_x N_x P_x$$

and the number expected to die is

$$N - \sum_x N_x P_x = \sum_x N_x (1 - P_x).$$

$P_x$ is estimated by

$$\frac{N_{x+1} \text{ this year}}{N_x \quad \text{last year}}$$

The *crude death rate* is then defined as this quantity divided by $N$, i.e.,

$$\text{Crude death rate} = \sum N_x(1 - P_x)/N.$$

The *crude birth rate*, which is discussed in the next section, is defined by

$$\text{Crude birth rate} = \frac{\text{Number born this year}}{N}$$

The estimates of the $P_x$ can also be used to estimate the mean or expected length of life of a baby just born. To see how some of these figures have varied in the United States this century, we show some values in Table 9.3. The effects of improvements in health science, sanitation, and hygiene are clearly seen, as would be the small likelihood of the average man enjoying a long retirement if the retirement age had stayed at 65.

**TABLE 9.3**

| Year | Crude death rate per 1000 population | Expectation of life length at birth | |
|------|------|------|------|
| | | male | female |
| 1900 | 17.2 | 46.3 | 48.3 |
| 1910 | 14.7 | 48.4 | 51.3 |
| 1920 | 13.0 | 53.6 | 54.6 |
| 1930 | 11.3 | 58.1 | 61.6 |
| 1940 | 10.8 | 60.8 | 65.2 |
| 1950 | 9.6 | 65.6 | 71.1 |
| 1960 | 9.5 | 66.6 | 73.1 |
| 1970 | 9.5 | 67.1 | 74.8 |
| 1976 | 8.9 | 69.0 | 77.0 |

## 9.3    BIRTH-RATE FORECASTING

Now consider the question, how many 6-year-old children will be entering school in 10 years' time? To make a forecast, a formula that can be used is

Number of children = (Number born in 4 years' time)
                        × (survival rate over first 6 years)
                        + (net immigration).

This is clearly a more difficult problem than that discussed in the previous section, as it deals with children yet to be born. To predict the number of children to be born in 4 years' time, a sensible method would be to estimate the number of women aged 15–44 that will be alive then and to multiply by a forecasted *fertility rate*.

There are two methods of defining a fertility rate, and they have different uses. The *general fertility rate* is defined as

General fertility rate
$$= \text{(Number of births in a year per 1000 women aged 15–44)}.$$

In 1975, this rate had the value 66.7 in the United States. The *total fertility rate* is an estimate of the number of children that a representative sample of 1000 women would bear in their lifetime. This estimate is based on present, age-specific birth rates, as follows.

Let $r_x$ equal the birth rate per woman aged $x$ at the start of the year ($r_x$ is said to be an age-specific fertility rate). Then a woman aged $Y$ would be expected to bear

$$r_Y + r_{Y+1} + \cdots + r_{44}$$

more children in the rest of her life. The total fertility rate is then defined as the sum of the $r_x$ for all $x$ values between 15 and 44 (or possibly 49). The total fertility rate assumes that the present age-specific fertility rates will continue unchanged in the future and ignores the possibility of a woman not surviving throughout the potential childbearing years. This total fertility rate is considered easier to interpret than some of the alternative measures. In colonial times, the average American woman bore about eight children, but infant mortality rates were also extremely high then. In the early 1970s, the rate fell to 2.1 and below in the United States. This is a particularly significant figure because, at this rate, enough girls are born to replace the generation of mothers that bore them. In other words, 1000 females must bear 2098 children so that there will be 1000 females for the next generation, as more males are born than females, at a ratio of about 51 to 49, and some females do not live to childbearing age. Although the total fertility rate is now below 2.1, it does not mean that the number of babies born will necessarily decline, as the children of the postwar baby boom are now reaching ages that traditionally have the highest age-specific fertility rates.

Suppose that the age-specific fertility rates $r_x$ have been estimated for the last twelve months and let $F_x$ be the number of females aged $x$ presently in the population. Then, by assuming that the $r_x$ values will continue into the future without altering, the expected number of children to be born next year is given by

$$\sum_x F_x r_x,$$

where the sum is over $x$ values from 15 to 44, say.

Similarly, the expected number of children to be born the following year is

$$\sum_x F_{x-1} P_{x-1} r_x,$$

where again $x$ goes from 15 to 44. The number of births expected the subsequent year is

$$\sum_x F_{x-2} P_{x-2} P_{x-1} r_x,$$

as $F_{x-2} P_{x-2} P_{x-1}$ is the estimate of the number of females that will be aged $x$ at the start of that year, and so forth.

It is reasonable to expect that these forecasts will be fairly accurate when forecasting just a few years ahead, but when considering, say, 25 years hence, very little confidence could be displayed. Not only are fertility rates very likely to have changed, but the estimate includes children by mothers that have yet to be born themselves, so the possibility of errors cumulating obviously increases.

It should now be clear how the population for some country in a future year is estimated: The likely number of those alive who survive until the year is calculated, and the predicted number of children born is then added for each year to make up the total. When forecasting from, say, 1970 to 2000, the children to be born are not only a major part of the projected population, but are also the most difficult part to estimate. In practice, death rates and immigration figures are fairly stable for at least the advanced countries, but the fertility or birth rates are changing quite quickly. To provide a sound long-range population forecast, it is necessary to forecast future fertility rates. To show how important fertility rates are, consider the following three projections:

(i)  Series I assumes a slight improvement in mortality, an annual net migration of 800,000 and fertility rates that move towards a level of 2700 children for every 1000 women of child-bearing age.

(ii)  Series II is the same as series I except that fertility rates go to 2100 children per 1000 women.

(iii)  Series II-X is the same as II but with no immigration.

(iv)  Series III is the same as I except that fertility rates go to 1700 children per 1000 women.

The U.S. census bureau continually makes projections of future population under a variety of assumptions about the movements in fertility rates. They have used the terms I–III for the above three scenarios. It must be emphasized that they are projections, being essentially conditional forecasts. To make true forecasts of population, a particular scenario has to be selected

TABLE 9.4[a]

| Series | 1980 | 1990 | 2000 | 2050 |
|--------|------|------|------|------|
| I | 226 | 258 | 287 | — |
| II | 222 | 245 | 262 | — |
| II-X | 220 | 237 | 249 | — |
| III | 220 | 236 | 245 | 270 |

[a] Figures taken from the *Statistical Abstract of the United States, 1976*, Washington, D.C.: U. S. Dept. of Commerce, U.S. Govt. Printing Office.

as being the most likely. The projected populations for the United States are (approximately, in millions) given in Table 9.4. Fairly small changes in family size are seen to make a tremendous difference in eventual projected population size, the difference between series I and III being roughly that between an average family's having three children or two. The actual census bureau projections are based on a more sophisticated model than that mentioned above, although the essence is the same. It is fairly clear that different subsections of the populations can be considered separately, based on race and geographical location, and married women can be considered separately from unmarried ones when using fertility rates. Precisely how useful this decomposition is in producing superior projections is not clear, as while a better model is certainly produced the estimates of essential values such as the age-specific fertility or survival rates may be less reliable.

It should be clear that to produce good population forecasts, future fertility rates need to be forecast. Once these are available, the projection procedure is fairly straightforward. The methods of forecasting fertility rates are similar to those discussed in earlier chapters when considering economic variables. The main methods seem to be the following:

(i)   Trend fitting and time series modeling, producing forecasts based just on previous rates.

(ii)   Anticipations data. In 1960, a survey of married women aged 18–24 showed that they expected to have an average of 3.1 children. It seems likely that this age group will actually end up with a fertility rate of 2.9. In 1967, a similar survey of women aged 18–24 showed that they planned to have 2.9 children on average. By 1972, however, the anticipated average by women then aged 18–24 was down sharply to 2.3.

(iii)   Causal models. By far the most satisfactory way to proceed is to find out why people's anticipations and behavior change, if possible to find the main causes of these changes, and to build a suitable model. Unfortunately, this appears to be a difficult and complicated task and one that is very far from being satisfactorily answered. Change in the age that women get married is obviously a factor, but is it a cause or merely an effect of more fundamental causes? Changes in job opportunities for women, the tendency for more women to want to work, improvements in birth-control techniques, and changes in moral attitudes are also doubtlessly important, but the full impact of these changes has yet to be appreciated. Economic reasons may also be relevant and the more general awareness of the population problem, with its consequent overcrowding may also have an impact. Doubtless there is no single main cause, but many causes are working simultaneously and almost certainly not in a linear or simple additive fashion.

Until satisfactory answers are found to the question of what makes fertility rates change, high quality long-range population forecasts will not be possible.

## QUESTIONS

1. Suppose that you are approached to forecast the population of a small country town and also of a popular ocean-side resort this year and also 25 years hence. Write an essay how you would approach this problem and the kind of data that you would require.
2. The diaper supplier wants to forecast how many babies will be born in each of the next four quarters in some region. Briefly outline how one might make forecasts based on each of the following approaches: trend-line fitting, indicators, survey and anticipations data, and seasonal time series modeling.
3. Given the following population figures for a small town:

| Age $x$ | Number in population ($N_x$) 1975 | Number in population ($N_x$) 1976 | Age $x$ | Number in population ($N_x$) 1975 | Number in population ($N_x$) 1976 |
|---|---|---|---|---|---|
| 1 | 1026 | 1033 | 4 | 980 | 990 |
| 2 | 1010 | 1020 | 5 | 971 | 980 |
| 3 | 992 | 1000 | 6 | 960 | 970 |

Forecast the number of children aged 6 who will enter school in 1977. Also forecast the total number of children aged 2–6 in 1977, assuming in both instances that there is zero net immigration.
Find the crude death rate for 1976 of children aged 1–5.

**4.** Considering further the small town mentioned in the previous problem, the accompanying table shows the number of women aged 14–23 in the town in 1975 and 1976 and also the number of births to each age group in 1975. Forecast the number of children born to women aged 16–23 in 1977 and the number born to women aged 22 in 1979.

| Age | No. of women (1975) | No. of births (1975) | No. of women (1976) |
|-----|-----|-----|-----|
| 14 | 6132 | 0 | 6120 |
| 15 | 6242 | 0 | 6100 |
| 16 | 6140 | 0 | 6201 |
| 17 | 6100 | 130 | 6020 |
| 18 | 6090 | 292 | 6030 |
| 19 | 6090 | 343 | 6003 |
| 20 | 6073 | 488 | 6005 |
| 21 | 6082 | 561 | 6000 |
| 22 | 6070 | 502 | 6010 |
| 23 | 6060 | 492 | 6010 |

## FURTHER READING

Pressar, R. (1972). *Demographic Analysis*, Chicago: Aldine-Atherton.
    Contains extensive discussion of population projection.

CHAPTER
# 10

# Technological Forecasting

A religious sect is predicting that the world will end at 10 P.M. tonight. For more details, watch the news at eleven.

T.V. news flash

To expect the unexpected shows a thoroughly modern intellect.

Oscar Wilde

## 10.1   INTRODUCTION

The majority of the forecasting methods considered in previous chapters have been concerned with short- and medium-term forecasts, the only exception being the trend-curve fitting procedures. Over periods of less than five years, it is reasonable to make forecasts against a background of no technical change, so that the objects on sale will not change dramatically and neither will productivity. Of course prices can change as well as the values of other important economic variables, but the forecasts will largely be concerned with reactions of economic variables to behavioral, policy, or exogenous variable changes. However, when considering longer-run forecasts, an assumption of no technological change becomes quite unreasonable. One may expect that over periods of twenty years or more ahead the major changes in the economy and society will be due to changes in technology or in largely exogenous variables such as population size, distribution, or climate. Population forecasting was discussed in the previous chapter, and current evidence suggests that there is no clearcut trend in climate, although there may be long swings which have important effects.

Technological forecasting is generally concerned with the fairly long term and asks what technology will be likely to be available in particular

177

years in the future and what the impacts of important technological developments and innovations will be. It is clearly related to problems of long-term
planning so that companies can try to identify new markets and the decline of
present markets and governments can foresee future bottlenecks in the
growth or development of society in some proposed direction. Although a
new field, technological forecasting is rapidly developing in importance and
use. A survey in 1971, for instance, of 162 major corporations in the United
States found that 71% of these companies used a formal system of long-range
planning or technological forecasting, employing on the average five people
and looking ahead, on average, seven years. As may be expected, companies
in high growth industries made much greater use of technological forecasting
than those in low growth industries. Like any new and potentially exciting
field, it has attracted both some extremely good researchers and many who
certainly do not deserve such an accolade. The obvious major problem with
the field is that it is inherently very difficult to evaluate the work of any individual or the usefulness of any technique. This difficulty of evaluation
occurs whenever long-term forecasting is attempted, as it takes so long to
decide if a forecast was adequate or not, and this means that it takes a great
deal of time to generate sufficient evidence for the quality of one method to
be seen to be better than another. It must be said that most of the techniques
available for technological forecasting are neither very sophisticated nor
highly developed. This is partly due to the evaluation problem just mentioned, but mostly to this kind of forecasting's being inherently difficult, as
might be imagined. However, if it can be done well, the potential rewards are
immense. As an illustration of both of these points, it is reported that in the
very early days of electronic computers a European electrical company asked
for a forecast of the potential sales of these new machines. The forecast made
was that there would never be more than twenty computers sold, and so the
company decided not to enter the field. Later events suggest that the forecast
was incorrect in that IBM did quite well by selling thousands of computers.
Of course, the company's decision may well have been the correct one, as
many manufacturers did start to make computers in the beginning and
nearly all lost a great deal of money.

   There are basically two approaches to technological forecasting, which
may be called exploratory and normative. Exploratory techniques provide
specific forecasts of what will happen, such as when a particular medical
breakthrough is thought most likely to occur. These forecasts can be in terms
of probability statements, such as "with probability 0.75 by the year 1993
automobile engines will be twice as efficient as now." One difficulty with such
forecasts is that they implicitly include a forecast of how much money is
going to be invested in trying to reach some goal. It seems possible that
rockets would have been less developed in 1970 if the United States had not

decided to put a man on the moon. Normative forecasts start with an objective for some future period and then by working back to present time and state of the art determine what areas or technological parameters need improvement and by how much, by what means the required improvements will be attained, and what the costs, consequences, and major potential bottlenecks will be in attaining the goal. Regulations about future automobile emissions fall into this category. The most successful example was the effort by NASA to put a man on the moon by a specific date and at a specific cost, both of which, it has been stated, were attained. It was known that certain developments in electronic miniaturization, rocket design, and new materials would be required, and by assigning good enough scientists and sufficient investment the intermediate goals were all attained in time for the final objective to be achieved. It was a truly remarkable piece of long-range planning coupled with excellent management and scientific research. In general, it is clear that normative and exploratory forecasts have to be linked, for it is pointless setting impossible objectives—such as having a colony on the sun by the year 2000, or eradicating all poverty, disease, and starvation on the earth by 1984. Some inventions and developments can simply be required and usually achieved by sufficient allocation of researchers, whereas others clearly cannot. However, there is a large penumbra of uncertainty consisting of developments that are neither clearly attainable or clearly unattainable, and penetration of this region is obviously of central importance in providing good technological forecasts.

Before discussing techniques for producing forecasts, it is worth asking the question whether there is any hope of predicting an invention or technological development. As might be expected, a wide range of views exists on this question. At one extreme, it is argued that invention is by its very nature unforecastable, being achieved by a flash of inspiration by some genius. At the other extreme, it is claimed that most inventions occur when in some sense "the time is right," as illustrated by several workers making the same invention or breakthrough at the same time, and that someone with sufficient knowledge could have observed precursors and thus forecast the invention. The truth is usually somewhere in between. It is certainly true that many inventions and breakthroughs do occur almost simultaneously. It is said that the telegraph, the reaper, the motion picture, the filament electric lamp, the sewing machine, and the elevator are all examples of inventions that occurred more than once, and many other examples exist. At least two instances come from the field of forecasting itself. Both Kolmogoroff, in Russia, and Norbert Wiener, in the United States, in the early 1940s developed the theory of optimum forecasts which was briefly mentioned in Chapter 4. At a less sophisticated level, the idea of combining forecasts, as discussed in Chapter 8 was suggested by Bates and Granger in 1969 and very soon after, and quite independently, by C. Nelson, using a different approach. Every research worker can supply similar examples. However, the fact that examples of simultaneous invention can be found does not necessarily mean that the inventions could have been predicted. There are many examples of what might be called the Pearl Harbor syndrome; situations in which it was later shown that information existed such that they could in theory have been predicted, yet in fact were not. Even after an invention has been made, it is not clear that it will be a success. In the early days of the automobile, most engineers were uncertain whether the electric car, the steamer, or the gasoline car would turn out to be the most successful.

The question of how well breakthroughs can be forecast, if at all, has still to be answered, and work is being conducted on the types of precursors that were available before the first release of nuclear power or the invention of the jet engine, for example. Once sufficient experience from the past has been gained, it may well be possible to monitor the research literature and the requests for patents so that improved forecasts are achieved.

Although breakthroughs in science and in other fields are naturally very important in the long run, they are perhaps less important when forecasting in the middle run, say from seven to twelve years ahead. Most of the changes in technology that will occur in the middle run will consist of developments of the present technology and of inventions that have already occurred and are being currently discussed in the research literature. There are eight basic stages in the development of a technological innovation:

*Stage 1*   the original scientific suggestion or discovery or the recognition of an achievable need or opportunity,
*Stage 2*   crystallization of a theory or design concept,
*Stage 3*   laboratory verification of the correctness of the theory behind the innovation,
*Stage 4*   laboratory demonstration of the successful application of the theory,
*Stage 5*   full scale or field trial,
*Stage 6*   commercial introduction or first operational use,
*Stage 7*   widespread adoption, and
*Stage 8*   proliferation, including adoption in areas other than that for which it was intended, plus impact on other products or parts of science.

By recognizing in which state a particular innovation now resides and by using case studies of the development of previous comparable inventions it may be possible to forecast when it will reach later stages. The full process, through all stages, will usually take at least 10 years, with 20–25 years being more likely. It has been suggested that the speed of an innovation going from stage 1 to stage 6 has been increasing, but it is not clear that this is true for the more complicated modern inventions, such as fission and fusion nuclear power, for example.

To give more structure to the procedures whereby forecasts are made about technological breakthroughs or developments, a variety of techniques has been suggested. The most important two, trend-curve fitting and Delphi, are described in the following two sections, and some of the other methods are summarized in the final section of this chapter.

## 10.2  GROWTH CURVES

For many purposes it is sufficient to forecast what the state of some technology will be in a specific year rather than how that state will be achieved. For example, a forecast that computing costs will be reduced will have many important implications for the ever increasing use of computers both in industry and in homes. It would not matter how this cost reduction is achieved provided that it does occur. Such a forecast could be based on observations of how costs have declined in the past. It could be noted that while in 1952 it cost $1.20 to do 100,000 multiplications on an IBM computer, six years later the cost had dropped to 26¢. By 1964 the same calculations could be executed for 12¢, by 1970 for 5¢, and in 1975 for just 1¢. By fitting a trend curve, such as one of those discussed in Chapter 2, to these figures, it would be easy to produce a forecast of future costs.

The question, as always, is which curve to fit. The most popular, by far, is the exponential curve, in which the logarithms of the values being fitted are explained by a linear time trend. Other popular curves are the linear, the logistic (also called Pear), and the Gompertz curves. It will be recalled from the discussion in Chapter 2 that these last two curves tend to an asymptote or upper limit. This upper limit may be estimated or it can just be selected from other considerations. For instance, if a curve is being fitted to the number of telephones per 1000 members of the population, then an upper limit of 800 might be selected and this will fix one of the parameters of the model. The obvious problem with this approach is that very poor forecasts result if this upper limit is badly selected.

Examples of exponential growth curves given by Martino (1972) include

(i)   the efficiency of light sources, in terms of lumens per watt, going from the paraffin candle in 1850, through the tungsten filament lamp in 1908 and the mercury lamp in 1936, to the gallium arsenide diode in 1960;

(ii)   the gross take-off weight of U.S. single-place fighter aircraft;

(iii)   the top speed of U.S. combat aircraft;

(iv)   the maximum thrust from U.S.-built liquid and solid propellant rocket engine;

(v)   electric power production in the United States;

(vi)   the installed technological horsepower per capita in the United States;

(vii)   the ratio of the size of random access memories, in bits, to access time in microseconds, for digital computers; and

(viii)   the time required for inversion of a 40 × 40 matrix by a digital computer.

With the exception of the last of these examples, the fitted exponential trends are upward. To illustrate the kind of result achieved, the logarithm of the ratio in (vii), denoted by $Y_t$, when regressed on time, gives

$$Y_t = -1080.82 + 0.5513t,$$

where $t = 0$ corresponds to 1945 and data up to about 1967 are used in the estimation. One way to interpret any such exponential growth curve is to use what is known as "the rule of 70." Suppose that the curve

$$Y_t = Ae^{bt}$$

is fitted to some data. On taking logarithms, the equation becomes

$$y_t = a + bt,$$

where $y_t = \log Y_t$, $a = \log A$, and one asks how long it takes for $Y_t$ to double in size. Some easy algebra gives the result that this doubling time is given by $0.6931/b$, which is often approximated by $0.70/b$. Thus, for the computer memory ratio, the doubling time is $0.70/0.55 = 1.23$ years. Thus, the ratio will expand eightfold in $3 \times 1.23 = 3.7$ years. This is a tremendous rate of growth, but not at all uncommon in technology.

It has been found that trend-curve fitting can provide useful forecasts, at least for the middle run. However, these forecasts are of technological parameters rather than of actual technology. No attempt is made to forecast how technological changes will be achieved. The curve fitting approach is also basically unsatisfactory in another way in that it is essentially based on an assumption that things will keep on going in the same way that they have in the past. Although this could often be the case, there may be information available suggesting that such an assumption is incorrect. Policy changes concerning environmental effects could limit growth in certain directions and the policy of reduced support to the U.S. space program may well be expected to reduce the growth in rocket maximum thrust, for example. Simply examing past data can miss such potential changes in growth. A method of expanding the information set to include such possible policy changes is discussed in the next section.

As an example of the dangers of uncritical use of growth curves, a speaker at an international conference on the quality of life stated, "Computerized estimates of the world's end need not be accurate. Had there been a computer in 1872 it would have predicted that by 1972 there would be so many horse-drawn vehicles that the surface of the globe would be covered with six feet of manure."

## 10.3 THE DELPHI METHOD

When trying to make a technological timing forecast, such as when some breakthrough will occur, it is clearly of little value to ask the opinion of anyone who is not an expert in the technological field concerned. Most people, including scientists in other fields, would not have sufficient technical competence or knowledge about current research or problems needing to be overcome to give a relevant forecast. If, however, it is possible to identify a group of experts, there still remains the problem of how best to extract a useful forecast from them.

One obvious procedure is to select the best expert—a genius—and ask that person for a forecast. Although this is basically a sound idea, it is difficult to achieve in practice. It is not easy to select the genius and different selections may not give similar forecasts. It is not sufficient to pick the best-known person in a field as this position may have been achieved through a sound marketing effort rather than real eminence or because of an important discovery ten years earlier, which does not necessarily mean that the person is still in the forefront of research or ideas. The most relevant single individual to make a forecast might well be some fairly young, unknown scientist who is about to make a real breakthrough, but it is usually virtually impossible to identify such a person. More established research workers are likely to be most concerned with developing earlier ideas rather than discovering new techniques.

If the single-genius method is risky, would a meeting of minds in a committee or seminar format be any more successful? Personal observation by the author suggests that most minds become moribund when on a committee for reasons that presumably only psychologists can explain. Many scientists are not used to defending their views verbally and so a small committee is likely to be dominated by a few superegoists who do not necessarily have superior forecasting abilities. Similarly, a large seminar involving, say, 100 participants may not be able to hear the views of more than a few. The other extreme from face-to-face meetings is to conduct a postal poll or survey. The problem here is that although all opinions now have equal weight, there is no opportunity for those with particularly convincing arguments to present them, so that the likelihood of a consensus opinion's being obtained is low.

A suggested procedure to circumvent most of these problems and to squeeze out reasonable forecasts from a group of experts was developed at the RAND Corporation in 1963. The necessary ingredients are a carefully selected group of experts and an organizer. At the first stage, a set of properly worded questions are given to each expert, such as the following:

Q.1.   When will a reliable automated language translator be available?

Q.2.   When will it be economically feasible to commercially produce synthetic protein for food?

Q.3.   When will it be possible to breed intelligent animals, such as apes, for low grade labor?

Q.4.   When will there be two-way communication with extraterrestrials?

Q.5.   In what year will the percentage of electric amongst all cars reach 50%?

To each such question the expert is supposed to give a specific date, usually in the form of a year, which he or she thinks is the most likely to be correct. An answer of "never" is also allowed. A somewhat different form of question that might be used is

Q.6.   What is the probability of a world war occurring in the next twenty years?

The answer may be any number between 0 and 1 inclusive.

Once the answers have been returned to the organizer, the next task is to summarize them, to obtain both an average forecast date and a measure of how much the experts disagree. A sensible way of doing this is to find the median year and the two quartiles of the distribution of forecasts. This is done as follows. Suppose that all of the years named are placed in order from the nearest to the furthest. If a year is named several times, then it appears that number of times in the list. The median year is such that half of the list lies on each side of it. The first quartile has a quarter of the list before it and three quarters after. The last quartile has three quarters before it and a quarter after. Thus, for example, assume twelve experts gave the following dates in order:

1979, 1980, 1983, 1985, 1986, 1987, 1989,
     ↑       ↑
    first quartile  median

1990, 1990, 1990, 2010, never.
     ↑
    last quartile

Then the median lies between 1987 and 1989 (and so is recorded as the average of these two years, i.e., 1988), the first quartile lies between 1983 and 1985 (and so is 1984), and the last quartile is between 1990 and 1990 (i.e., 1990). The median guess, or forecast, is thus 1988 and represents an average value, and the interquartile range (IQR) is 1984–1990 and is a measure of the extent of agreement or disagreement of the experts. The use of these measures is recommended because of their ease of calculation and interpretation and because the reply "never" creates no problems with the analysis.

As an example, a sample of people attending a forecasting conference in 1967 replied to question Q.5, generating a median of 1990 and an IQR of 1985–2012. Such replies are frequently represented diagramatically as shown in Fig. 10.1.

The forecasts produced at this stage represent simply the result of a survey of possible experts and, although possibly useful, allow no form of debate. Rather more sophistication occurs at the second stage, where the experts are sent the results of the initial survey and asked if, given this extra information, they wish to alter their views. An expert who finds his view to be quite different from that of everyone else might decide that his views cannot be supported and so change his forecast toward the median. There is, however, no pressure for him to so change his viewpoint. He may well think that everyone else is out of step. Any expert who wishes to maintain a viewpoint or forecast outside of the interquartile range is invited to state briefly the main reasons for holding such a viewpoint.

Returning to the question of when electric automobiles would make up 50% of all automobiles, in the second round the experts changed their opinions somewhat, giving a median now of 1995 and an IQR of 1985–2020. The organizer of the experiment summarized the arguments in favor of an earlier date. "The first use will be for local travel, which will rapidly exceed 50%, in view of urban development. Developments in nuclear power cost-effectiveness and energy storage point to an earlier date." The arguments in favor of a later date ran, "Pollution will force improvements in the combustion engine. Batteries don't provide enough power or range. Battery recharging is too inconvenient. The oil industry will adjust this."

Once more, the participants are sent a summary of the second stage, their revised aggregated forecasts, plus the summaries of arguments for holding extreme views, and again they are asked to provide revised forecasts. They

*Fig. 10.1*

can also provide further arguments for holding a particular viewpoint and try to combat the arguments for the opposite viewpoint. For the electric car question, the third round produced little change, with a median of 1995 and an IQR of 1985–2011. The counterarguments in defense of an earlier date included, "The later-date arguments overlook the political pressure. Battery and fuel cell improvements will, in the 1970s, provide sufficient power and range. Inconvenience will be minimized because recharging can be automatic upon garaging." Those in defense of a later date included, "If it were not for pollution, this would occur even later than 2000. Energy storage would have to improve by 10 orders of magnitude. Consumers buy cars for long-distance, high-speed driving."

The sequence of questioning could continue almost indefinitely, with developing arguments, provided the participants' patience remained, but cost constraints usually stop the sequence after three or four rounds. For the forecasting conference views on electric cars, a fourth and final question produced a median of 1995 with an interquartile range of 1985–2000. A review of these results and arguments ten years later shows a great deal of sense to have been generated. The lack of development of a greatly improved battery still prevents electric cars' becoming popular, and a median of 1995 appears reasonable, despite considerable changes in attitude towards electric cars due to concern about dependence upon foreign oil.

The original large-scale Delphi experiment was conducted by Gordon and Helmer at the RAND Corporation around 1965 and the technique was immediately widely accepted as being both sensible and potentially useful. The panel used in this first study consisted mainly of highly intelligent, well-respected scientists, social scientists, and intellectuals, who were asked to provide forecasts on a very wide range of topics, most of which were outside the field of expertise of the majority of the panelists. Some of the forecasts made in 1965 concerning scientific breakthroughs are given in Table 10.1.

**TABLE 10.1**

| | Question | Median | Interquartile range |
|---|---|---|---|
| 1. | Economically useful desalination of seawater | 1970 | 1970–1983 |
| 2. | Automated language translators | 1972 | 1968–1976 |
| 3. | New organs through transplanting or prosthesis | 1972 | 1968–1982 |
| 4. | Reliable weather forecasts | 1975 | 1972–1988 |
| 5. | Controlled thermonuclear power | 1985 | 1980–2000 |
| 6. | Feasibility of limited weather control | 1990 | 1987–2000 |
| 7. | Economically useful farming of ocean to produce at least 20% of world's food | 2000 | 2000–2017 |
| 8. | Use of drugs to raise level of intelligence | 2012 | 1984–2023 |

Some of these forecasts now seem optimistic and others still reasonable. These figures illustrate a problem common to all long-term forecasting techniques: How can they be evaluated? It can take many years until one knows whether or not the forecast proves to be accurate. Although this problem is insurmountable, it is possible to conduct experiments that throw some light on the value of the Delphi technique. One such experiment goes through the full set of stages but using questions of fact rather than forecasts. The questions are selected so that the experimenter can know the true answer but the panelists will merely have an opinion and are very unlikely to know the truth. The kinds of questions used are illustrated by the following:

(a)   How many divorces, in thousands, were there in the United States in 1960?

(b)   How many prime numbers are there between 1000 and 2000?

(c)   What was the year of birth of the inventor of FM radio?

(d)   What is the area of Los Angeles county, in square miles?

(e)   How many telephones were there in Africa in 1965?

(f)   How many women Marines were there at the end of World War II?

Table 10.2 gives an example of the results obtained.

Although the experiments are hardly ideal, and the participants are rarely "experts," they do provide some interesting results, which may be summarized as follows:

(a)   There was a tendency to converge, although the movement occurs less in the median than in reduction in the interquartile range.

(b)   Panelists holding views outside the interquartile range were very much more likely to alter their views, toward the median, than other panelists. Thus, if the true answer fell inside the original IQR, there would appear to be a tendency for the panel to reach a consensus somewhere near the

**TABLE 10.2**

| Question | Median and IQR | | | | True answer |
|---|---|---|---|---|---|
| | Round 1 | Round 2 | Round 3 | Round 4 | |
| (a) | 500 | 500 | 500 | 400 | 393 |
| | 100–1000 | 250–750 | 350–750 | 400–500 | |
| (b) | 130 | 150 | 150 | 150 | 135 |
| | 50–200 | 100–200 | 118–200 | 120–200 | |
| (c) | 1893 | 1890 | 1890 | 1890 | 1890 |
| | 1884–1900 | 1885–1898 | 1885–1898 | 1885–1895 | |
| (d) | 1600 | 1800 | 2000 | 2000 | 4060 |
| | 500–4000 | 1200–4000 | 1500–3000 | 1500–2500 | |

truth. However, if the truth lies outside the original IQR, it is unlikely that it will be approached in later rounds.

(c)   There is a tendency for participants to change their views toward the median opinion rather than toward the true value.

(d)   If participants are allowed to rank themselves as "experts" or not on a particular question, the expert panel does no better than the full panel.

(e)   If two panels are used, the one receiving feedback, i.e., information about the results of previous rounds, forecasts better than that not getting this information.

(f)   A Delphi panel is much more likely to converge towards the truth than a panel involved in face-to-face discussion.

Although the results of such experiments do confirm that Delphi is a sensible procedure, the actual value of the technique still needs evaluating by observing the eventual accuracy of the forecasts made. The success or lack thereof of a particular Delphi forecasting survey naturally depends on the care with which the panel is selected, the questions formulated, and the arguments summarized. It is important for inexperienced survey directors to undertake a small pilot study before the full-scale survey is conducted, so that ambiguously worded questions are avoided for example.

There are many possible criticisms of the Delphi approach, and doubtless ways of improving it can be found. One criticism is that most of the participants appear to be playing a game rather than thinking deeply about their position, trying to defend their views, or attacking the views of others. A method of generating more active participation might involve using groups of experts already committed to a position. For example, suppose a technological forecast is required about the relative importance of future energy sources. Groups active in conducting research into nuclear energy, solar energy, tidal sources, and oil shale usage could each be asked to state their reasons for being optimistic about their own specialization and the relative disadvantages of the alternative sources. These arguments could then be circulated to the other groups, who would try to defend their own positions and undermine those of the competing groups. This procedure, which might be called Competive Delphi, could produce acrimonious arguments but also deeper expert thinking about the various problems to be solved. Whether or not it would eventually produce a forecast about the portfolio of energy sources that the nation would be using in the future is less certain.

## 10.4  OTHER TECHNIQUES

Just a few of the many other available techniques will be reviewed in this section. Most of them are even less scientific than those already described in this chapter. They are inclined to involve considerable subjective judgement and may not provide very reliable forecasts if used individually. However, they will sometimes release a research worker's thought patterns from the inhibitions that are often present and thereby enable him or her to produce more realistic long-range forecasts.

### 10.4.1    Forecasting by Analogy

When considering a particular forecasting problem it is occasionally possible to find a situation in an earlier time and perhaps in a different location, society, or technology that has many similar features to the situation being investigated. By studying the analogous situations, the timetable or sequence of events that occurred in the earlier case may be helpful in the later case. For example, if a community is planning to build from scratch a good quality university to teach 6000 students, it may well be worthwhile looking at the experiences of those building a similar university in some other state. The times required to recruit suitable faculty; to plan, design, and build the teaching facilities; to order, have delivered, and debug a computer system; and to collect together an adequate library need to be known before the university can fully open its doors. The observed times taken by other new universities would clearly provide valuable information when making forecasts. It is unlikely that the forecasts will be exact because the analogy will not be complete. For example, that other universities have been set up may make the buying of a workable computer system easier but the finding of available back issues of academic journals for the library more difficult. The decision whether a proposed analogy is apt or not has to be subjective. Presumably the lessons learnt in building a new university in an adjacent state will be more appropriate than experiences with building a new hospital locally, for example.

Examples of the use of analogies can be found in the fields of weather and stock market forecasting. In the 1960s, one method used to forecast British weather a month ahead was to compare the current weather map with all previous maps for similar parts of the year, using a computer. If, for example, the map for March 23, 1962, was found to be most similar in appearance to that of April 2, 1953, then the forecast for the month starting March 24, 1962, would be the same as what actually occurred in the month starting April 3, 1953. Experience with this procedure indicated that it is slightly better than choosing at random, which, given the well-known complexity of Britain's weather, is not totally unimpressive. For the stock market, a group of analysts known as chartists plot a stock price index or the price of a particular company's share against time and look for certain patterns. These patterns or shapes are given names such as "head and shoulders," and it is claimed that when such a shape occurs the market index or the price of the share is inclined to go in a specific direction afterwards. The value of this method of forecasting stock market prices is still controversial; there is little evidence that chartists all retire rich, although they may retire somewhat richer than the average speculator.

These are examples of unambitious analogies; the following example is more controversial. Fifteen or so years ago the problem of how to dispose of the incredible amounts of garbage generated by a large city was an important and worrisome one. Advances in technology have now made garbage a desirable product, to produce energy, animal feed, and raw materials. Some cities, in a sense, cannot get enough. Can the same sequence occur with radioactive waste, the disposal of which is causing so much heartache to some governmental agencies now? It might be suggested, from the analogy, that a technology will soon arise which will convert this waste into useful, and safe, materials so that the demand will be for more of it rather than less.

The difficulty in finding reliable analogies is an obvious problem, but in some circumstances use of analogies may enhance the available information set upon which a forecast is made in a useful way. Certainly historians would like this to be generally agreed upon, as it increases the importance and acceptance of their discipline.

### 10.4.2   Precursor Events

The identification of precursor events in a technology and their use for forecasting is similar to the use of leading indicators in time series forecasting, as discussed in Chapter 7. If the introduction of an innovation in one technology or society is frequently signaled by a similar innovation in another technology or society, this observation clearly has forecasting value. Examples would be developments in commercial aircraft design first appearing in military aircraft, developments in transmission, engine, or brake design in family cars first being seen in racing cars, or innovations in marketing usually first appearing in the United States and later occurring in Europe and Australia. Managers and research workers in some areas will usually be aware of such precursor events, but a search for others may sometimes prove worthwhile. One more, the identification of what events are relevant and how the information should be incorporated is generally necessarily very subjective.

### 10.4.3   Scenarios

Starting with some specific situation, such as the observed present, a scenario attempts to set up a logical sequence of events to indicate how some future state or situation can evolve step by step. As alternative developments occur, such as a breakthrough happening early or late, a set of alternative scenarios will usually arise. Thus, in considering future electricity production procedures, a "most probable" scenario might involve phasing out oil, phasing in more coal-burning plants in the short term, building more fission nuclear plants in the middle run, and relying on solar, geothermal, and fusion plants in the longer run. However, alternative and quite different scenarios would result if some states, or the federal government, restricted the building of nuclear plants, if more strigent air-pollution policies limited the use of coal or oil, if Australia decided never to export its large store of uranium, or if a breakthrough occurred in fusion technology and allowed commercial use of this technology in ten year's time. The use of the most probable scenario, or "surprise-free" viewpoint provides a basis against which to compare other alternative scenarios. The primary purpose of these scenarios is not strictly to predict the future but rather to facilitate a systematic exploration of branches or networks of critical events within some explicit time frame. By considering alternative scenarios, governments, states, or companies can devise contingency plans to meet these possible situations. Clearly, more attention will be given to the more probable scenarios, although lower probability but high impact situations should not be ignored in long-range planning.

Scenarios can be prepared either just for specific technologies, such as electricity production, water supply and quality, or military arms development, or for whole societies, such as the Saudi Arabian economy or the whole world. When this is attempted, it is not sufficient simply to run through sequences of possible events for each main part of the society or for each main technology as the interrelation, or cross impacts, of these events also need to be considered. Developments in one field may greatly affects developments in another. For example, it may be thought that the general acceptance of electric automobiles is dependent on the invention of a superior method of storing electricity than is provided by either conventional batteries or their foreseen developments in the shortrun. Thus electricity storage technology affects automobile technology. Similarly, a breakthrough in one field may increase the probabilities of innovative events in other fields. A formal way of proceeding is to attempt to estimate these cross-impact probabilities, using a Delphi procedure perhaps, and then to build scenarios taking these probabilities into account. Use of these ideas, either formally or not, should both increase the plausibility and self-consistency of the resulting scenario and also encourage the inclusion of all the critical and most relevant factors.

Scenarios are sometimes written by individuals, but more recently they have often become team efforts, bringing together opinions of experts in a variety of fields. This is particularly relevant when considering a bundle of alternative scenarios.

## 10.5   EXAMPLES OF SCENARIOS

As an example of scenario construction, consider the following evolution of the labor market in a developed economy. It may be expected that in the next decade there will be increased women's participation in the work force, in that there will be a substantial growth in the proportion of women in the age group 20–60 who earn wages for 20 or more hours per week. The similar proportion for men will decline slightly, but overall the total work force will increase. Relaxation of retirement rules will allow some people to extend their working life by five or so extra years, but many others will decide to retire early, although some of these will eventually attempt second careers. The declining birth rate will lead to a decrease in the number of school leavers entering the work force each year, and this will lead to a lessened seasonal component in the unemployed figures. Overall, there will be an increased demand for jobs. Automation will remove some jobs from the market, but other developments, particularly in the service industries, will create jobs. However, to meet the extra demand for jobs there will be a reduction in the average work week. Employers will find that they are employing more workers but for fewer hours each. Overtime will decline dramatically, and the pattern of hours worked during the day will become more varied.

During the following decade these tendencies will continue, but later retirement will become more common due to decreasing social security retirement benefits and improvements in health of the older sections of the work force. The money available for social security has been a continuing problem because of the general aging of the population, although it will be considerably alleviated by the increasing women's participation rate. Married couples both of whom are eligible for retirement benefits will observe that their combined benefits are less than that of two single persons, as the government relies on the "two can live as cheaply as one" adage. Consequently, the number of divorces involving couples in the 50–70 age group will increase considerably. Very much more attention will be paid to the legal problems of "common-law marriages," and, due to continuing changes both in the law and in attitudes, marriage rates will decline for all age groups. Partly as a consequence of this development, birth rates will decline further and many teachers will be required to retire early.

This is not intended to be a forecast of what will occur. It does emphasize some of the factors that will be important, such as women's participation rates, retirement, automation, birth rates, length of work week, and so forth. By making different assumptions about these factors, different scenarios result. If one is an administrator concerned with social security, for instance, the implications of these various scenarios should be of the greatest importance. The administrator would also require that the probability of its actually occurring be attached to each alternative scenario. This could either be his own subjective probability or could be obtained by using a Delphi-type panel.

A second and more carefully constructed example of a set of scenarios is that discussed by Herman Kahn (1976). Over period as long as 200 years, the important issues include population growth, the availability of scarce resources, economic growth, and the effects of technological innovations. Two extreme viewpoints are called the *neo-Malthusian* and the *technology-and-growth* positions. The first is a modern version of Malthus' argument that population will eventually grow faster than food supply, with consequent starvation for the poor. The opposite view is that technological developments will meet all needs, population will be controlled, the more advanced nations will develop superindustrial and then postindustrial economies, and the rest of the world will not be far behind. Two alternative versions of each of these viewpoints may be taken, the position of

A   the strong neo-Malthusian,
B   the moderate neo-Malthusian or guarded pessimist,
C   the guarded optimist, or
D   the technology and growth enthusiast.

These viewpoints provide the following alternative bases around which scenarios could be constructed

### 10.5.1   The Strong Neo-Malthusian

(i)   There is a finite pie of nonrenewable resources to be divided up. These resources will reach critical levels within 50 years. Any economic growth that makes the rich richer can only make the poor poorer.

(ii)   The effect of technology and capital is largely illusory and counterproductive. Proposed technological solutions to problems of pollution or scarce resources are shortsighted illusions that only compound the difficulties. Any future economic development should be restricted to the Third World.

(iii)   In management and decision making, failure is almost certain. The complexities, rigidities, and ideological differences among nations and their institutions make it inconceivable that present human organizations, even with computer assistance, could sufficiently comprehend and effectively act to solve our most important problems. More emphasis is needed on the community and regional level, much less on big business, big government, and big organizations generally.

(iv)   There is a steady depletion of resources, including foods, fuels, and minerals. All signs point to catastrophe for the medium- and long-term future.

(v)   Current growth is carcinogenic. Current population and economic production are akin to a spreading cancer. They are already more than the earth can sustain in a steady state. Future economic or population growth will hasten and increase the magnitude of the future tragedy.

(vi)   New discoveries of resources, new technologies, and new projects may postpone the immediate need for drastic actions but not for long. The postponement could make the eventual collapse more severe.

(vii)   Income gaps and poverty will grow worse.

(viii)   Industrialization of the Third World would be a disaster and further growth of the developed world even worse.

(ix)   The quality of life has already been ruined, particularly in the developed nations.

(x)   The long-range outlook is bleak and desperate. Grave and even draconian measures are justified now to alleviate the extent and intensity of the future collapse.


## 10.5.2   The Guarded Pessimist

(i)   The future supply and value of both old and new materials are necessarily uncertain. Prudence requires immediate conservation of remaining resources.

(ii)   Despite some exceptions, the future will generally bring diminishing marginal returns from new investments, and the effort required for economic gains will increase dramatically. Until practical solutions to the problems of pollutions and shortages appear, we must turn away from technology and investment.

(iii)   There will be a likely failure in attempts to manage resources, control pollution, and resolve social conflicts due to the increasing complexity of these problems.

(iv)   The basic problem of limited resources may be insoluble, and so a more cautious approach to growth seems clearly desirable.

(v)   There is a large potential for disaster in growth. Because of rapidly increasing population, even current levels of production must lead to exhausted resources and hazardous pollution. Few positive human values would be served by continued mindless growth.

(vi)   Innovation and discovery will become increasingly ineffective. The basic solution is to limit demand rather than encourage a desperate search for new inventions, which could make basic problem even worse in long-run.

(vii)   Income gaps and poverty are increasing and could become threatening. A more equitable income distribution has become an urgent matter.

(viii)   Undeveloped nations would be better off preserving their cultural, environmental, and ecological values rather than entering headlong into industrial development.

(ix)   The quality of life is in conflict with much growth.

(x)   The long-run outlook is of contingent disaster. Although it is not possible to predict which disaster is most imminent, many possibilities exist even if we are careful and prudent today. Drastic actions should be taken soon to manage our resources and population more prudently.

### 10.5.3   The Guarded Optimist

(i)   There is a growing pie to be shared out due to increased productivity. Progress in one region encourages similar developments elsewhere; thus as the rich get richer the poor also benefit. Some caution with regard to growth is necessary in selected areas.

(ii)   Despite some dangers, only new technology and capital investment can increase production, protect and improve the environment, hold down the cost of energy, minerals, and food, and provide economic surpluses with which to improve living standards in the less developed countries. We must be alert for problems resulting from inadequately understood innovations, inappropriate growth, and natural causes.

(iii)   Decision making should be fairly successful. Normal economic mechanisms can make most private organizations adequately responsive to most problems.

(iv)   Resources should generally be sufficient. Given slow but steady technological and economic progress and an ultimate world population below 30 billion, it should be feasible to attain economic living standards markedly better than current ones.

(v)   Concerning growth, we are on a probable transition to stability. There will be enough energy, resources, and space for a stable population to occur at a better standard of living provided that a relatively small number of people put forth the necessary efforts and others do not interfere.

(vi)   Innovation and discovery are usually effective, do help solve current problems, although sometimes creating new ones, and provide some insurance against bad luck or incompetency.

(vii)   The threat of worldwide absolute poverty and starvation is likely soon to be forever abolished. Some income gaps will increase and others decrease, but both rich and poor will have increased real income.

(viii)   Industrialization of the less developed countries should and will continue, technical assistance being provided by the rich nations.

(ix)   There will be more gains than losses in the quality of life, particularly in terms of the environment, health, and safety.

(x)   The long-range outlook is a contingent success, the ultimate prospect being far superior to a world of poverty and scarcity.

### 10.5.4   The Technology and Growth Enthusiast

(i)   The important resources are capital, technology, and educated people and there are no meaningful limits to growth in sight. The perennial doomsayers have always been scandalously wrong.

(ii)   Technology and capital can solve almost all problems. Some current problems have resulted from careless application of technology, but none are without remedy. It is not paradoxical that the technology which has caused some problems can also solve them; it just requires mankind's attention and desire. The eventual colonization of the solar system will provide virtually unlimited living space.

(iii)   Decision making is not a serious problem. We flatter ourselves that current issues are more important and difficult than ever: Actually there is nothing very special happening.

(iv)   The earth is essentially bountiful in all of the important resources. Trust in the economics of the market system and have confidence in emerging technological solutions.

(v)   Growth is desirable and healthy and no obvious limits are apparent. Even with current technological potential, growth (except perhaps in a few of the poorest nations) is and will be purely a matter of human choice, not of natural limitations. Problems always exist but solutions always emerge, often as a result of the dynamism of growth.

(vi)   Innovation and discovery are mankind's greatest hope and man is now entering the most creative and expansive period of his history.

(vii)   Income gaps and poverty are a misformulated problem. All countries can expect to become wealthy in the next 200 years and income gap is a false issue, some inequalities being inevitable in a dynamic society.

(viii)   Industrial development is necessary for wealth and progress.

(ix)   The quality of life is a meaningless phrase and issue.

(x)   The long-range outlook is one of high optimism and confidence. Mankind's ultimate goals cannot be known, but they include a solar civilization and a utopian notion of the quality of life on earth.

None of these viewpoints is strictly a scenario as it stands, as they need fleshing out with specific sequences of events. For example, the following scenario presented by Kahn corresponds approximately to the Guarded Optimist viewpoint. In this scenario a superindustrial economy is one whose enterprises are extraordinarily large, encompassing, and pervasive forces in both the physical and societal environments; a postindustrial economy is one in which the task of producing the necessities of life has become trivially easy because of technological advancement and economic development.

1956–1995. Four decades of worldwide and rapid economic and population growth; the initial emergence of a superindustrial economy, technological crises, and many other transitions, e.g., inflection points in world population and possibly also gross product curves—a decline in the rate of growth. In 1996 there are 4.1 billion people, and the Gross World Product (GWP) is $5.5 trillion, corresponding to an annual income of $1300 per capita. The first steps into space.

*1996–2025.* Another three decades for the initial emergence of postindustrial economies in European and non-Communist Sinic cultures, perhaps also in the Soviet Union. The full development of superindustrial societies and cultures in advanced countries. The first serious move to colonize space. A Gross World Product per capita of $2500.

*2026–2175.* 150 years for the emergence of postindustrial economies almost everywhere on earth. Possibly the establishment of an independent dynamic solar system society. By 2175 world population at 15 billion people (with a likely range of 7.5–30 billion), a per capita Gross World Product of $20,000 (range $7000–$60,000), and GWP at $300 trillion, give or take a factor of 5.

If this becomes true, prospects for mankind will be encouraging, to say the least. Again, it must be emphasized that this is a scenario and not a forecast, since it is designed to illustrate a possible future, to awaken minds to these possibilities, and to point out some bottlenecks that could occur in the future to delay mankind's objectives. Scenarios could be argued to be unscientific in that they are likely to deal in generalities without working out all the detailed implications. An approach that is in some sense more scientific is considered in the next chapter.

## APPENDIX: SOME PROBABLE AND POSSIBLE SCIENTIFIC INNOVATIONS

The following are just a few of the expected or possible scientific and sociological changes that we can look for over the next 20–40 years:

1. Improved superperformance fabrics.
2. Major reduction in hereditary and congenital defects.
3. Effective appetite and weight control. Nonabsorbable sugar achieved by molecule alteration.
4. New and useful plant and animal species.
5. Nuclear reactors that cannot be used for the manufacture of atomic weapons.
6. Three-dimensional photography, movies, and television.
7. Electrical transmission of newspapers.
8. Substantial decrease in hours spent sleeping due to controlled relaxation.
9. Cheap and widely available major war weapons and systems.
10. Drugs to permanently raise the level of human and animal intelligence.
11. Ability to choose sex of unborn children.
12. Semiautomation of repairs.
13. Physically nonharmful methods of overindulging.
14. Chemical alteration of personality, applied to convicted criminals.
15. Extensive use of robots in the house.
16. Photon rockets.
17. Chemical methods for improving memory and learning.
18. International citizens.
19. New methods for rapid language teaching.
20. Home computers to run finances, to plan meals, and to communicate with the outside world.
21. Synthetic blood substitute.
22. Electrical control of pain.
23. Electronic sensors provide artificial "eyesight" for the blind.
24. Artificial growth of new limbs and organs.
25. Long-term suspended animation.
26. Automated highways.

A few very unlikely developments are

1. Antigravity transportation systems.
2. Compulsory genetic manipulation to improve the quality of the human race.
3. Practical and routine use of extrasensory phenomena.
4. Lifetime immunization against practically all diseases.
5. Interstellar travel.

## QUESTIONS

1.  A large soap manufacturer is worried by the rumor that a new type of shower is being investigated that uses low frequency vibrations. It is thought that the new technique could completely clean the occupant of the shower without the use of any soap or water. How would you try to investigate for the manufacturer the timing of the introduction and potential success of this invention?

2.  A manufacturer of an electric automobile, for purposes of future planning and design, would like an estimate of when a battery will be available with twice the present capacity, in terms of the amount of electricity stored, and at a quarter of the present size. Describe ways in which he can obtain such an estimate. Also discuss briefly the factors he should consider when trying to forecast sales for an automobile using such a battery.

3.  "The future of a society, an economy or a firm is too dependent on the decisions and desires of real individuals for a mechanical model based on mathematics, statistics, or computer simulation to be able to provide adequate forecasts. A clearly superior strategy is to base forecasts on mental modeling, analogies, opinions, expectations, anticipations, and rational thought." Comment.

4.  Because of the fast growth of knowledge in most academic subjects, a consultant's report suggests that all university degrees should lapse after ten years, to be renewed if a further six-months study at a university is undertaken. A university wants to study when such a scheme may be instituted and what the effect would be on its student numbers in future years. Discuss how you would provide forecasts for the university.

5.  Write three alternative scenarios about how your local community might look in twenty years time, including a wild one of the "gold discovered in Central Park" variety.

6.  Consider your favorite sport. Write a scenario about how it could change or develop over the next 30 years, considering the effects of new rules and new technological developments from the viewpoint of both the players and the spectators.

7.  Write a criticism of the following scenario:

    In the mid-1980s the governments of both Britain and the United States, consisting largely of those who had been radicals in the 1960s, become particularly sympathetic to the masses of the world who are starving. Consequently, they decide to try to increase agricultural production in their countries. One aspect of this policy is a new law which prevents any land currently used for agriculture or forestry to be converted to any other use. There follows a decline in the construction of new houses and a sharp increase in housing prices. Old houses are pulled down in groups and replaced by high rise apartment buildings. The higher population concentration in cities leads to increases in pollution and crime. The new law also means that many speculator farmers who own land on the outskirts of cities are replaced by real, and more efficient, farmers. This leads to an increase in food production, which results in lower food prices. Americans begin to eat more and this leads to increases in deaths due to heart and blood circulation problems.

## FURTHER READINGS

Gabor, D. (1963). *Inventing the Future*, London: Secker and Warburg.
Kahn, H. (1976). *The Next 200 Years: A Scenario for America and the World*, New York: Morrow.
Kahn, H., and A. J. Wiener (1967). *The Year 2000*, New York: MacMillan.
Martino, J. P. (1972). *Technological Forecasting for Decision Making*, New York: Amer. Elsevier.

# 11

# World Models

This is the first age that's ever paid much attention to the future, which is a little ironic since we may not have one.

Arthur C. Clarke

The problem is not whether you can see the handwriting on the wall, but whether you can read it.

Evan Esar

## 11.1  INTRODUCING WORLD MODELS

For some years now there have existed models of the economy of a single nation, the econometric models discussed in chapter 5, and more recently these national models have been linked together to form an international model, called LINK. Although important difficulties have been encountered, both in model specification and in estimation, worthwhile progress has been achieved. A considerably more ambitious project involves modeling not merely the world's economy but all of the major variables of world society, including wealth, population, pollution, food, and resources. The first serious project of this kind originated with Jay Forrester (1971) at MIT and produced a sequence of models of increasing complexity culminating in WORLD 2 and WORLD 3. Part of this work was sponsored by an organization known as the Club of Rome. The models have become known under various names, including that of the sponsors, Limits to Growth, and World Dynamics. The modelers included several control engineers, and this fact has effected both the approach used in forming the model and the language describing it. The goals were described in one account by the modelers in the following terms,

Every physical quantity growing in a finite space must eventually exhibit one of three basic behavior modes: a smooth transition to a steady state, oscillation around an equilibrium position, or overshoot and decline. The WORLD 3 model was designed to investigate which of these behavior modes is most likely to characterize the evolution of population and capital on this finite earth and to identify the policies that would increase the probability of an orderly transition to global equilibrium.

In forming the model, emphasis is placed on the interrelationship between the major variables. The world society is considered to be a closed system, so that feedback relationships can be found between many variables. For example, the rate of increase of population could depend on pollution levels, but pollution depends on production and production on population. The main feedback loops of the two WORLD models are shown in Fig. 11.1. The boxes represent the main subsystems of the world system. The arrows show the assumed causal links between them, and the broken arrows show links included only in WORLD 3. Some of the causal relationships are positive, so that an increase in capital investment leads to increased living standards and an assumed increase in population, and some are negative so that pollution leads to a reduction in population. The relationships may involve lags and many are taken to be nonlinear. Each of the main subsystems of population, pollution, geographic space, agriculture, nonrenewable natural resources, and capital investment are modeled separately and may involve several variables. The following are the main assumptions in each of the subsections:

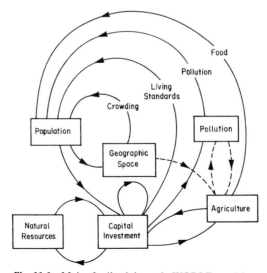

*Fig. 11.1*   Major feedback loops in WORLD models.

(i) Nonrenewable resources. On aggregate, the world has a 250 years supply of minerals, at current consumption rates, the minerals are perfectly substitutable, and the economic cost of exploiting the remaining deposits will increase significantly.

(ii) Population. The difference between birth and death rates is negative for low per capita nonfood consumption, increases as consumption increases, and becomes positive just below 1970 world average levels.

(iii) The agricultural subsystem. Food is produced from arable land and agricultural inputs, such as fertilizer and seed; food output increases as these inputs increase, but there are decreasing returns; newly developed land is expensive to obtain but enters at the current average land fertility; arable land erodes due to intense cultivation; capital-intensive use of land leads to persistent pollution of the land; land yield is reduced by air pollution; and arable land disappears when built upon, a process occurring more rapidly as wealth increases.

(iv) Capital and industrial output. The average life of industrial capital now and for an indefinite period is assumed to be a constant, 14 years; the industrial capital output ratio is a constant with a value of 3 and diminishing returns will not affect investment in the industrial sector; finally, the marginal utility of food and services as a fraction of industrial output is also a constant and does not change over time.

(v) Pollution. The generation of persistent pollution is the result of industrial and agricultural activities: There exists a delay between the time a persistent pollutant is generated and the time it appears as a harmful substance; the time required to absorb a unit of pollution increases as the total level of pollution increases.

An example of the type of equation found in the model is

Change in population = [(birth rate) − (death rate)] × (present population)

where both birth and death rates are specific, nonlinear functions of material standard of living (nonfood consumption per capita), food production per capita, population density, and level of pollution. The forms of the relationships are not estimated directly from data but are selected subjectively both so that the views of the modelers are represented and so that if the model is run using starting-up values for 1900, the plots of the variables fit adequately well to what actually occurred from 1900 to 1970. Once the full set of equations has been set up, the starting-up values can be inserted and the "standard run" of the model is then observed, in which it is assumed that no changes in the equations occur in the future. The conclusions from the standard run of WORLD 3 suggest that population will rise to a peak of perhaps six billion in the year 2020 and will thereafter decline. This decline in population is caused

by falling natural resources, which become increasingly more costly to extract
as their quantity declines. This means that more capital has to be allocated to
extraction of natural resources and less is then available to industrial output
and food. Thus, both industrial output per capita and food per capita reach
peaks at about 2000 and decline rapidly thereafter. Pollution levels increase
steadily until just before the year 2000 A.D. They then increase dramatically to
very high levels until about 2040, when they start to decline. By the year 2100,
industrial output and food per capita will be below 1900 levels, but population level will be much higher as pollution and natural resources will be only
about 20% of 1900 values. The plot of the **WORLD** 3 standard run is shown
in Fig. 11.2. The reasons for this prediction of world cataclysm from the
model are easily found. It is assumed that, if left unchecked, population and
capital levels will increase exponentially. However, such growth cannot occur
because of the finiteness of the earth and its resources, the impossibility of
providing enough food for the people and enough materials for the industrial
processes, even if the latter are run cheaply by ignoring pollution problems.

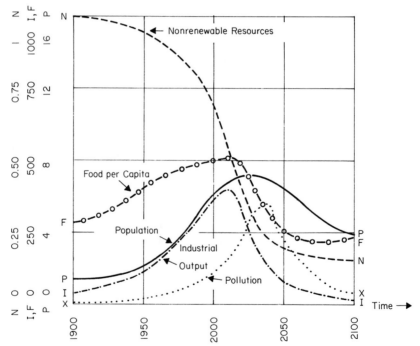

**Fig. 11.2**  Standard forecasts from WORLD model. *N*, nonrenewable resources (fraction
remaining); *F*, food per capita; *P*, population (billions); *I*, industrial output per capita; *X*,
persistent pollution.

The physical limitations will constrain the exponential growth curves and, when the crunch does eventually occur, the controls on society act with such lags and inefficiency that production, for example, does not simply level off but actually crashes down from its peak value. If the assumptions about exponential growth in population and consumption are allowed to stand, it is easily shown from the model that a very similar scenario occurs, at only a slightly later date, if the assumed amount of available nonrenewable resources is dramatically increased or if some recycling of these resources is allowed. In general, the predictions from the model, all of which are strictly conditional forecasts, are very depressing and suggest that the human race as a whole is facing a desperate situation in the early part of the next century.

To prevent the predicted catastrophy, the model suggests that population control by itself may not be sufficient and that natural resource usage rate, pollution generation, food production, and gross investment will also have to be drastically reduced for a "global equilibrium" to be achieved.

## 11.2   EVALUATION

As might be expected the scientific community at large was hardly enthusiastic about the prediction of a doomsday so near in the future. There was an immediate dislike to the conditions of the model and the reality of its basic assumptions was attacked. There followed more careful analysis of the most important assumed feedback relationships, and some were found to be contrary to some empirical evidence or to modern theory. Finally, the whole system was run using rather different formulations to test the stability of its conclusions. Of course, the major problem with such models is to know how to evaluate them. An obvious start is to ask how realistic the assumptions are, how well it fits known data, and how sensible are the forecasts it makes. The economists, and particularly the econometricians, were most disturbed by the specification of the model and of the way it had been constructed. The fact that parameters had not been formally estimated from data was severely criticized, and the quality of the models was hardly enhanced by the remark by the original modelers that only 0.1% of the data necessary to build such a model from fact was actually available. The econometricians were also unimpressed by the size of even WORLD 3, which appeared very complex to the laymen, politicians, and media and yet only consisted of less than 50 equations, all of which were assumed to hold without error. It was argued that if it requires over 200 equations to properly model the economy of a single nation, it can hardly be possible to capture the true nature of the whole world society with just a few equations. The economists also found fault with the economic laws being called upon in the model. No price system was used to allocate resources and capital investment occurs in the model in a rather unconvincing fashion totally unrelated to potential rates of return. The implicit production function in the WORLD 2 model also had strange properties. It had a form such that if one were making pig iron and doubled both the number of blast furnaces and the number of ore fields, then the amount of pig iron produced would quadruple. Most economists would guess that in such circumstances, pig iron production would approximately double. The importance of this assumption is seen by noting that in the critical parts of the model forecasting period the above example is run backwards, so that a halving of both capital and resources divides output by 4. This pessimistic assumption obviously makes the system grind to a halt rather quickly.

One other important equation in WORLD 2 received a great deal of attention. It was assumed that as consumption per capita increased, so did the difference between birth and death rates and, conversely, as consumption decreased this difference also automatically declined. As was suggested in Chapter 9, the relationship between birth rate and the economy is by no means determined and is probably not a stable one. In any case, looking at current figures for birth rates in developed and undeveloped countries does not support the WORLD 2 assumed relationship. Some of these criticisms were partially met by altered specifications in WORLD 3 but many parts of the model remained controversial.

The results of running the models with different specifications did not resolve the question of their quality. Some workers found that the assumptions could be altered considerably without changing the conclusions appreciably. Others found the results much less stable, particularly if it is assumed that resources are recycled, population is controlled, and sufficient technological progress is introduced, the doomsday then postponed indefinitely. One group ran the model backward from 1900 and found that population should have been considerably higher in 1880 than it actually was, so that the model exploded when run in the reverse direction. There is considerable controversy about the appropriateness of such a test. It is certainly true that econometric models have not been subjected to such tests.

It soon became clear that most research workers who carefully investigated the MIT models found them flawed, and some highly critical remarks surfaced, such as "Malthus in, Malthus out," "Malthus with a computer," and the comment that the models are "bad science and therefore bad guides to public policy." In fact so one-sided did the discussion become that it turned from criticism of the actual models to worrying about whether it is even worthwhile trying to build quantitative models of world society. The discussion was not decisive but the most influential contestants supported the idea of attempting to construct such models. Even if the predictions made by the WORLD models are not accepted as being particularly realistic, the models have certainly forced consideration of the most important problems facing mankind. The more thought given to the problems of overpopulation, food and space shortages, and the repletion of resources, the more chance there is of reducing the impact of these problems in the future. The MIT experience has emphasized both these questions and the difficulties that will be encountered when worldwide models are attempted. The main difficulties are lack of knowledge about important social and demographic relationships, such as that between birth rate and the growth of the economy, and the problem of forecasting technological innovation and development, as has been emphasized in the previous two chapters. These difficulties will certainly not prevent other models being constructed and, one hopes, as knowledge is accumulated those models will evolve towards one that will provide both convincing forecasts and also useful policy suggestions.

## 11.3 FOOD FOR A DOUBLING WORLD POPULATION

The advent of the WORLD models has stimulated other models with wide scope. An example of a model that is less ambitious than those discussed in the previous two sections but which may well have greater impact is MOIRA—a Model of International Relations in Agriculture. It uses economic theory, plus some statistical modeling, to examine the effects of food production and of a doubling of world population over the period 1975–2010 and also to investigate what can be done to mitigate the problems that will obviously arise. It is based on such facts as that the industrialized nations have under 30% of world population but consume over half of the world's food supply, so that in the developing nations over 70% of the world's population have to survive on under half of the available food. Those that starve, or survive but are greatly undernourished, do so because they cannot afford food, not because it is not potentially available for them. Currently, there is sufficient food for everyone at an acceptable level if only it were distributed evenly. It has also been estimated that if all potentially productive land throughout the world were used in the most efficient manner possible, food production could reach 25 *times* present levels. Although such an increase could only be realized by considerable planning and huge inputs of capital, both physical and human, such figures do suggest that the population of the world should not face starvation problems due to an inability to produce food. The ability of most of the world to be able to pay enough to persuade farmers to produce the required food is a much bigger problem and is the main question that **MOIRA** investigates.

To simplify the situation, the model considers just consumable protein derived from vegetables, so that raising cattle is considered a protein loss or inefficiency in the production system. The world is divided into 106 geographic units but the results are then aggregated and presented for just ten world regions. Each unit is divided into twelve income classes, six in the agricultural sector and six in nonagriculture. The behavior of the food consumers are described in terms of a consumption function, so that demand for food is explained in terms of income and food price levels. The socialist block of countries is assumed to be neutral with regard to imports and exports. The exogenous variables, determined outside the system, are economic growth in the nonagricultural sector, population increase, income distribution within geographical units, and prices of agricultural inputs, such as fertilizers.

Assuming that population doubles over the period considered, that is, each region's population continues to grow at current rates and that there is also a steady growth in nonagricultural production, the model suggests that, while there will be the obvious increase in demand for food, production will not increase sufficiently to meet this demand, and so a relative scarcity will develop, driving up prices to two-and-one-half times as high in real terms by 2010. During this period the number of people who have less than the minimum necessary amount of food for a healthy life will quadruple to 1.5 billion—almost a quarter of the world's population. Members of the nonagricultural sector will be particularly affected. These consequences contrast with those for the wealthy countries, where food consumption per capita will increase, widening the present gap in standard of living between the countries that have and those that have not.

If nonagricultural production increases at a slower rate than assumed in the above scenario, **MOIRA** suggests that food production will double along with the population, but the number starving will also increase because of the assumed rigid income distribution.

The objective in building such models is not really to make forecasts but to check out the effects of alternative policies that might be attempted to alleviate the world's food shortage problems. A number of policies are considered, including measures to achieve redistribution of the available food in the world, such as a decrease in food consumption by the wealthy countries, food purchases by an international food aid organization financed by the wealthy countries which would distribute this food to the underfed population groups, measures to control world food prices, and measures intended to stimulate food production in the developing countries. These policy measures were first considered individually and then in combinations. If applied individually, a reduction in food consumption by wealthy countries has bad effects on total food production due to reduction of demand, but an aid program has great temporary benefits, although in the long term it may not encourage sufficient development in food production in the poorer countries. Stabilization of the world market price at a relatively high level does enable a gradual improvement of the food supply per capita of poor countries, but the extent of hunger is not very sensitive to such a policy. Regulation of the world market does not render food aid unnecessary, but seems to be better than a complete liberalization of international trade in basic foods, since in this latter case food production in the developing countries will grow more slowly than if policies remain unchanged. The most effective policy is to encourage more efficient food production throughout the world, so that the wealthy countries should provide suitable encouragement in terms of capital inputs, research, and know-how, combined with some price maintenance and food aid in the early part of the period. If the model is correct such a policy, together with further attempts to control population growth, should reduce the problem of undernourishment of a large proportion of the world's population, although part of the problem will remain.

MOIRA can be criticized in various ways, particularly for some of the assumptions made, but initial reaction to the model is that it is basically sound and the doubtful assumptions are not of considerable importance and can be fairly easily circumvented in later, improved versions of the model. It seems very likely that models of this kind will eventually have considerable impact on the form of international agreements and therefore be highly relevant for long-term forecasting.

## FURTHER READINGS

Bruckman, G. (1976). "A Pre-evaluation of Moira," *Technological Forecasting and Social Change* 10, 21–26.

De Hoogh, J. *et al.* (1976). "Food for a Growing World Population," *Technological Forecasting and Social Change* 10, 27–51.

Forrester, Jay W. (1971). *World Dynamics*, Cambridge, Massachusetts: Wright-Allen Press.

Meadows, D. H. *et al.* (1972). *The Limits to Growth*, New York: New Amer. Library.

Meadows, D. H. *et al.* (1974). *Dynamics of Growth in a Finite World*, Cambridge, Massachusetts: MIT Press.

Semitechnical and detailed accounts of the world dynamics models.

Nordhaus, W. D. (1973). "World Dynamics: Measurement without Data," *Economic Journal* 83, 1156–1183.

Severe criticism of the economic content of the models.

Sussex Science Policy Research Unit (1973). "Malthus with a Computer," and other chapters, *Futures*, Volume 5.

Wide ranging criticism of many aspects of the models.

# 12

# Techniques Old and New

I always avoid prophesying beforehand because it is much better to prophesy after the event has already taken place.

Winston Churchill

Prophesy is a good line of business, but it is full of risks.

Mark Twain in *Following the Equator*

## 12.1   FORECASTS FROM THE PAST

It has probably always been realized that the person who can somewhat predict what is about to occur will have an advantage over those who cannot correctly forecast. Examples of these forecasts, or prophecies, are found in written records from the earliest times. Probably any intelligent person can provide forecasts of some quality, but in an attempt to get a further edge some very curious information sets have been utilized. The haruspex looked into animal's entrails, the palmist at hands, and the astologer at the stars. Other methods have included cartomancy, using playing cards or the more powerful Tarots; numerology, which manipulates numbers, letters, and words; crystallomancy, whose proponent goes into a trance and looks into a crystal ball; geomancy, done by throwing dice, small bones coins, match sticks, or dominos; and taseology, which uses tea leaves, coffee grounds, or even sand or pebbles. Spiritualists have used various mediums, such as a planchette or ouija board, while others have looked into ancient books, such as *I Ching* or the *Bible*, or even at the pyramids. Such methods of sirying not only are from the past, but are arts still practiced and apparently still believed in. Many people believe those techniques are merely superstitious mumbo jumbo, while others plead that such judgments should not be made without a proper attempt at evaluation. Astrologers, for example, point out that a study made by Gauquelin in 1966 of 25,000 prominent citizens of Western Europoean countries found that significant numbers of scientists, doctors, atheletes, and executives were born during the rising and setting of Mars and extra politicians and writers during the moon period. They ask if it is merely coincidence that two Nobel prize winning physicists, Albert Einstein and Otto Hahn, were both born on the 14th of March 1879, that two similar Irish writers, James Stephen and James Joyce, were both born at 6:00 A.M. on the 2nd of February 1892, and that two of the New York Metropolitan's famous tenors, Beniamino Gigli and Lauritz Melchior, were both born on the 20th of March 1890. There is ample evidence that one's birthdate partly determines a person's academic achievements, since a class will include students with almost a whole year's difference in maturity. A somewhat different example comes from the observation that during the Vietnam war men born earlier in the year had almost twice the probability of being drafted than those born later in the year, due presumably to an error in the selection procedure. Whether or not such facts are sufficient for an approach such as astrology to be taken seriously has to be a personal judgment. The majority of those taking a scientific approach appear not to be convinced. To properly evaluate any such technique a correctly designed experiment needs to be conducted in which a sequence of forecasts is made, measured against what actually occurs and compared with forecasts from other techniques, if possible. This is rarely attempted.

The accumulated prophecies from the past do appear to give us plenty to evaluate. Some of the prophecies made are quite impressive. For example, Mother Shipton of Knaresborough, in England, was apparently making prophecies in the early fifteenth century, and her work was certainly known by 1641. One of her more famous pieces goes

Carriages without horses shall go
And accidents fill the world with woe.
Around the earth thoughts shall fly
In the twinkling of an eye.
The world upside down shall be
And gold be found at the root of a tree.
Through hills man shall ride
And no horse be at his side.
Under water men shall walk,
Shall ride, shall sleep, shall talk.
In the air men shall be seen
In white, in black, in green.
Iron in the water shall float

As easily as a wooden boat.
Gold shall be found and shown
In a land that's not now known.
Fire and water shall wonders do,
England shall at last admit a foe.
The world to an end shall come
In eighteen hundred and eighty-one.

Apart from the final lines, where she becomes more specific about timing, the statements are fairly unambiguous and could apply to the early twentieth century.

A second famous piece by Mother Shipton has

Over a wild and stormy sea
Shall a noble sail,
Who to find, will not fail
A new and fair countree
From whence he will bring
A herb and a root
That all men shall suit
And please both the ploughman and king,
And let them take no more than measure
Both shall have the even pleasure
In the belly and the brain.

It is easy to associate "a noble" with Sir Walter Raleigh, the country with America, the "herb" with tobacco, and the "root" as the potato.

Most of the famous forecast producers are much less easily interpreted. The sayings of the oracle at Delphi are famous for their ambiguity. The most famous and prolific prophet was probably Nostradamus. He was born in St. Remy, France, in 1503, and produced hundreds of prophetic quatrains in his 63 years. Books are still continually being produced attempting to interpret the statements. The interpretations given often reflect the interpreter's own background. For instance, in a book published in the United States the quatrain

The populous places shall be deserted
A great division to obtain fields
Kingdoms given to prudent incapable
When the great brothers shall die by dissension

is thought to refer to the Civil War in the United States, while writers in other countries could think that it refers to their own civil wars. Nostradamus seems to be frequently concerned with wars, plagues, fires, and other unpleasant events, and he is very rarely specific about when these events are to occur. An exception is the statement that "In the year 1999 and seven months, from the skies shall come an alarmingly powerful kind," which is certainly precise enough. A "forecast" that some event will occur, but at a totally unspecific time is of very little value. If one adds difficulty in interpreting exactly what the forecast means, the value is reduced even further. These difficulties are found in most of the ancient prophecies, which makes their evaluation so difficult. Further, only the apparently more significant or successful prophecies have been remembered and the rest have been forgotten and discarded. This bias has to be remembered when an apparently impressive example from the past is presented. In more modern terminology, it is unclear if the prophecies are actually forecasts or merely scenarios.

There are plenty of examples of specific forecasts made in the distant past which are now easily evaluated and there are plenty of examples of very unsuccessful predictions, including one by an Astronomer Royal that space travel is impossible made just a few years before the first moon walk, or older ones that humans could never survive speeds of greater than 25 miles per hour, which was a concern before the first passenger trains started to run. Other forgettable forecasts include that by the historian Henry Adams made in 1903, fixing "1950 as the year when the world must go smash," and a statement in the 1899 Literary Digest that the automobile or horseless carriage "is at present a luxury for the wealthy: and although its price will probably fall in the future, it will never come into as common use as the bicycle," an error compounded in 1902 by Harpers Weekly in saying that "the actual building of roads devoted to motor cars is not for the near future, in spite of many rumors to that effect." It is natural to wonder which of the futuristic statements being made currently will provide similar examples of totally incorrect forecasts in a text written 50 years hence.

Finally, it might be noted that many of the techniques developed for forecasting can equally well be used for backcasting, that is, for estimating the state of the world before the earliest data in the information set. One of the most famous backcasts, and certainly the most precise, was the estimate made by Archbishop James Ussher, a seventeenth century Irish churchman, who after studying the Bible decided that the earth was created in 4004 B.C., on Sunday, October 23rd at 9:00 A.M. More recent estimates put the creation at least four billion years earlier, which suggests the Archbishop produced a forecast error of record size.

## 12.2  CHOOSING METHODS

The preceding chapters have introduced a variety of forecasting methods, usually the best known and most respected. There are plenty of methods that have not been discussed and new ones are being proposed regularly. These alternatives range from the highly sophisticated to the very unsophisticated, from the sublime to the ridiculous. An example of a method at one of these extremes is known as the "one-percent method." Suppose that you want to forecast the GNP of Mexico but find the task difficult. The one-percent method suggests that you find a component of the variable that represents about 1% of the total and which is fairly easy to forecast, then make a forecast of this component, and finally, multiply your forecast by 100 to get a forecast value for the whole variable. There has been no serious attempt to evaluate this procedure, but its quality can be anticipated. Some other methods are based on more sophisticated statistical or economic techniques, such as Markov chain models or input–output matrices. The first of these is most relevant for event forecasting and is analogous to using an AR(1) model, while the second may be thought of as an alternative to econometric modeling, as it does interrelate various sectors of the economy, though generally ignoring many important sectors, such as the financial and monetary, and using few, if any, lags.

The three main current or likely developments, with clear potential for producing improvements in forecasts, are the following:

(i) Multivariate generalizations of the Box–Jenkins type of statistical modeling described in Chapter 3, using just the data to pick a model rather than some causal theory, such as would be provided by an economist. Automated methods are already being introduced as commercial services to build univariate ARIMA models, and doubtless these will be generalized to deal with two or a few series. Other methods of dealing with several series try to simplify the situation by representing these series in terms of just a few others, using procedures such as principal components and factor analysis.

(ii) Nonlinear statistical models, both univariate and multivariate. The real world is almost certainly nonlinear and so one would expect nonlinear models to be necessary to properly model it. One problem is that the class of nonlinear models is immense, but for analysis, or identification, of a model a limited class is required. A class which involves a certain amount of non-linearity, but is capable of analysis and has been shown to produce improved forecasts on occasion, is that of the bilinear models, an example of which is a series generated by

$$x_t = \varepsilon_t + a\varepsilon_{t-1}x_{t-2}.$$

One surprising feature of some model of this class, including the example just given, is that they identify as white noise, using the methods discussed in Chapter 3, and yet they are forecastable from their own past, although in a nonlinear manner.

(iii) Changing parameter models. The models discussed in earlier chapters generally assume that the parameters do not change through time, which means that the series are stationary. In the real world, an assumption of stationarity is unlikely to be true: Relationships between variables change over time and parameters will probably change. If they change slowly, or smoothly, it may well be possible to model this and produce a more complicated but more realistic model. In some cases, the parameters may alter in accordance with the value taken by some other variable. If the actual form of the model is known, the changing parameter model can be efficiently estimated and forecasts formed easily using an algorithm known as the Kalman filter. The main difficulty is selecting the proper model.

All of these techniques, and others like them, are in early stages of development and the extent of their practical value is still being determined. Full accounts of these methods are beyond the scope of a textbook, but one can forecast that a textbook twenty years hence will find it necessary to discuss at least some them quite fully.

A professional forecaster clearly cannot rely on just a single technique and should both be aware of several current methods and also attempt to keep up, at least somewhat, with new developments. The only problem with knowing many alternative forecasting techniques is that one has to choose between them. Few people would want to apply every known technique to each forecasting problem they face. To help decide which method, or small group of methods, to employ, the overall decision can be broken down into a series of smaller and, hopefully, easier decisions. At each decision stage, the main posibilities can be listed to help selection. When all these subdecisions have been made, many possible forecasting techniques will have become irrelevant and one can list those that do remain available. In technological forecasting, this technique is known as morphological analysis. The various stages in the analysis of forecasts, together with the available choices, are shown in Table 12.1. Most of the entries should be self-explanatory given the contents of the preceding chapters, but in some cases some amplification is required. The types of information sets considered are (i) single series, in which a series is forecast just from its own past; (ii) noncausal, in which the series is forecast also from other series which are not really causal but may help predict, such as leading indicators; (iii) causal, which involves series that do cause according to some theory or statistical test; and (iv) enhanced causal, which uses both causal and other variables, such as anticipations data. The decision concerning "transformation" is whether to analyze the raw data or whether the data should first be transformed, by using the logarithm of the data or in rate of return form, for example.

If several different methods of forecasting are available, a decision has to be made about synthesis. By "one step" is meant just using whichever single method seems best; in "two step" a second round of analysis is considered,

**TABLE 12.1**

*Forecasting Morphology*

1. *Recognition of type of forecasting problem*

Timing     Event     Point     Trace

2. *Preanalysis decisions*

Information set
  (i) Length            short series               long series

| | | | |
|---|---|---|---|
| (ii) Depth | One series¯ | Two series | Few series | Many series |

| | | | |
|---|---|---|---|
| (ii) Depth | One series¯ | Two series | Few series | Many series |
| (iii) Type | One series | Noncausal | Causal | Enhanced causal |
| Horizon | Short term | Middle term | Long term | |
| Cost | Low cost | Medium cost | High cost | |

3. *Analysis decisions*

| | | |
|---|---|---|
| Trend | Trend | No trend |
| Seasonal | Seasonal | No seasonal |
| Transformation | Transformation | No transformation |
| Form | Linear | Nonlinear |
| Stationarity | Time invariant | Time-varying parameters |
| Analysis | List techniques available | |
| | (alternative identification, estimation methods) | |

4. *Synthesis decisions*

        One step     Two step     Many step

5. Post analysis decisions

| | | |
|---|---|---|
| Updating | None   Occasional | Continual |
| Tracking | Automatic monitoring | No automatic monitoring |
| Evaluation | None   Casual | Intensive |

such as combining the consistent forecasts; and by "many step" synthesis is meant a deeper analysis of the relationships between methods, such as applying single or multiple time series modeling techniques to the residuals from econometric models.

The postanalysis decisions include the problem of how frequently to update one's model as new information becomes available, whether a track is kept automatically of the type and size of forecast errors being made, and how intensively the forecasts are being evaluated.

Table 12.2 shows some examples of different decision sets and the consequential alternative techniques that are available. Example A shows a low cost, single-series situation with few data, B is a higher cost, single-series case and leads to the ARIMA models, C is a multiseries situation with few or no data or cost limitations, and the two sections of D have either time-varying parameters or nonlinearity. Some groups of decisions lead to cases where there are probably no methods available. For instance, if one specifies that there is little data, requires low cost, and suggests that nonlinear, time-varying

**TABLE 12.2**

*Examples of Decision Sets and Resulting Techniques*

| Information set | A | B | C | D | |
|---|---|---|---|---|---|
| (i) Length | Short series | Long series | Long series | Long series | |
| (ii) Depth | One series | One series | Many series | One series | |
| (iii) Type | One series | One series | Causal | One series | |
| Horizon | Short term | Short term | Short/middle term | Short term | |
| Cost | Low cost | Medium to high cost | High cost | High cost | |
| Trend | Trend | Trend | Trend | Trend | |
| Seasonal | Seasonal | No seasonal | Seasonal | No seasonal | |
| Transform | No transform | No transform | No transform | No transform | |
| | | | | D1 | D2 |
| Form | Linear | Linear | Linear | Linear | Nonlinear |
| Stationary | Time invariant | Time invariant | Time invariant | Time varying | Time invariant |

*Alternative Techniques*

|  | Naive models<br>Adaptive methods | Automatic AR models<br>Automatic ARMA models<br>Stepwise autoregressive<br>Box–Jenkins ARMA models, etc.<br>Estimated by:<br>search estimates<br>maximum likelihood estimates<br>Bayesian estimates<br>robust estimates | Econometric<br>Factor-analysis time series<br>Automatic AR models<br>Many estimating techniques<br>Time series–econometric | Kalman filtering<br>Time-varying AR<br>Harmonizable | Bilinear<br>Bounded processes |
|---|---|---|---|---|---|
| Methods available | | | | | |
| Synthesis | One step | Two step (combining) | Synthesis (TSAR) | One step | One step |
| Updating | No updating | Occasional updating | Occasional updating | Continual updating | Occasional |
| Tracking | Trigg track | No automatic tracking | No automatic monitoring | No monitoring | No monitoring |
| Evaluation | No evaluation | Intensive evaluation | Casual | None | Casual |

models are most appropriate, then he should be not surprised that the cupboard is bare.

Although morphological analysis does help with the choice of a method, there still may remain a few alternative methods available. It will be up to the individual to use the techniques with which he is most comfortable or several methods together with a combining procedure. It is certainly true to say that not all forecasters will reach the same conclusion or the same model, so the possibility that experience, ability, or good luck will allow an individual to produce a better forecast than his competitors still remains.


## 12.3  THE MANAGEMENT OF FORECASTS


Forecasts are made to be used. In most companies or organizations there are the producers—the forecasters—and the users—who may be called the management—who incorporate the forecasts in their decision making process. There is often some tension in this situation. The producers may feel that management is unappreciative and makes insufficient use of the forecasts, whereas the managers may think that the forecasts are insufficiently accurate and can be easily improved. The tension can often be reduced by extra communication and by some knowledge of the other group's tasks. Management should be aware of the information set being utilized and have some appreciation of the techniques being used. The forecaster should be aware of how his forecasts will be used and of the inherent difficulties in the decisions to be made. It is also important for the forecaster to give some indication of the uncertainty attached to his figures, and he should resist the temptation to be overly optimistic in his estimate of the confidence bands around the forecast. It is equally important for management to supply the forecasters with all relevant information for incorporation into the forecasts rather than retaining some pieces for their own use. The most important thing of all is for both sides to agree on precisely what is being forecast and why.

Both groups do have certain responsibilities to ensure that good quality forecasts are produced. The forecasters have to be aware of the properties of the data being used, such as the precise definition, whether, and how, it has been seasonally adjusted, and how it is upgraded as new information becomes available. It is also necessary for the forecasters to attempt to keep up with new developments in the field. Management has to provide the environment and facilities to ensure that the forecaster operates as effectively as possible, known technically as prophet maximization.

## QUESTIONS

1. How true is it to say that the more data analysis attempted, the better the quality of the forecasts achieved, in general?

2. A company director wants to employ you to forecast the monthly inventory levels for the firm, which manufactures a single product. However, he is unclear what facilities to provide you with, this being the first formal forecasting project undertaken by the firm. Discuss the kinds of decisions that need to be made, including those about what information to utilize and how much money to spend, and the implications of these decisions.

## FURTHER READINGS

Granger, C. W. J., and A. P. Andersen (1978). *An Introduction to Bilinear Time Series Models*, Gottingen: Vandenhoech and Ruprecht.

Granger, C. W. J., and P. Newbold (1976). *Forecasting Economic Time Series*, Chapter 11, New York: Academic Press.

# Index

223